2025年度版

静岡県・静岡市・浜松市の

英語科

過 去 問

協同教育研究会 編

協同出版

本書には，静岡県・静岡市・浜松市の教員採用
試験の過去問題を収録しています。各問題ごとに，
以下のように5段階表記で，難易度，頻出度を示し
ています。

難 易 度

非常に難しい ☆☆☆☆☆
やや難しい ☆☆☆☆
普通の難易度 ☆☆☆
やや易しい ☆☆
非常に易しい ☆

頻 出 度

◎ ほとんど出題されない
◎◎ あまり出題されない
◎◎◎ 普通の頻出度
◎◎◎◎ よく出題される
◎◎◎◎◎ 非常によく出題される

はじめに～「過去問」シリーズ利用に際して～

　教育を取り巻く環境は変化しつつあり，日本の公教育そのものも，教員免許更新制の廃止やGIGAスクール構想の実現などの改革が進められています。また，現行の学習指導要領では「主体的・対話的で深い学び」を実現するため，指導方法や指導体制の工夫改善により，「個に応じた指導」の充実を図るとともに，コンピュータや情報通信ネットワーク等の情報手段を活用するために必要な環境を整えることが示されています。

　一方で，いじめや体罰，不登校，暴力行為など，教育現場の問題もあいかわらず取り沙汰されており，教員に求められるスキルは，今後さらに高いものになっていくことが予想されます。

　本書の基本構成としては，出題傾向と対策，過去5年間の出題傾向分析表，過去問題，解答および解説を掲載しています。各自治体や教科によって掲載年数をはじめ，「チェックテスト」や「問題演習」を掲載するなど，内容が異なります。

　また原則的には一般受験を対象としております。特別選考等については対応していない場合があります。なお，実際に配布された問題の順番や構成を，編集の都合上，変更している場合があります。あらかじめご了承ください。

　最後に，この「過去問」シリーズは，「参考書」シリーズとの併用を前提に編集されております。参考書で要点整理を行い，過去問で実力試しを行う，セットでの活用をおすすめいたします。

　みなさまが，この書籍を徹底的に活用し，教員採用試験の合格を勝ち取って，教壇に立っていただければ，それはわたくしたちにとって最上の喜びです。

協同教育研究会

C O N T E N T S

第１部

静岡県・静岡市・浜松市の英語科出題傾向分析

静岡県・静岡市・浜松市の英語科　傾向と対策

中学校

　2024年度も2023年度に引き続き，学習指導要領に関わる問題が1題，英語教育に関する作文が2題，読解問題2題が出題されている。2021年度からリスニング問題が廃止され，大問数も減った。配点は，大問1〜大問3は各10点。大問4，大問5は各15点。合計60点。記述問題の割合がかなり多い。

　学習指導要領に関わる問題は，基本的な内容と言える。また，英語教育に絡めて，英作文が2題出題されている。1題は，「初心に帰る」という語句の説明，もう1題は，英語が話せない生徒の悩みにどのようにアドバイスするかを書くというもの。語数はともに80語以上と指定されている。近年，静岡県ではこれくらいの英文量が作文で求められている。80語であれば，4，5文が目安になると思われる。簡潔な文で，意見を明確に表現することを念頭に，字数の感覚がつかめるよう何度か実際に書いてみることが大切である。なお，解答欄には6行にわたり，ラインが設けられている。

　読解問題2題の英文の長さは，それぞれ500語程度，600語程度である。設問が空所補充，内容一致文選択，説明記述問題，英問英答などで構成されている。難解な文章ではないが，英文自体が比較的長く，選択肢や設問の英文と合わせると読むべき英語の量はやや多い。新聞や雑誌のコラムやエッセイ等は楽に読みこなせるように学習しておくことが必要である。解答にあたりたびたび本文に戻って確認することがないように，文章構成を分析するとともに，どこにどんな情報が書かれているか，トピックセンテンス，サポーティングセンテンスやキーワードなどをチェックしながら1回目を素早く読み，全体が把握できたうえで解答に臨むのが効果的である。過去問題を解くほか，大学入試レベルの長文問題集で数をこなしておくとよい。

高等学校

　2024年度も2023年度に引き続きリスニング問題4題，読解問題2題が出題されている。配点は，大問1から順に，16点，12点，10点，22点，20点，20点。難易度の高い問題が多く，時間との戦いであることに加えて，相当の集中力・持続力が求められる。リスニングの占める割合がかなり高いので，それなりの対策が必要である。

　リスニング問題は，対話や英文を聞いて，その内容に関する質問の答えとして適切なものを選ぶ選択式問題，内容一致文選択問題，図表を見て解答する選択問題など様々な形式から成る。特に後半は例年，ニュースなどからの抜粋で，リスニング問題としてはかなりの長文で，内容も難易度が高い。TOEFLテストのリスニングセクションや英語検定準1級以上のリスニングテストの対策CD等を使い，ある程度長時間にわたるリスニングをこなして慣れておく必要がある。さらに，新聞や雑誌，研究論文などで社会・経済・環境・教育などに関する情報や語彙をストックして，様々な話題に対応できるようにしておくことも必要である。内容の素早い把握が，予測しながら落ち着いて聞くことにつながる。リスニングの最後の大問4は，英問英答と英作文を兼ねての出題になっている。問いは「SDGsの課題を1つ選び生徒に対し教師の立場でどのように説明するか」というものであった。おそらくこの解答に最も時間を要すると思われる。語数は指定されていないが，公開解答は144語である。内容10点，文構造4点，語彙と文法2点と採点の基準が示されている。

　読解問題は2題。解答形式はほとんどが選択式で，内容一致文や英問英答などから成る。難解な文章ではないが，900語と1200語程度と英文量も多いので，一読して内容をつかみ，どこに何が記述されているかすぐ遡って見つけられるよう，トピックセンテンス，サポーティングセンテンス，キーワード，キーフレーズなどを的確に把握しながら読む学習を重ねることが必要である。過去問題を解くほか，大学入試レベルの長文問題集や英字新聞などを利用して，速読力をつけることも必要である。

過去5年間の出題傾向分析

中学＝● 高校＝▲ 中高共通＝◎

分類	設問形式	2020年度	2021年度	2022年度	2023年度	2024年度
リスニング	内容把握	●▲	▲	▲	▲	▲
発音・アクセント	発音					
	アクセント					
	文強勢					
文法・語法	空所補充					
	正誤判断					
	一致語句					
	連立完成					
	その他					
会話文	短文会話					
	長文会話					
文章読解	空所補充	●▲	●▲	●▲	●	●▲
	内容一致文	●▲	●▲	●	●▲	●▲
	内容一致語句	▲	▲			
	内容記述	●			●	
	英文和訳					
	英問英答	●▲	●▲	●▲	●▲	●▲
	その他	●▲	●▲	●▲	●▲	●▲
英作文	整序	▲				
	和文英訳					
	自由英作	●▲	●▲	●	▲	▲
	その他	●▲	▲			
学習指導要領		●	●	●	●	●

第2部

静岡県・静岡市・浜松市の教員採用試験実施問題

2024年度　実施問題

【中学校】

【1】次の文は，「中学校学習指導要領(平成29年3月告示)第2章　第9節　外国語　第1　目標」「中学校学習指導要領(平成29年3月告示)第2章　第9節　外国語　第2　各言語の目標及び内容等　英語　3　指導計画の作成と内容の取扱い(1)ア」の記述である。(　　)に当てはまる語句として適切なものを以下の語群から選び，記号で答えなさい。

第1　目標

　外国語によるコミュニケーションにおける(　1　)を働かせ，外国語による聞くこと，読むこと，話すこと，書くことの(　2　)を通して，簡単な(　3　)などを理解したり表現したり伝え合ったりするコミュニケーションを図る(　4　)を次のとおり育成することを目指す。

　　　　　　「中学校学習指導要領(平成29年3月告示)第2章　第9
　　　　　　節　外国語　第1　目標」

第2　各言語の目標及び内容等
英語
3　指導計画の作成と内容の取扱い
　(1)　指導計画の作成に当たっては，小学校や高等学校における指導との接続に留意しながら，次の事項に配慮するものとする。
　　ア　単元など(　5　)や時間のまとまりを見通して，その中で育む(　4　)の育成に向けて，生徒の(　6　)の実現を図るようにすること。その際，具体的な(　7　)等を設定し，生徒が外国語によるコミュニケーションにおける(　1　)を働かせながら，コミュニケーションの(　8　)や(　9　)，

状況などを意識して活動を行い，英語の音声や語彙，表現，文法の知識を(10)の領域における実際のコミュニケーションにおいて活用する学習の充実を図ること。
「中学校学習指導要領(平成29年3月告示)第2章　第9節　外国語　第2　各言語の目標及び内容等　英語3　指導計画の作成と内容の取扱い(1)ア」

＜語群＞

ア　場面	イ　四つ	ウ　五つ
エ　技能	オ　課題	カ　見方・考え方
キ　情報や考え	ク　相手	ケ　思いや考え
コ　言語活動	サ　内容	シ　主体的に学習に取り組む態度
ス　資質・能力	セ　目的	ソ　交流活動
タ　主体的・対話的で深い学び	チ　教科書	ツ　基礎

(☆☆☆◎◎◎)

【2】外国人の友達からきた次のメールに，あなたは返信しようとしています。返信文を以下の条件に従って英語で書きなさい。

Dear ○○,

 初心にかえる

Hi, how have you been?

I have a question. I saw this phrase yesterday and I didn't understand the meaning.

Could you explain this meaning and when does this phrase come to mind?

Take care,

◇◇

＜条件＞

・80語以上の英語(?,." "などの記号は語数に含まない)で書く

・あいさつなどは省き，本題から書き始める

・「初心にかえる」という語を使用する場合は，1語として書く

"Shoshin ni kaeru"

(☆☆☆◎◎◎)

【3】 "Give Your Opinion" という投稿サイトに，日本人の学生が次のような投稿をしました。

> I like English very much, but when I try to have a conversation with someone in English in person, I can't speak it well. How can I improve my English-speaking ability?

あなたはこれに対して投稿しようとしています。次の条件に従って英語で書きなさい。

＜条件＞

・80語以上の英語(?,. " " などの記号は語数に含まない)で書く

・投稿者の悩みを解決するための具体的な案について書く

・その具体案を提案した理由を書く

(☆☆☆◎◎◎)

【4】次の英文は，Ａさんが英語の授業を構想する際に読んだ雑誌の記事(以下，「本文」という。)である。本文を読み，以下の問いに答えなさい。

本文

　Sipping her yuzu tea in a buzzy café, 20-year-old university student Marin Minamiya is exactly what you'd expect of a fashionable young Japanese woman. Her hair is long and shiny. Her fingernails are painted a sparkly gold. She laughs easily and punctuates her conversation with breathless, OMG-style exclamations. What you don't expect is this: A few weeks later, she will be wrapped in up to seven layers of clothing, slogging through minus-70-degree temperatures, in an attempt to ski to the North Pole.

　Minamiya—bubbly exterior, steely core—is one of Japan's youngest and most high-profile adventurers. 【　①　】 At 18, she became the youngest woman ever to climb 8,163-meter Mount Manaslu in the Nepalese Himalayas. At 19, she was the youngest Japanese person, man or woman, to climb Mount Everest. When we meet, in February this year, she is in the middle of training for the North Pole trip, the final leg of her attempt at the famously (　②　) Explorers Grand Slam. To date completed by just 51 people worldwide, this demands that participants reach both poles and climb the tallest mountains on seven continents. If Minamiya reaches the Pole, she will be the youngest Asian to have completed the challenge.

She'll make the attempt on the North Pole in early April, as part of a small group—but exploring can be a lonely life. Minamiya is often not just the only woman in a group but also the youngest overall. Women can be competitive and men prejudiced: One male Japanese climber once said he was insulted just to be introduced to her.

"People are often really surprised when they learn about what I do," she says. "They say, 'Oh my gosh' and can't imagine me climbing a mountain, especially when I'm wearing my normal, everyday clothes. They ask me why I do it—and I want to tell them the reason, but it's not easy to say in one sentence."

Minamiya's longing to climb started as a way to connect with others. She was an only child, and her father's work as a financial trader meant the family was always on the move. At the age of 12, after time living in Malaysia, Shanghai and the Chinese city of Dalian, Minamiya moved with her family to Hong Kong, where she went to an English-speaking school for largely expatriate children. She had a difficult time there, she recalls: A culture of overreliance on technology meant there was very little human interaction. Every course was taught on laptops, and at lunchtime, Minamiya ate on the first floor while FaceTiming with her best friend, who sat on the eighth.

Things at home weren't any better. Her father was rarely there, and her mother had stayed behind in Japan. Then, when she was 13, her teachers started taking groups of 50 students on trips to the mountainous interior of Lantau, Hong Kong's largest island. On the mountainside, the group had to collaborate, with the participants helping one another navigate across the unfamiliar landscape and coming together to plan the group meal. "For the first time, there was a human bond between us," she says.

Climbing also gave the adolescent Minamiya a sense of perspective, a view of the wider world that she found invaluable. When she reached her first mountaintop with her schoolmates, she looked east across the waters of the South China Sea to the "concrete jungle of Hong Kong." In that moment, she saw the stresses of her preteen life for what they were. "We thought, Oh my gosh, our existence is so tiny. All these daily issues don't (③)."

After that, Minamiya climbed dozens of mountains around Hong Kong, before joining a friend and two teachers on a 14-day climb to the Annapurna base camp in Nepal. There — still only 13 — she glimpsed Mount Everest looming over a valley and vowed to climb it one day. She then completed an arduous ascent in Argentina.

Her parents divorced when she was 17; climbing high kept her (④), giving her a much needed sense of control. "I knew the one thing that would get me back on track was climbing," she says. "It has always been like meditation for me. It's not only about healing—it's about self-empowerment and self-awareness. I just thought, 'I have to get out of here and find myself, through basing myself on a mountain.'"

She experienced a different kind of grounding too. While she was descending Mount Amida in Nagano in March 2015, the snow beneath her crumbled, and she fell 250 meters, head-first. That's nearly as bad as falling off the Eiffel Tower. "I really thought I was going to die," she says, but then adds, "When I was falling, I screamed and prayed to God, saying, 'I don't want to die yet, please help me.'" Right after her prayer, her crampons got caught in the snow, and she stopped falling.

She spent the night in a snow hole she'd dug for herself, before an emergency search team in a helicopter rescued her. 【 ⑤ 】 She cried for days afterward in an empty house; her parents hadn't visited her in hospital. Yet she completed her record-breaking Mount Everest ascent just 14 months later. "The accident made me realize that people die extremely easily," she says. "That made me propel myself even further."

Where does a woman who's reached both ends of the earth propel herself next? Assuming she makes it back from the North Pole, Minamiya's next plan is to sail around the world — this time, she hopes, not alone. She's looking for a companion to sail with "who is definitely committed, has a dream of their own, is excited about life — and basically has the same goal as me, which is to help others reach their full potential." It doesn't seem like an accident that she's choosing an adventure that requires another person to come along for the ride. I hope she finds someone.

(Newsweek, March 17, 2017 一部改)

1　本文の内容に合うように，【 ① 】【 ⑤ 】に入る最も適する英語を次のア～オより一つずつ選び，記号で答えなさい。

　ア　Climbing mountains wasn't any feat.

　イ　The accident made her vulnerable in a different way.

　ウ　Minamiya juggles time spent on expeditions with studying at the university.

　エ　Minamiya thought that she had become somebody completely new.

　オ　During her teens, she quietly broke a string of records.

2　本文の内容に合うように，(②)(③)(④)に入る最も適する英語を次のア～エより一つずつ選び，記号で答えなさい。

　②　ア　successful　　　　イ　straightforward
　　　ウ　grueling　　　　　エ　insignificant

　③　ア　pose a challenge　イ　mean a thing
　　　ウ　make an impact　エ　resolve my doubts

　④　ア　grounded　　　　イ　unstable
　　　ウ　immature　　　　エ　ready

13

3　本文の内容に合うように，次の質問に6語以上の英語で答えなさい。

(1)　Why are people often really surprised when they learn about what Minamiya does?

(2)　When did Minamiya get inspired to climb Mount Everest?

(3)　For the next plan of sailing, what kind of companion does Minamiya hope to find?

4　Aさんは，世界に発信する日本人というテーマでMinamiyaさんを紹介するために，伝えたいことをまとめた。次はその一部である。本文の内容に合うように，(　①　)〜(　③　)に入る英語を書きなさい。ただし，(　①　)〜(　③　)は，異なる英語を使用すること。

=The person who sends a message to the world=

Marin Minamiya

◆Background

→　Minamiya moved around Asia with her father's job.

→　When she went to an English-speaking school for largely expatriate children, she could hardly (　①　) with her classmates.

◆Climbing and her

→　To build (　②　) with others, her longing to climb started.

→　When her teachers took groups of 50 students on trips to the mountainous interior of Lantau, she felt there was a human (　③　) between them for the first time.

5　次の英文は，Aさんが，Minamiyaさんについてもっと知りたいと思い，読んだインタビュー記事の一部である。この英文において，Minamiyaさんが，最も伝えたいことを以下のア〜エの中から一つ選び記号で答えなさい。

I would like to encourage young girls to pursue anything, whatever it is that they want to do. Believe in your potential and believe that it's infinite. All the limitations and barriers out there ─ if you do think that they're barriers, you put it on yourself. I think it's all in the mind. And don't be afraid to be the only girl in certain situations, and you'll definitely learn to manage, so go for it.

(CNN ENGLISH EXPRESS, October, 2019 一部改)

ア　Know your own limitations.
イ　Turn to others for help.
ウ　What will be, will be.
エ　Never place limits on yourself.

(☆☆☆◎◎)

【5】ALTが英語教員Bさんに ICT 活用について次のような発言をした。それに対する意見を述べるため，Bさんはある文献(以下本文)を読んだ。英文を読み，その後の問いに答えなさい。

We can see so many technologies moving at such a pace・・・. Students are already tech-savvy. I think that deploying devices is ideal. Students will be active learners by using technology on their own.

ALT

＜文献＞

With the rapid growth of online testing, schools have also rushed to buy educational technology that supports these assessments. Since some states require online assessments, districts have essentially been forced to add large numbers of devices. So far, the emphasis of this type of technological integration has overwhelmingly been on the assessment side, and the instructional side has gotten lost in the process. This has led to devices in schools being [①] somewhat randomly－tossed around with little precision yet done with the hope that it'll enrich current growth far and wide. In many cases, the devices become simplistic instructional add-ons or gap fillers for time, yielding little to no instructional benefit.

We must also question the pedagogical practice of teaching and learning in a traditional format and then assessing digitally. We believe that such assessments require an additional skill set. In cases where assessments are fully digital but are rarely used during the learning process, students are likely to perform at a lower level.

The research is clear. Technology by itself does not, and will not, transform teaching and learning. In fact, like any tool, when used poorly, it can have negative consequences. We believe that

· Simply adding the latest technology to traditional learning environments can have a negative effect on teaching and learning.

· Technology can accelerate great teaching practices, which can in turn support equity and create greater opportunities for all students.

· Technology can amplify poor teaching practices and increase the amount of time students spend on low-level learning tasks.

· Assessing students in an online format but consistently using traditional instructional methods during the learning process can yield lower results. Online assessments require a digital skill set and comfort level that may not be present for students who have learned in a very different fashion.

A 2014 report by the Stanford Center for Opportunity Policy in Education and the Alliance for Excellent Education set out to study the effective use of technology, particularly with students who are most at risk (Darling-Hammond et al., 2014). The report verified that early versions of technology-based instruction that were structured like "electronic workbooks," where students passively moved through a digital curriculum, showed little effect on achievement. The report cited one particular study that evaluated the impact of math and reading software products in 132 schools across 33 districts, which found no significant difference on student test scores between classrooms that used the software and classrooms that didn't (Dynarski et al., 2007). The report also cited another large study that evaluated the effectiveness of students' [②] to a phonics-based computer program, which also found no effect in terms of gains on reading comprehension tests (Borman, Benson, & Overman, 2009). Time and again, the "digital drill and kill" or use of technology as an electronic workbook shows little to no effect on student learning.

So what does the effective use of technology actually look like? What is worth the investment of time and money? There are three important variables for the successful infusion of technology, particularly with at-risk students who are learning new skills.

Interactive Learning: The interactive use of technology can enhance student learning and, ultimately, achievement by providing multiple ways for learners to grasp traditionally difficult concepts. Interactive learning opportunities have become more robust as adaptive content and systems have evolved in recent years. In these systems, the content levels up and down based on a student's ability; in other words, it adapts to a student's level of need. When leveraged for interactive learning, students become active users — not passive consumers of content.

Use of Technology to Explore and Create: When students are given the opportunity to leverage technology to explore and create, new learning can be accelerated. When this is the case, students are able to create and develop new content rather than absorb content passively. When empowered to explore and create, students also demonstrate higher levels of engagement, more positive attitudes toward school, higher levels of skill development, and self-efficacy.

【 ③ 】 : When students have ubiquitous access, particularly in

17

environments with 1:1 student-to-device ratios, digital experiences can be blended into the learning environment to extrapolate concepts and maximize learning opportunities. In these environments, students can access the "right blend" of direct instruction and technology-accelerated learning. Student voice and choice play an important role while the teacher gives the needed level of direct support.

Technology use is most productive when experiences combine the "structured learning of information with collaborative discussions and project-based activities that allow students to use the information to solve meaningful problems or create their own products, both individually and collectively" (Darling-Hammond et al., 2014).

Displaying lesson notes on an interactive whiteboard, answering multiple-choice questions in an online platform, typing documents that are saved to the cloud, reading a textbook on a mobile device, or looking up facts online may make certain tasks more efficient, but they do nothing to challenge or redefine an outdated pedagogy. Leveraging technology to create a more teacher-centric environment is detrimental to student learning and undoubtedly fails to create the personal and authentic learning opportunities students need. Intentionally designed schools refuse to utilize technology for technology's sake. These schools purposefully use technology as the right tool, at the right time, to create the needed access and opportunity.

(出典： LEARNING TRANSFORMED:8 Keys to Designing Tomorrow's Schools, Today, Sheninger, Eric C., & Murray, Thomas C., 2017　一部改)

1　本文の内容に合うように，[　①　][　②　]に最も適する英語を次のア～エより一つずつ選び，記号で答えなさい。

① ア　spread out　　　イ　passed through
　　ウ　handed in　　　エ　entered in
② ア　regulation　　　イ　obstacle
　　ウ　concealment　　エ　exposure

2　【　③　】にはその後に続く内容を説明する見出しが入ります。

18

【 ③ 】のタイトルとして最も適する英語を次のア～エより一つ選び，記号で答えなさい。

ア　Right Blend of Teachers and Technology

イ　Right Blend of An Outdated Pedagogy and A Digital Pedagogy

ウ　Right Blend of Learning and Accessing

エ　Right Blend of Digital Experiences and Digital Supporting

3　本文の内容に合うように，次の質問に6語以上の英語で答えなさい。

(1)　According to the author, when are students likely to perform at a lower level?

(2)　According to the author, how can achievement help enhance learners to grasp traditionally difficult concepts?

(3)　Give an example written in this passage of teaching methods that makes certain tasks more efficient but does nothing to challenge or redefine an outdated pedagogy.

4　文献を読んだ英語教員Bさんは文献を基に次のようにALTに伝えました。(①)～(③)にあてはまる適切な英語を書きなさい。

I think that deploying technology without considering how to use it effectively for maximum educational benefit will (①) a detrimental effect on student learning. Some reports verified that the "digital drill and kill" or use of technology as an electronic workbook showed little to no effect on student learning and students became passive learners.

The technology itself is not effective. The technology with (②) can be effective. I don't think that students will be active learners by using technology on their own. With technology, we teachers can (③) students to have the personal and authentic learning opportunities they need.

英語教員
Bさん

＜条件＞

・語数は問わない

・(①)～(③)は全て異なる英語を使用すること

(☆☆☆☆◎◎◎)

【高等学校】

【 1 】 Listen to the dialogues and questions. Choose the most appropriate answer from the three choices, (A), (B), and (C). You will hear the dialogues and questions only once.

Dialogue 1

Mary: John, Dad's birthday is next month.

John: What shall we buy for him?

Mary: Hmm... How about this tie? Navy blue is his favorite, isn't it? It's 150 dollars.

John: Yes, it is a good color. I think he will like it. But isn't it a little expensive?

Mary: Look at this advertisement! This week only, this store is giving a 10 % discount to customers that spend more than 100 dollars.

John: Really? That's good news.

Mary: The advertisement also says if we pay through the app, they give us another 10 % discount.

John: That's a 20 % discount, then. Let's do that and I'll pay you half the cost later.

Q1.　How much will John pay afterward?

　(A)　60 dollars.

　(B)　75 dollars.

　(C)　120 dollars.

Dialogue 2

Taro: Would you like to see some photos of when I traveled in west England?

Hanna: Yes, I'd love to.

Taro: One of my best memories was when I traveled in Bristol, which is a classical port city. It is famous for its beautiful cathedrals and has the biggest suspension bridge in the UK. Please look at these.

Hanna: Wow, this bridge looks so big!

Taro: Yes, it is. It is the Clifton Suspension Bridge, where cars and trucks can drive.

Hanna: Really?

Taro: Yeah, and another thing that I was interested in was the art. There are many colorful paintings and graffiti on the walls of houses and buildings in the city. I noticed a piece that famous artists painted. I guess their name is Ba...Ba...

Hanna: Who is it?

Taro: Oh, I can't remember. But it is on the tip of my tongue... it sounds something like Bank...

Q2. According to the conversation, which is NOT true about the city?

   (A)   Bristol is a historical port city that has some beautiful cathedrals.

   (B)   Bristol has a well-known suspension bridge where vehicles cannot pass.

   (C)   Bristol has many colorfully-painted walls of houses and buildings.

Dialogue 3

Paul: What are these?

Anna: These are cutting-edge goggles that you can use to dive into the world of virtual reality. Would you like to try them on?

Paul: Yes, please! ...Wow, awesome! It looks so real.

Anna: Do you like it? Technology progresses day by day, doesn't it?

Paul: It is always changing our lives.

Anna: Yes, smartphones are another good example. Smartphones have changed our lives dramatically since they were invented about 2 decades ago. Now I cannot do without my smartphone. Robots are also an example. Many people have cleaning robots at home, which were considered unusual a few years ago.

Paul: Exactly. Do you think virtual reality will also become more common in the future too?

Anna: Yes. Actually, it is already common in some fields such as computer games and pilot training systems.

Paul: Wow. I wonder what our lives will be like in the next 20 years.

Q3.　Which is true about their opinions on modern technology?

(A)　Smartphones are too convenient for us to live without them.

(B)　Virtual reality will be outdated in the near future.

(C)　Robots will replace us at our jobs in the future.

Dialogue 4

Alex: Oh, my gosh!

Lucy: What's wrong, Alex?

Alex: My data seems to be completely wrong. I've just realized that the data I used was from File 7. It should be File 17...

Lucy: What? Are you sure?

Alex: Unfortunately, yes. I checked it over twice when I made it, but I don't know why I still made a mistake. What should I do?

Lucy: We cannot continue the project using the wrong file. First, you should tell our boss about it as soon as possible. The sooner, the better.

Alex: Yes, I agree. He will yell at me, but I am more concerned for our team. I mean, we have to start the work over because it is already in process. I have to apologize to our team members.

Lucy: Things happen. They will be OK. Let's go to talk to our boss first. I will go with you.

Alex: Thank you, Lucy.

Q4.　What is happening now?

(A)　Alex intentionally used the wrong file and Lucy is trying to fix it.

(B)　Lucy is persuading Alex to say sorry to the team members first.

(C)　Alex caused a problem and Lucy is giving some advice.

Dialogue 5

Ken: I wonder when the deadline for the first draft of the paper is.

Sophie: It is October 17th, I think. Let me have a look at my planner.

Ken: OK.

Sophie: Yes, I was right. We have 1 week left until the first draft is due. And the deadline for the second draft is October 31st.

Ken: We are going to be busy. Do you think we can make it?

Sophie: Yes, we can. We have gotten through a lot of difficulties, haven't we? If we can't, we won't graduate from university.

Q5.　How many weeks are left until they have to hand in the second draft of the paper?

(A)　2 weeks.　　(B)　3 weeks.　　(C)　4 weeks.

October

Mon	Tue	Wed	Thu	Fri	Sat	Sun
						1
2	3	4	5	6	7	8
9	10	11	12	13	14	15
16	17	18	19	20	21	22
23	24	25	26	27	28	29
30	31					

Dialogue 6

Father: It is about time we let our daughter have a smartphone since we promised to do so when she enters high school.

Mother: Well then, we should decide on rules for how she uses it. She is getting a smartphone for the first time, and she is still too young to be exposed to the world of the Internet. It will be risky for her and for us without rules.

Father: I know we need to set rules, but I think we should discuss rules with her first. It is a good opportunity for her to think for herself. Including her in the discussion can help her to be responsible and independent.

Mother: OK then, let's do that.

Q6.　What are the parents likely to do next?

   (A)　They are going to decide on the rules without their daughter.

   (B)　They are going to discuss the rules with their daughter.

   (C)　They are going to let their daughter decide on the rules by herself.

Dialogue 7

Mom: These cars won't move at all. We're stuck in a traffic jam and it's already 8:30. You should have listened to me when I told you to hurry up!

Son: I'm sorry, Mom. Last night I planned to prepare for the school trip in the morning, but I woke up late.

Mom: How could you think that preparing on the morning of the school trip is a good idea? Anyway, your bus is leaving the station soon, it's ten to nine? Right?

Son: No, Mom. That is the time we gather at the station. The bus is supposed to leave 10 minutes after that.

Mom: Oh, that's better! Still, we may not be able to make it.

Son: Hey, Mom. I just got an e-mail saying that the teachers have delayed the gathering time by 20 minutes because of the traffic jam. The departure time will be 10 minutes after that.

Mom: Thank goodness for the traffic jam.

Q7.　What time will the bus leave the station?

   (A)　9:20　　(B)　9:40　　(C)　10:20

Dialogue 8

Sarah: Do you think money can buy happiness?

Eric: What?

Sarah: I found an interesting article on the Internet, and I want to know what you think.

Eric: Tell me about it.

Sarah: One professor compared the people who spent their money on themselves with the people who spent their money on others and measured how happy they were. His research study included people from a variety of backgrounds, such as undergraduate students and factory workers.

Eric: So, what was the result of the study?

Sarah: In one of his experiments, some people received 5 dollars and others received 20 dollars. Some of them were asked to spend the money on themselves and others were asked to spend it on someone else like friends or family. In the end, the professor found that people who spent their money on others felt happier than people who spent it on themselves and how much money they spent was not important.

Eric: Interesting!

Sarah: Yes, it is. The result implies that...

Q8.　Which of the sentences is most appropriate to continue the conversation?

　　(A)　"Saving for a rainy day"

　　(B)　"More money, more problems"

　　(C)　"Giving is receiving"

(☆☆☆☆○○○)

【2】You are a high school English teacher, and you are looking for some materials to use for your English class. You come across two audio lectures titled lecture A and lecture B. Listen to the lectures. Choose the most appropriate answer from the choices below. You will have 20 seconds to prepare before listening to each lecture. You will hear the lectures only once.

[Lecture A]

How many times a day do you laugh? Did you do anything fun today? To lead a better and healthier life, we need "fun". Now, let me tell you how fun affects us.

What is the feeling of having "fun"? There are three factors that are consistently present in "fun". And those three factors are playfulness, connection and flow.

So, by playfulness, I mean having a lighthearted attitude of doing things without caring too much about the outcome. When we have fun, our guard is down, and we're not taking ourselves too seriously.

Connection refers to the feeling of having a special, shared experience. And I do think it's possible, in some circumstances, to have fun alone. However, in the majority of the stories that I've heard about other people's most fun memories, another person was involved.

And then flow is the state where we are so engaged and focused on whatever we're doing that we might even lose track of time. You can think about an athlete in the middle of a game, or a musician playing a piece of music. It's when we're in the zone. It's possible to be in flow when you're not having fun, like when you're arguing with someone, but you cannot have fun if you're not in flow.

So, playfulness, connection and flow all feel great on their own. But when we experience all three at once, something magical happens ―we have fun: Having fun feels good and is good for us.

Now, how do we have more fun? To start, reduce distractions so you can increase flow. Anything that distracts you is going to kick you out of flow and will prevent you from having fun. And the number one source of distraction for most of us, these days is our phones. So, I challenge you to keep your phone out of your hand as much as possible. You will increase connection by interacting with people in-person, instead of digitally.

(SOURCE: *Why having fun is the secret to a healthier life?*, Catherine Price, TED TALK, REVISED https://www.ted.com/talks/catherine_price_why_having_fun_is_the_secret_to_a_healthier_life/comments)

How fun affects us

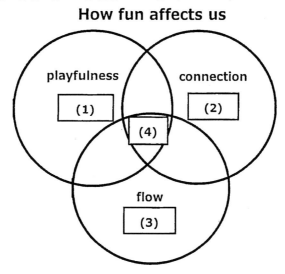

Q1. Place the explanations associated with each factor in the blanks (1)− (4).

  (A) concentrating on what we are doing

  (B) feeling good and being good for us

  (C) spending time with others

  (D) thinking less about the outcome

Q2. In his speech, to have more fun, one thing that he did NOT suggest was ...

  (A) avoiding something that interrupts us.

  (B) using digital devices.

  (C) interacting with people in reality.

[Lecture B]

We are losing our ability to consciously listen. Roughly 60 percent of all of our communications is spent listening, yet we retain just 25 percent of what we hear.

There are a lot of reasons for this. First, there are many ways to record what we hear — written, audio, and now video recording. Secondly, the world is so noisy all the time. There are many background sounds going on all day, and what's worse is that many people take refuge in headphones. Unfortunately, this turns a public space, with many people, into tiny private bubbles. And of course, nobody's listening to anyone else.

We're also becoming impatient. We don't want eloquent speeches any more, we want short and simple ones.

This is a serious problem. Listening is our access point to understanding. Conscious listening always creates conscious understanding. And without conscious listening, scary things can happen — we end up in a world where we don't listen to each other at all, which leads to misunderstandings, fights, discriminations, and even wars.

(SOURCE: *5 ways to listen better*, Julian Treasure, TED Global 2011 REVISED

https://www.ted.com/talks/julian_treasure_5_ways_to_listen_better/transcript)

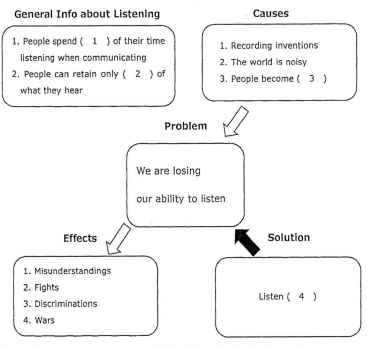

General Info about Listening

1. People spend (1) of their time listening when communicating
2. People can retain only (2) of what they hear

Causes

1. Recording inventions
2. The world is noisy
3. People become (3)

Problem

We are losing our ability to listen

Effects

1. Misunderstandings
2. Fights
3. Discriminations
4. Wars

Solution

Listen (4)

Q1. Choose the appropriate words for blanks (1)－(4).

1 (A) a quarter (B) half (C) more than half

2 (A) less than a quarter (B) a quarter (C) a half

3 (A) hopeless (B) emotionless (C) restless

4 (A) actively (B) passively (C) carelessly

Q2. Choose the most appropriate statement that the speaker is most likely to make next.

(A) Now, I'd like to tell you how to train your own conscious listening.

(B) Now, I'll tell you the reason why we should understand the serious problem.

(C) Now, I'll let you know conscious listening is crucial in making a good speech.

(☆☆☆☆◎◎◎)

【3】 You are a university student listening to the lecture about language learning strategies and taking notes. Choose the most appropriate answer from the three choices, (A), (B), and (C). You will have 40 seconds to prepare before listening to the lecture. You will hear the lecture only once.

Today, I'll talk about language learning strategies. As you listen to my lecture, follow along using the worksheet.

Successful language learners consciously incorporate effective strategies into their language learning.

Although there is widespread agreement among language researchers and teachers on the benefits of using language learning strategies, there is much less agreement on how to encourage a student to employ these strategies. The first study explored which strategies college students frequently use by conducting survey and interview with a focus group of students. The instructor asked the students to discuss the various learning strategies that they knew about or had used while learning English, then had them evaluate those language learning strategies on a Likert scale.

Table 1 shows the result of the survey regarding their use of learning strategies. The top two strategies are about having opportunities to talk with native English speakers. Many of the students believe using the language is the best way to improve their own communicative language skills. Interestingly, reading favorite books in the target language was not considered as an effective way to memorize phrases.

Let's move to Table 2. It shows the use of different learning strategies. Kenta said "I made a lot of friends with this school's exchange students and I tried to speak English with them". According to Kumiko and Mika, they also both had foreign friends that they talked to in English. Kumiko talked to her English-speaking friends every day.

Mika used her smartphone to study English. She said, "Sometimes I record myself reading my English diary". Taku liked to listen to podcasts and watch YouTube videos.

Taku and Kumiko both liked to watch online videos and TV with English subtitles. Taku said "I really like Anime".

They both also read aloud and believed it helped them. Taku reported that he read aloud at home and sometimes recorded it on his smartphone to check his accuracy. He believes focusing on grammar is important to acquire languages.

Kenta, Kumiko, and Mika all believed that they learned English better by actually focusing less on grammar and more on just trying to communicate. In essence, comprehensible output was more important to them than accuracy.

Another survey was conducted to determine which methods students recalled using in their English classes. You can see the options in Table 3. According to the results, more than half of 3rd year junior high students recalled often changing English sentences into Japanese to deepen their understandings. A strategy used during class was learning vocabulary and sentence structures first, then doing grammar excises. Less than a quarter of the students answered that they recalled often talking about their own ideas and thoughts in English.

Based on the survey and interview data, we could see that advanced-level students were conscious of when and how they used learning strategies in order to help themselves learn English. Advanced learners may not need to use the same learning strategies that they used as beginners, but the data in this study showed that these students were using specific learning strategies to maintain their level or to improve it.

In conclusion, as English teachers, it is our job to assess what it is that our students need in order to help them achieve success.

(SOURCE 1: *A Closer Look at Language Learning Strategies.* Wood, J. C., JALT Post Conference Publication, 2020, REVISED)

(SOURCE 2: 「英語学習に関する継続調査」から考える指導のありかた, 上智大学・ベネッセ英語教育シンポジウム2018 *https://www. arcle.jp/report/2018/pdf/0207_02s.pdf*)

31

Worksheet

The purpose of the 1ˢᵗ study: | X |

1ˢᵗ Survey

Table 1. The Rank of the Use of Learning Strategies

1. Talking with English speakers
2. | Y |
3. Watching movies with English subtitles
4. Repeating what characters say in English movies
5. Memorizing phrases, not only words

⋮

Table 2. The Use of Learning Strategies

	Kenta	Kumiko	Mika	Taku
Active use of the language				
Utilizing technologies				
Watching movies and TV programs				
Reading and writing				
Focusing not too much on grammar				

2ⁿᵈ Survey

Table 3. The Activities Used in Junior High Schools

Translation
Learning vocabulary and sentence structures
Expression of their ideas and feelings
Grammar exercises

The conclusion of the lecture: | Z |

Q1.　What is the appropriate option for | X |?

(A)　To raise awareness of utilizing learning strategies while learning one's first language

(B)　To examine how language teachers use language learning strategies to improve their communicative skills

(C)　To research what strategies students used to learn English

Q2.　What is the appropriate option for | Y |?

(A)　Listening to music

(B)　Learning sentence structures

(C)　Making friends with foreign students

Q3.　Of the four students in the table 2, how many students used "Focusing not too much on grammar" strategy in the categories shown in the table? Choose the appropriate option.

(A)　2　　(B)　3　　(C)　4

Q4.　Choose the graph which matches the result of the second survey on activities in junior high schools?

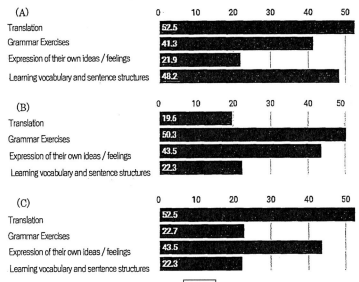

(A)

	0	10	20	30	40	50
Translation	52.5					
Grammar Exercises	41.3					
Expression of their own ideas / feelings	21.9					
Learning vocabulary and sentence structures	48.2					

(B)

	0	10	20	30	40	50
Translation	19.6					
Grammar Exercises	50.3					
Expression of their own ideas / feelings	43.5					
Learning vocabulary and sentence structures	22.3					

(C)

	0	10	20	30	40	50
Translation	52.5					
Grammar Exercises	22.7					
Expression of their own ideas / feelings	43.5					
Learning vocabulary and sentence structures	22.3					

Q5.　What is the appropriate option for ☐ Z ☐ ?

(A)　Language teachers don't have to pay attention to how advanced learners use the language learning strategies.

(B)　Language teachers need to take a close look at their students to help students utilize learning strategies.

(C)　Language teachers should let their students choose the strategies, regardless of whether they achieve their goal.

(☆☆☆☆◎◎◎)

【4】 University student, Aoi, is interested in effective English teaching. He asked Professor Brown to elaborate on it more. Listen to their dialogue and answer the questions below. You will have 20 seconds to prepare before listening. You will hear the dialogue twice.

Question 1

Aoi: Professor Brown, what do you think is the most important thing to do to effectively teach English?

Brown: In the new national curriculum for English education, fostering communication skills is a main goal for effectively teaching English. In addition to knowledge and comprehension, it is essential for students to think about something and express it by themselves.

Aoi: Communication skills! So, in order to encourage students to think and express their ideas, teachers should use a variety of teaching methods, right?

Brown: Exactly. What do you think English teachers can do to help students to learn proactively, interactively, and deeply?

Aoi: I understand the importance of learning proactively, interactively, and deeply, but I don't know how to enforce these three learning traits during a lesson, Professor.

Brown: I know it's difficult. Since you would like to be an English teacher, it is crucial for you to think about the answer to the question. I'll give you a hint. In the report, "Reiwa no Nihongata Gakkou Kyouiku", the board of education shows that both personalized and collaborative learning are essential methods to fostering the three learning traits.

Aoi: I see. I understand to help students to learn proactively, interactively, and deeply, teachers should use both personalized and collaborative learning methods.

Q1.　According to the professor, what are the answers? Listen and find the answers, then fill in the blanks on the answer sheet.

(1)　What is a main goal of English education in the new national curriculum for English education?

[　It is fostering (　　). 　]

(2)　To foster proactive, interactive, and deep learning, what kind of learning methods should teachers use in the report, "Reiwa no Nihongata Gakkou Kyouiku"?

[　They should use (　　) and (　　) learning.　]

Question 2

Brown: By the way, I conducted a discussion class with Fujisan high school students using the SDGs logo last week. Almost all the students chose No. 14 and talked about plastic bottle problem.

Aoi: Really?

Brown: It's good to know that high school students are aware of environmental problems. High school students can only think about things around them, but there are many other issues in the world that we should discuss.

Aoi: Yes! We should become more aware of what is happening in the world.

Brown: That's the point! I have another discussion class next week with the same students. Can you come with me and tell one of your concerns about the social problems related to SDGs? If you do so, the students' views will widen. We want to encourage diverse opinions.

Aoi: I'd love to go with you! I will email you tonight and let you know what I will talk about.

Brown: I'm really looking forward to reading it. Write one of your concerns about the SDGs that you want them to discuss in class. Please tell them why you think the issue is important and explain more about the topic to the students. Make sure you include the reason and explanation.

(ORIGINAL)

Q2.　If you were Aoi, what would you write to Professor Brown? Choose

35

one topic from below and write what you would like to tell the students.

(SOURCE: https://chubu-sdgs.com)

Q2　To Professor Brown,

　　Thank you for letting me go with you. I'm really looking forward to talking with high school students. I wrote my idea about what I would like to tell them. Could you please read it and check if it is ok for your class?

```
┌─────────────────────────────────────────────────────┐
│ ········································· │
│ ········································· │
│ ········································· │
│ ········································· │
│ ········································· │
│ ········································· │
└─────────────────────────────────────────────────────┘
```

(☆☆☆☆☆◎◎)

【5】 You are planning to teach a debate class as a high school teacher. The students will exchange their opinions in English on the following topic: COVID-19 had a harmful influence on people's careers. You are making a worksheet for the students to organize the information based on the article below. Read the article and choose the most appropriate answers from the choices below.

The negative impact of COVID-19 on careers

For many, COVID-19 has had a negative impact on several aspects of work, including the decline in meaningful day-to-day interactions, market instability, and a potential double-dip recession. According to our research, 75% of respondents reported that they still feel powerless to change things. This hints at a newfound sense of global uncertainty, as professionals are placed under increasing pressure to adapt to their circumstances and foster resilience in order to thrive at work.

Many respondents expressed feeling anxiety over working longer hours during the pandemic, and also suggested that they have struggled to stop work from bleeding into their personal time. Other studies reported finding that during lockdown, employees worked 48.5 minutes longer every day and

37

participated in more meetings. Our research found that across generations, burnout is also an abiding theme, as is a feeling that plans and career growth have stalled.

The pandemic has also landed a substantial body blow to many of the methods traditionally used to exert influence in business. The respondents who remained employed during the pandemic expressed anxiety over how the loss of mobility and valuable networking opportunities, has slowed their cash flow and delayed important plans. With 9 in 10 people living in countries that have had some form of travel restriction, many have found their business opportunities curtailed and spheres of influence shrunk.

Our research also reflects a sense of disconnection from the workplace ─ particularly among baby boomers whose recent isolation has, in some cases, pushed them into early retirement. Other reports also suggest that nearly half of today's newly remote workers worry that their sense of belonging suffers when they're stuck at home.

The positive impact of COVID-19 on careers

At the same time, many people feel that COVID-19 has had a positive impact on their careers. While some respondents felt restricted, more than half (51%) of the total respondents reported having simultaneously found new clarity in this regard. By claiming ownership over their skill development and embracing remote work, respondents have also been able to take more control (38%) of their careers and professional growth.

For many, the 'new normal' has enabled organizations to pinpoint growth opportunities and advance digitization. According to our research, both Generation Z and millennials expressed excitement at how companies have been advancing cutting-edge technologies and fostering digital collaboration. 75% of employees had been able to maintain or improve their productivity while working remotely, which then attracted additional support from their organizations.

Lockdown has also afforded respondents greater control over their time, and the opportunity to reevaluate their priorities. Millennials, Generation X, and baby boomers all expressed that they appreciated the opportunity to reconnect with what's important to them, with parents feeling particularly grateful. Nearly half of newly remote workers say they now spend the time that they once needed for commuting with their families. 86% of workers even expressed satisfaction with their new work-life balance.

Our research suggests that millennials (especially those who aren't parents) have used their time to contemplate a career change or focus on pursuing their studies. Over half of tertiary-educated young people, globally, have already pursued new training courses during the pandemic. A look at the top trending competencies towards the end of 2020 revealed that, broadly relevant skills such as teaching, writing, team building, and project delivery — those detached from any single sector or job title — are increasingly prioritized in leading economies. A combined arsenal of both technical and soft skills can empower today's professionals — not only to prosper in their current positions, but to build sustainable careers that are resilient to the most drastic changes. Ultimately, it appears that we stand on the cusp of a new era of upskilling and personal development. The majority of professionals who are continuing their learning and development have a stronger appetite for learning than they did before COVID-19 appeared. Now is the time to prepare for an uncertain future.

(https://www.getsmarter.com/blog/market-trends/the-great-career-reset-the-positive-and-negative-impact-of-covid-19/ revised)

Worksheet:

Topic of the debate: COVID-19 had a harmful influence on people's careers.	
Affirmative side	Negative side
Data (1)	Data
Argument① Employees worked longer and had more meetings.	Argument③ (3)
Argument② (2)	Argument④

Q1.　In the worksheet, which graph is appropriate for [　(1)　]?

(A) Respondents whose companies were affected by COVID-19.

(B) People who found that their business opportunities were growing.

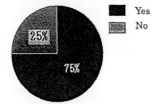

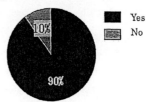

(C)People who worry about their sense of belonging while working from home.

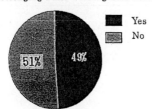

Q2.　In the worksheet, which statement could be [　(2)　] on the Affirmative side?

(A) Employees worked for 48.5 minutes longer a month during lock down.

(B) Burnout did not contribute to a feeling that plans and career growth stalled.

(C) Because of some form of travel restrictions, many people found that their business opportunities and areas of influence lessen.

Q3. In the worksheet, which statement could be [(3)] on the Negative side?

(A) With the 'new normal,' companies cannot pinpoint growth opportunities or advance digitization.

(B) Almost half of newly remote workers say they now spend the time they once needed for commuting with their families.

(C) A sense of disconnection from the workplace has pushed baby boomers into early retirement.

Q4. To counter Argument① on the Affirmative side in the worksheet, which statement could you use?

(A) Work remotely has enabled over half of workers to have more time to spend families.

(B) Three-quarters of employees improved their productivity while working remotely.

(C) More than half of young people who graduated from college globally have pursued new training courses during the pandemic.

Q5. After the debate, you had your students write an essay with their personal experience. The topic of the essay is whether COVID-19 had a harmful influence on their life. Read one of the essays and point out an unnecessary sentence to support his or her opinion from (A)〜(F).

> I don't think that COVID-19 had a harmful influence on my life.
> First, (A)I spent more time with my family. (B)My parents worked remotely and they didn't need to drive for a lone time. (C)However, it was difficult for me to travel and I couldn't meet my grandparents.
> Second, (D)thanks to digitization, I can study more effectively. (E)For example, I can hand in my assignment easily with convenient applications. (F)In addition, I can practice English conversation online to improve my English skills.
> That's why COVID-19 had a positive influence on my life.

(☆☆☆☆◎◎◎)

【6】 You are a first-year high school English teacher. You find an article about inquiry-based language learning. Read the article and choose the most appropriate answers from the choices below.

[1]　Japanese policy makers for English language education "highlight the need for Japanese universities to cultivate students with the necessary English skills to participate in the global market" (Chin Leong, 2017). The development of business-related language skills can be facilitated by inquiry-based learning, which challenges learners to engage with real-world problems. In modern learning environments, teachers can also utilize technology to help students move beyond the confines of their classroom walls into real-world learning environments. Together, inquiry-based learning and technology can aid the development of language skills and facilitate students' transitions from local students to global professionals. This article proposes a design for inquiry-based language learning in the context of intermediate to advanced language programs at Japanese high schools and universities.

[2]　Inquiry-based learning is a process by which students critically engage with resources related to a real-world problem. The process is aimed at

fostering the skills for developing disciplinary knowledge (Laurillard, 2012). In inquiry-based language learning, learners' development of knowledge arises from critical engagement with the language which appears in resources related to real-world problems.

[3]　According to van Joolingen et al., the inquiry process consists of five successive stages: 1) analysis, 2) hypothesis generation, 3) experiment design, 4) data interpretation, and 5) conclusion. Analysis might consist of "breaking down" a language, to better understand it. Hypothesis generation would then involve learners creating questions related to topics of their own choosing. In their experiment design, learners can decide what types of linguistic data to collect and how. Data (i.e., language) interpretation involves comparison (synthesizing data), critical thinking (evaluating data), and demonstration of the language function in focus for assessment. Finally, useful concluding tasks include reflections upon what was learnt and difficult, and how such difficulties may potentially be overcome in the future.

[4]　In an inquiry design, learning resources consist of what is available to students both within and outside the classroom. Rather than resources from experts, teacher-provided resources serve as models of examples. Therefore, teachers must carefully choose several resources and prepare students to select and analyze appropriate options. This approach will equip students to learn independently.

[5]　A hotly-debated, focal principle of inquiring learning design is guidance, or the degree of scaffolding provided. On the one hand, Hmelo-Silver et al. argue that inquiry learning needs to be highly scaffolded and should therefore be strongly guided. On the other hand, Laurillard suggests that the more scaffolding a learning approach entails, the more it reduces learning. Regardless, students still need a high degree of guidance in language functions that have been newly learnt. Therefore, inquiry-based learning requires a high degree of scaffolding.

[6]　The pedagogical design proposed here (see Appendix 1) focusses on

persuasive language. The design is suitable for intermediate to advanced learners of English at senior high school and university levels. The unit consists of ten core lessons, followed by student presentations, and then a final reflection lesson. Moreover, the unit is divided into six task stages, which are based on the inquiry process stages proposed by van Joolingen et al., outlined above in the section on Inquiry-Based Learning Design Philosophy. In Task Stage 1, students nominate and discuss topics within the domain of current social issues in the media. In Task Stage 2, persuasive language concepts are introduced. In Task Stage 3, students analyze news media text related to the selected topic and exchange their opinions in class. Task Stage 4 has students work in pairs to find additional topic-related resources suitable for supporting their own viewpoints on the topic. In Task Stage 5, students present their own TED Talks-styled presentations, using persuasive language tools with the aid of visual resources. All the students have a chance to give a presentation in front of other students. For the sixth and final task stage, students contribute to a class blog to reflect on what they learnt throughout each stage of the inquiry process.

[7] This approach works outside of the confines of the traditional classroom construct. Students can present not only to the class but also to the wider school community and upload their videos on YouTube. This leads to students receiving feedback from a real-world audience beyond their classroom.

[8] Finally, students are tasked with contributing to a class blog using Kialo(https://www.kialo.com/) to reflect upon what they have learnt in the inquiry process. This activity garners peer feedback for the benefit of and application to future learning. The teacher can summarize student contributions using Voyant Tools (https://voyant-tools.org/), to quickly present student ideas to the class and help students remember what they have learnt more effectively than through more conventional means. The reflection process is useful for students to apply what they have learnt to future inquiry

units and to language-related challenges. Feedback is also useful for making adjustments to the pedagogical design and improving the approach to future inquiry-based study.

(SOURCE: Andrew Pitman (2022). Preparing Local Students for the Global Workplace Through Inquiry-Based Language Learning. JALT Publications The Language Teacher - Issue 46.3; May 2022. REVISED)

Appendix 1

Model Inquiry-Based Language Learning Pedagogical Design
(Based on Laurillard, 2012)

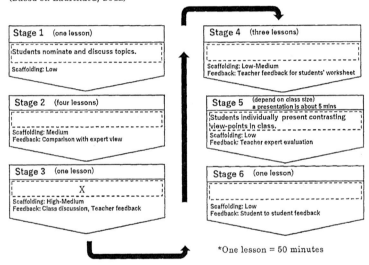

Q1. According to paragraph [1] and [2], what is the benefit of inquiry-based language learning?

(A) Students can improve their language skills without taking classes.

(B) Students can get business experience directly related to their future jobs.

(C) Students can deepen their knowledge of global issues for their future careers.

(D) Students can gain higher computer skills for the global marketplace in the future.

Q2. According to paragraph [3] and [4], which of the following is NOT the characteristic of inquiry-based language learning?

(A) Data is analyzed in various ways to prove if the hypothesis is correct.

(B) Final reflection leads to knowing how to overcome the difficulties faced on learning.

(C) Learning is conducted by following materials that were carefully selected by experts.

(D) Learning will greatly help students develop their independent learning skills.

Q3. According to paragraph [5], which of the following best describes the author's opinion to the degree of scaffolding provided in inquiry-based learning?

(A) As Hmelo-Silver et al. suggested, greater guidance should be given to students.

(B) As Hmelo-Silver et al. suggested, less guidance should be given to students.

(C) As Laurillard suggested, greater guidance should be given to students.

(D) As Laurillard suggested, less guidance should be given to students.

Q4. Which of the following best fits ⌈　X　⌋ in Stage 3 in Appendix 1?

(A) Students reflect on their learning.

(B) Teacher introduces language function.

(C) Students do further research for resources to support their ideas.

(D) Students compare and evaluate the texts through discussion in class.

Q5. If you adopt the author's model in your class, which of the following are true? Choose two options.

> Your class
>
> Grade: 2nd grade   Class size: 35 students
>
> English level: intermediate   Length of lesson: 50 minutes

(A) Since this model requires a high level of English proficiency, you must first improve your students' English language skills.

(B) You need to spend more than thirteen lessons including core lessons, presentation and reflection in order to introduce this model in your class.

(C) You need to support your students in analyzing the content of the articles at Task Stage 3.

(D) At any task stage, you must have time for feedback in class in order to wrap up what students have learned.

(☆☆☆☆☆○○)

解答・解説

【中学校】

【1】 1 カ   2 コ   3 キ   4 ス   5 サ   6 タ   7 オ
8 セ   9 ア   10 ウ

〈解説〉外国語科の目標は,「簡単な情報や考えなどを理解したり表現したり伝え合ったりするコミュニケーションを図る資質・能力を育成すること」であることを,しっかり理解しておこう。この資質・能力を育成するために,(1)「知識及び技能」,(2)「思考力,判断力,表現力等」,(3)「学びに向かう力,人間性等」の3つの柱が設けられている。学習指導要領を参照し,これらの3つの柱の内容を精読しておくこと。また,英語の指導計画の作成と内容の取扱いについては,指導計画に当たっての留意事項について出題されている。生徒の主体的・対話的で深い学びの実現を目指した授業改善を進めること,外国語科の特質

に応じて効果的な学習が展開できるように配慮すべき内容が示されて
いる。選択肢の数が多く，やや紛らわしいものも含まれているため，
正確に暗記しておくことが求められる。なお，「外国語科」の目標及
び「英語」の目標を，混同せずに覚えておきたい。

【２】(解答例)　The phrase *"Shoshin ni kaeru"* basically means "Going back
to basics". For example, when we start learning a new language, we feel
excited and motivated. However, as we find it difficult, we tend to give up
learning. *"Shoshin ni kaeru"* comes to mind when we want to call attention
to regain our fresh feeling we used to have at the start of learning. This phrase
can be used not only for ourselves but also for others. We can encourage
people to restart and keep focused on something again with this phrase. (87
words)

〈解説〉「初心に帰る」とは「原点に戻る」ことであると説明している。
例えば新しい語学の学習を始めるときは熱意や意欲があるが，難しい
と学習をあきらめてしまいがちである。このフレーズはそんなときに，
学び始めの頃の気持ちを取り戻し再スタートするよう促すときに使う
と説明している。

【３】(解答例)　To improve your speaking ability, you have to practice
listening and reading at the same time. Because, listening is the base of
speaking, and reading aloud helps build confidence in speaking. First, listen to
native speakers' English as much as possible. TV shows, your favourite
movies, dramas should be available. Second, Read English aloud every day.
Any topics you like in the magazines, newspapers will work. Third, try role
playing with your class mates to introduce yourself. Be sure to use grammar,
vocabularies, phrases you have learned in class. Finally, do not be afraid of
making mistakes when speaking. Creating relaxed atmosphere is essential to
have an enjoyable conversation. (110 words)

〈解説〉解答例では，スピーキング能力を向上させるには，同時にリスニ

ングと音読の練習が必要であると述べている。リスニングはスピーキングの基礎であり，音読はスピーキングへの自信につながるからである。これらのほか，学校で習ったことを使ってクラスメートとのロールプレイングを勧めている。また，会話の際は失敗を恐れずリラックスした雰囲気で臨むことをアドバイスしている。

【4】1 ① オ ⑤ イ 2 ② ウ ③ イ ④ ア

3 (1) Because they can't imagine her climbing a mountain.

(2) When she was 13, she got inspired to climb Mount Everest.

(3) She hopes to find a companion who is definitely committed, has a dream of their own, is excited about life and basically has the same goal as her, which is to help others reach their full potential. 4 ① interact

② relationships ③ bond 5 エ

〈解説〉1 ① 空所の後で「彼女は18歳の時に標高8,163メートルのマナスルに登った最も若い女性となった」「彼女は19歳の時にエベレストに登った最も若い日本人になった」という最年少記録が述べられていることよりオが適切。 ⑤ 空所の後で「誰もいない家でその後彼女は何日も泣き続けた」とあり精神的に弱くなっていたことが読み取れ，イが適切である。The accidentは前の段落で述べられている250メートルの高さを頭から落ちてしまった出来事を指す。 2 ② 直後のExplorers Grand Slam「探検家グランドスラム」を修飾する空所に当てはまるのはウのgrueling「辛い，過酷な」である。 ③ 空所の直前にOur existence is so tiny「我々の存在はとてもちっぽけなものである」とあり all these daily issues don't (③)「これらの日常の問題の全ては大したことではない」といった内容にすることで意味がつながる。よってイのmean a thingが適切である。否定語＋mean a thingで「少しも意味がない」の意。 ④ 空所直後のgiving her a much needed sense of control「とても必要とされている，物事をコントロールしている感覚を彼女に与えた」とあり，空所は同様の意味であるアのgrounded「地に足のついた」が適切。 3 (1) 設問の答えは第4段落2文目に書か

49

れている。設問文はWhyが使われているため理由を表すBecauseで書き始める。　(2)　設問の答えは第8段落2文目に書かれている。設問文はWhenが使われているため，答えとしてWhen she was 13, と時期を明確に示す。　(3)　設問の答えは最終段落3文目に書かれている。設問文で用いられている疑問文を平叙文にしたShe hopes to find a companion who〜と書き出し，who以下は本文の表現をそのまま用いればよい。 4　①　空所を含む文については第5段落4文目で言及されている。空所に入るのは動詞であり，本文のthere was very little interactionはcould hardly interactと言い換えられる。　②　空所を含む文については第5段落1文目で言及されている。as a way to connect with others「他人とつながる手段として」はTo build relationships with others「他人と関係を築くために」と言い換えられる。　③　空所を含む文については第6段落最終文で言及されており，本文のthere was a human bondがそのまま解答となる。　5　Minamiyaさんのインタビューでは，自分の潜在能力を信じて，恐れず自分のしたいことに挑戦してみるよう応援メッセージを彼女が送っていることが読み取れる。このメッセージとして適切な選択肢はエ「自分自身に制限を設けるな」となる。

【5】1　①　ア　　②　エ　　2　ア　　3　(1)　Students are likely to perform at a lower level in cases where assessments are fully digital but are rarely used during the learning process.　　(2)　By providing multiple ways for learners.　　(3)　(解答例)　・Display lesson notes on an interactive whiteboard.　・Answering multiple-choice questions in an online platform.　・Typing documents that are saved to the cloud.　・Reading a textbook on a mobile device.　・Looking up facts online.　から1つ 4　①　have

②　traditional teaching　　③　encourage

〈解説〉1　①　空所の後のtossed around with little precision「ほとんど精度のない検討がされる」と同じ意味の内容が空所＋somewhat randomlyとなることが読み取れる。よってアのspread outが適切。being spread out somewhat randomly「いくぶんランダムに広がる」といった意味になる。　②　studentsがa phonics-based computer program「フォニックス(音声学)をベースにしたコンピュータプログラム」に触れるという内容になると考えられるので，エのexposure「さらされること」が適切。　2　空所を含む第8段落の" right blend" of direct instruction and technology-accelerated learningという語句に着目する。direct instruction「直接的な指導」は教師による指導を指すため，教師と技術の正しい融合という意味のアが適切と判断できる。　3　(1)　設問の答えは第2段落最終文に書かれている。設問文はWhenが使われているが，本文のIn cases where〜がそのまま解答として用いることができるため，本文の表現をそのまま用いればよい。　(2)　設問の答えは第6段落1文目に書かれている。設問文はHowの疑問文であるため，手段を表すByを用いて本文の表現By providing multiple ways for learners.とする。　(3)　設問の答えは最終段落に書かれている。例を挙げるよう設問で求められており，該当箇所は冒頭から列挙されている5つのうち1つを記述すればよい。　4　①　空所を含む文については第3段落のSimply adding〜で言及されている。「考えなしにテクノロジーを導入しても有害な効果をもたらす」という意味であり，空所にはeffectの動詞となるhaveが適切。　②　設問2や第8段落で見てきたように，教師による指導とテクノロジーの融合が大きな効果をもたらす。教師による指導はいろいろな表現が考えられるが解答例ではtraditional teachingとしている。　③　冒頭で述べられたALTの発言Students will be active learners by using technology on their own.への反論である。Bは，テクノロジーと併せて，教師は生徒がアクティブ・ラーナーになるように生徒の学びを奨励することができると考えている。よって，encourageが適切である。

【高等学校】

【1】Q1　(A)　　Q2　(B)　　Q3　(A)　　Q4　(C)　　Q5　(B)
　Q6　(B)　　Q7　(A)　　Q8　(C)
〈解説〉Q1　Johnの最後の発話で，150ドルの父へのプレゼントは20％割

引になり，半分は払うと言っているので，60ドル払うつもりであることが読み取れる。　Q2　Taroの3回目の発話で「自動車やトラックが通れるつり橋」と言っているため，(B)が不適切である。　Q3　Annaの3回目の発話I cannot do without my smartphone.より，(A)が当てはまると判断できる。　Q4　Lucyの最後の発話で，上司にまず報告をしようとAlexにアドバイスをし，報告に一緒についてきてくれることが読み取れるため，(B)ではなく(C)が適切。　Q5　Sophieの1回目の発話より，最初の論文のドラフトの締切が10月17日であることがわかる。また，2回目の発話より，あと1週間あるということから，現在は10月10日であることがわかる。さらに，2回目の発話で次の締切が10月31日であることから，設問の解答は3週間となる。　Q6　父親の2回目の発話で，スマートフォンの使い方のルールを娘と一緒に話し合うと言っているため，(B)が適切。　Q7　母の2回目の発話より，駅への集合時間が8：50で，息子の2回目の発話より，出発がその10分後の9：00というのが本来のスケジュールであるとわかる。そして息子の最後の発話で，集合時間が20分遅れの9：10になり，出発がさらにその10分後の9：20になったと読み取れる。　Q8　Sarahの4回目の発話で，自分のためにお金を使う人より，他者のためにお金を使った人の方が幸福度が高いと述べられており，(C)が適切と読み取れる。

【２】[Lecture A]　Q1　(1)　(D)　　(2)　(C)　　(3)　(A)　　(4)　(B)
Q2　B　　[Lecture B]　Q1　(1)　C　　(2)　B　　(3)　C　　(4)　A
Q2　A
〈解説〉[Lecture A]　Q1　(1)　playfulnessの記述は第3段落1文目にあり，(D)が当てはまる。　(2)　connectionの記述は第4段落にあり，他者との関わりを意味するため，(C)が当てはまる。　(3)　flowの記述は第5段落1文目にあり，時間を忘れて物事に熱中することを意味するため，(A)が当てはまる。　(4)　playfulness, connection, flowの3つがそろった状態の記述は第6段落にあり，(B)が当てはまる。　Q2　最終段落5文目で，携帯電話を手の届かないところに遠ざけるのを勧めるという記

述がある。よって，これと反対のことを述べている(B)が正解となる。
[Lecture B]　Q1　1　第1段落2文目でListeningはコミュニケーションの約60％を占めると述べられており，(C)が当てはまる。　2　第1段落2文目で，空所に入るのは25％であることがわかり(B)が入る。
3　第2・3段落で，世界は音にあふれており人は他者の言うことを聞かなくなり，また我慢ができなくなっていると述べられている。よって(C)が当てはまると判断できる。　4　最終段落で，お互いに相手の話を聞かなくなる時の悪い結末が述べられており，その解決策としては「能動的に話を聞くこと」であると判断できる。　Q2　本文を通して，意識して人の話を聞くことの重要性が述べられており，(A)が適切と判断できる。

【3】Q1　(C)　　Q2　(C)　　Q3　(B)　　Q4　(A)　　Q5　(B)
〈解説〉Q1　first studyについて述べられているのは第3段落2・3文目で，英語学習の際の学習戦略を調べているため(C)が適切。　Q2　第4段落2文目で，学習戦略の上位2つは，ネイティブの英語話者と話すことだと述べられている。選択肢よりそれに当てはまるのは(C)であると判断できる。　Q3　第9段落よりケンタ，クミコ，ミカの3人は，文法にあまり重きを置かない学習をしていることが読み取れる。　Q4　第10段落最終文で，英語で自分の意見や考えを話したことを思い出すと答えた生徒は4分の1(＝25％)以下であったと述べられている。これに一致するグラフは(A)となる。　Q5　最終段落で，生徒が学習で成功するために必要としていることに注意を払うのが，英語教師の仕事であると述べられており，これに当てはまるのは(B)となる。

【4】Q1　(1)　It is fostering communication skills (in English).
(2)　They should use (personalized) and (collaborative) learning.
Q2　(To Professor Brown, Thank you for letting me go with you. I'm really looking forward to talking with high school students. I wrote my idea about what I would like to tell them. Could you please read it and check if it is ok

for your class?) I am concerned about gender equality, SDGs No.5. I often hear news about the gaps between men and women. For example, the percentage females working in management positions and in politics, in Japan is very low compared to other countries. Actually, all the politicians in my city are men. Male politicians might not consider the needs of pregnant women or mothers with small children. I chose to discuss this issue with you because it is directly connected to your future. About half of you are female. How would you feel if your bosses were all men when you start at a company? Do you think you could be a boss someday? I don't think so. I know some women who have wonderful leadership. Whether someone will be a good leader is not judged by gender. I strongly believe we should not face gender discrimination. (144 words)

〈解説〉Q1　(1)　ブラウン教授の最初の発話で，fostering communication skills is a main goal for effectively teaching Englishと述べられている。(2)　ブラウン教授の最後の発話で，both personalized and collaborative learning are essential methods to fostering the three learning traitsと述べられている。　Q2　解答例ではNo.5のgender equalityを選び，日本では他国に比べて女性の管理職の割合が低いことや，政治家は男性ばかりであることに言及している。性差別をなくすことが，半数が女性である目の前の生徒たちの将来に直結する議論すべき問題であり，性差別はあってはならないことを説明している。

【5】Q1　(C)　　Q2　(C)　　Q3　(B)　　Q4　(B)　　Q5　(C)

〈解説〉Q1　COVID-19時代の悪影響を肯定する面として，第4段落では，半数近くの人は，リモートワークで家に閉じこもっていることから会社への帰属意識を心配していると述べられている。このことを示すグラフは(C)が適切と判断できる。　Q2　第3段落最終文で，移動の制限の影響として，ビジネスの機会や勢力圏の縮小が述べられており，(C)が適切と判断できる。　Q3　第7段落3文目で，リモートワークで削減した通勤時間を家族との時間に費やすことができる，という良い面が

述べられており，(B)が適切と判断できる。　Q4　第6段落最終文で，75％(＝4分の3)の人はデジタル化が進んだことでリモートワークでも生産性が落ちることはなかった，という良い面が述べられており，この内容がArgument①の反論として適切である。　Q5　選択肢の中で，(C)のみがCOVID-19による悪影響を述べており，エッセイ全体の趣旨から外れるため，これが不適切と判断できる。

【6】Q1　(C)　　Q2　(C)　　Q3　(A)　　Q4　(D)　　Q5　(B), (C)
〈解説〉Q1　inquiry based-learningの利点としては，第1段落4文目のfacilitate students' transitions from local students to global professionals「地元の生徒からグローバルな専門家への生徒の移行を促進する」や，第2段落3文目のlearners' development of knowledge arises from critical engagement with the language which appears in resources related to real-world problems「学習者の知識の発展は，現実世界の問題に関連するリソースに登場する言語への批判的な取り組みから生まれる」より，(C)が適切と判断できる。　Q2　第4段落2文目で「専門家からのリソースよりもむしろ教師が提供するリソースのほうが事例モデルとして役に立つ」と述べていることから，専門家からの情報は有効ではないということが読み取れる。よって「専門家が選んだ教材で学習を行う」という内容の(C)は不適切だと判断できる。　Q3　第5段落2文目でHmelo-Silver et al. は，inquiry learningは支援される必要が大いにあり，しっかり導入することを主張している。一方で3文目では，Laurillardはinquiry learningをしっかり支援すればするほど学習が減少する，と別の観点を述べている。さらに，4文目では，どちらにせよ生徒は新しく学ぶことに対して大きな指導が必要であると述べられている。以上を踏まえると，2文目と4文目の内容を反映したAが最も適切だと判断できる。　Q4　第6段落半ばのTask Stage 3の記述「選択した話題に関係するニュースメディアの文章を分析して，授業内で意見を交換する」に着目する。この内容に合致するのは(D)となる。　Q5　本問では，不適切な選択肢を見つけて消去するほうが容易である。(A)は，設問に

おけるYour classのEnglish levelがintermediateという条件に対し，this model requires a high level of English proficiencyが矛盾するため不適切である。また，(D)はAt any task stage, you must have time for feedback in classとあるが，Appendix 1のStage 1にはFeedbackの項目がないため，不適切である。残った(B)や(C)に，本文の内容と一致しない点は見当たらないため，この2つを正解と判断する。

2023年度　実施問題

【中学校】

【1】次の文は,「中学校学習指導要領(平成29年3月告示)第2章　第9節　外国語　第2　各言語の目標及び内容等」の記述である。【　】に当てはまる語句として適切なものを以下の語群から選びなさい。また,　□□□□のA,Bに入る育成を目指す資質,能力を書きなさい。

⌐ A ⌐

(1)　英語の特徴やきまりに関する事項

　　実際に英語を用いた【　1　】を通して,小学校学習指導要領第2章第10節外国語第2の2の(1)及び次に示す言語材料のうち,1に示す五つの領域別の目標を達成するのにふさわしいものについて理解するとともに,言語材料と,【　1　】とを効果的に関連付け,【　2　】コミュニケーションにおいて活用できる【　3　】を身に付けることができるよう指導する。

⌐ B ⌐

(2)　情報を【　4　】ながら考えなどを形成し,英語で表現したり,伝え合ったりすることに関する事項

　　具体的な【　5　】等を設定し,コミュニケーションを行う目的や場面,状況などに応じて,情報を【　4　】ながら考えなどを形成し,これらを【　6　】に表現することを通して,次の事項を身に付けることができるよう指導する。

＜語群＞

ア　配慮し　　イ　目標　　ウ　表現力　　エ　自分の意見
オ　積極的　　カ　課題　　キ　自分の思い　ク　論理的
ケ　態度　　　コ　精選し　サ　実際の　　シ　理論的
ス　整理し　　セ　主体的　ソ　言語活動　タ　技能

チ　実践的な　　ツ　積極性　　テ　知識

(☆☆☆○○○)

【２】あなたは，"What have you learned from a mistake or a failure?" という
テーマで，英字新聞のReaders' Columnに投稿しようと考えている。
　このテーマについて，あなたの具体的な経験の内容と，そこから学
んだことを80語以上の英語(?,."" などの記号は語数に含まない)で書
きなさい。

(☆☆☆☆○○)

【３】次のメッセージが伝えていることを教育に置き換えて考えるとどう
いうことか，あなたが考えたことを，そう考えた理由を含めて，80語
以上の英語(?,."" などの記号は語数に含まない)で書きなさい。

> Give a man a fish and you feed him for a day; teach a man to fish and
> you feed him for a lifetime.
>
> (old proverb)

(☆☆☆☆○○○)

【４】次の英文Aは，「世界の偉人」についてスピーチを考える際に，興
味をもって読んだ文章である。また，英文Bは，英文Aに登場する
Mr.Yasinが，インタビュー動画で話している内容である。英文A,
B(以下，「本文」)を読み，以下の問いに答えなさい。
【英文A】

Most parents agree that kids grow up far too quickly. And they grow out of
their clothes even quicker. But 3-year-old Momo is wearing clothes that
(　①　).
Petit Pli is an origami-inspired range of outerwear for kids. Designed by
Royal College of Art graduate Ryan Mario Yasin, the pleated design expands
in multiple directions, and also contracts back to its original size.

"It's windproof, waterproof, with a hydrophobic coating. And the best part is that it's designed for continuous fit adjustment, so it'll never be a little bit too short or small or a little bit too long. It's always changing its shape and morphing with the child even in motion," said Mr. Yasin, Creator of Petit Pli.

Kids like Momo are always (②), and need clothing that can keep up. "As the child is running around, the pleats are deforming in both directions either folding together or expanding, and moving in synchrony with the child. And that way, it's the most comfortable jacket in motion," he said.

Petit Pli - French for "little pleat" - has been designed for children aged from four months to three years. The patent-pending design has been (③) tested to prove the pleats won't fall out with use. They're also machine washable.

Mr. Yasin says Petit Pli could reduce waste in the clothing industry since a single garment will last much longer.

He's now working on different sizes and designs, and looking for partners to help bring Petit Pli to market. While the futuristic-looking designs might raise a few eyebrows, Mr. Yasin hopes that eventually... they'll grow on you.

　　　(出典：The Japan Times / The STRAITS TIMES, July 26, 2017　一部改)

【英文B】

Narrator: London based-up start-up Petit Pli has developed sustainable children's clothing to fit babies through to toddlers. The clothes boast an innovate pleat system that expands in multiple directions. The material can also contract back to its original size ready to be handed down to younger siblings.

Mr. Yasin: So one of the main inspirations behind this was my background as an aeronautical engineer where I specialized in deployable structures for nanosatellites. This involved a lot of research into origami structures and folds and stowing away as much materials as possible into a small gap and then having that deploy out in space and that has really filtered down into this design.

Narrator: A child of nine months can continue wearing the same item of clothing until the age of four going through seven distinct sizes. It not only helps mom and dad save money, but it also reduces the environmental impact of the fashion industry.

Mr. Yasin: Petit Pli exists because the fashion industry is the world's second largest polluter and we already know what one of the resolutions is and that is to extend the life and the use of clothes and that's the best way we can reach our Carbon, Water and Waste Mission targets by 2030. Petit Pli has done this by focusing on a very niche user group which is children and designing clothes from the ground up with them.

（出典：Reuters, 2021, 一部改）

1　本文の内容に合うように，①に入る最も適する英語を次のア～ウより一つ選び，記号で答えなさい。

　　ア　"help" her while sleeping

　　イ　"change" its color hy her body temperature

　　ウ　"grow" as she does

2　本文の内容に合うように，②，③に入る最も適する英語を次のア～エより一つずつ選び，記号で答えなさい。

　　　②　ア　in fashion　　　イ　on the move　　　ウ　in need

　　　　　エ　at the end

　　　③　ア　rigorously　　　イ　inexactly　　　ウ　slightly

　　　　　エ　sparingly

3　なぜ，Petit Pliは "it's the most comfortable jacket in motion" であると述べられているか。Petit Pliの特徴を踏まえた理由を英語で抜き出しなさい。

4　下線部の内容について，スピーチの中で分かりやすく伝えようと考えている。本文の内容に最も適する英語を次のア～ウより一つ選び，記号で答えなさい。

　　ア　At first people may be surprised at the style of Petit Pli because they have never seen clothes like this before. However, they will start to like

60

it little by little.

イ　People will realize that Petit Pli is really cool and useful, and it'll become popular very soon.

ウ　Petit Pli's design will be changed in the future because the appearance of the clothing is a little bit weird. More people will come to love it as a result.

5　本文の内容に合うように，次の質問に4語以上の英語で答えなさい。

(1)　Who can use Petit Pli?

(2)　What kind of background influenced Mr. Yasin to create Petit Pli's clothes?

6　次の英文は，実際のスピーチの内容の一部である。あなたならどのように伝えるか，スピーチ内の空欄に英文を補いなさい。ただし，本文の内容を含め，スピーチの流れに沿うよう，2〜4文程度の英文とする。

I'm interested in new designs for clothing and ways of saving our environment. When I read the articles about Mr. Yasin, his new ideas caught my eye. What I was impressed with the most is that he's taken advantage of his ideas about clothing to save the environment. His new idea might be a flagship to the future field of fashion.

I'll tell you why his idea has been contributing to the future.

I was impressed that he tried to save the environment like this.

・・・・

(☆☆☆☆○○○)

61

【5】次の英文は，英語教員Aさんが，英語の授業づくりについて学ぶた
めに，ALTから借りて読んだ本の一部である。英文(以下，「本文」と
いう。)を読み，以下の問いに答えなさい。

'Autonomy' is currently a buzzword in educational psychology － it is
【　①　】 － and during the past decade several books and articles have been
published on its significance in the L2 (a foreign/second language) field as
well (see Benson 2001, for a recent review). Allowing a touch of cynicism, I
would say that part of the popularity of the concept amongst researchers is
due to the fact that educational organisations in general have been rather
resistant to the kind of changes that scholars would have liked to see
implemented, and research has therefore increasingly turned to analysing how
to prepare learners to succeed in spite of the education they receive. The other
side of the coin is, of course, that the theoretical arguments in favour of
learner autonomy are convincing and that there is some evidence that learners
who are able to learn independently may 【　②　】 greater proficiency.

The relevance of autonomy to motivation in psychology has been best
highlighted by the influential 'self-determination theory', according to which
the freedom to choose and to have choices, rather than being forced or
coerced to behave according to someone else's desire, is a prerequisite to
motivation. Autonomy is also related to group dynamics in that the group's
internal development and growing maturity go hand in hand with the
members taking on increasing responsibility and control over their own
functioning. From the point of group dynamics, involved students are
increasingly autonomous students.

What are the main ingredients of an autonomy-supporting teaching
practice? Without being comprehensive, I have found the following points
crucial:

Increased learner involvement in organising the learning process:

The key issue in increasing learner involvement is to share responsibility
with the learners about their learning process. They need to feel that they are

— at least partly — 【 ③ 】 . You can do a number of things to achieve this:

Allow learners choices about as many aspects of the learning process as possible, for example about activities, teaching materials, topics, assignments, due dates, the format and the pace of their learning, the arrangement of the furniture, or the peers they want to work with. Choice is the essence of responsibility as it permits learners to see that they are in charge of the learning experience. The difficult thing about such choices from our perspective is, however, that in order to make students feel that they are really in control, these choices need to be genuine, 【 ④ 】 the fact that students may make the wrong decision. The only way to prevent this is to 'nurture' our students' ability to make choices by gradually expanding their opportunities for real decisions, first asking them to choose between given options from a menu, then to make modifications and changes, and finally to select goals and procedures completely on their own.

Encourage student contributions and peer teaching. In my experience learners are very resourceful about finding ways to convey new material to their peers, if only to show that they can do a better job than the teacher! Some of my best seminar classes at university level have been the ones where I assigned complete sets of material to small student teams (usually a pair of students) and left it to their own devices how they went about teaching it to the others.

Encourage project work. When students are given complete projects to carry out, they will function in an autonomous way by definition: the teacher is 【 ⑤ 】 and students are required to organise themselves, to decide on the most appropriate course of action to achieve the goal, and to devise the way in which they report their findings back to the class.

When appropriate, allow learners to use self-assessment procedures (cf. Ekbatani and Pierson 2000). Self-assessment raises the learners' awareness about the mistakes and successes of their own learning, and gives them a concrete sense of participation in the learning process. I realise, of course, that in most school contexts self-assessment may not be sufficient and students are also to be assessed by you, the teacher ― in such cases they may perhaps be involved in deciding when and how to be evaluated.

(出典：Motivational Strategies in the Language Classroom, Zoltán Dörnyei, 2012　一部改)

1　本文の内容に合うように，【　①　】【　③　】【　⑤　】に入る最も適する英語を次のア～エより一つずつ選び，記号で答えなさい。

　　ア　not part of the immediate communication network
　　イ　also discussed under the label of 'self-regulation'
　　ウ　often limited in number and variety
　　エ　in control of what is happening to them

2　本文の内容に合うように，【　②　】【　④　】に入る最も適する英語を次のア～エより一つずつ選び，記号で答えなさい。

　②　ア　deny　　　　　　イ　lessen　　　　　ウ　ease
　　　エ　gain
　④　ア　appealing for　　イ　assisting for　　ウ　allowing for
　　　エ　arranging for

3　本文の内容に合うように，次の質問に6語以上の英語で答えなさい。

　(1)　Based on the idea of the self-determination, what do the learners need for their motivation?
　(2)　Why is choice the essence of responsibility?
　(3)　How do teachers gradually expand their students' opportunities for real decisions?

4　本文の内容に最も適する英語を次のア～エより一つ選び，記号で答えなさい。

　ア　The author of this book believes learners can't find ways to tell new material to their peers.
　イ　No one has argued the importance of autonomy around the L2 field.
　ウ　Through the group's internal development, learners' maturity will be

grown, and learners will turn to be independent.

 エ Learner's motivation is dependent on someone's instructions.

5 本文を読んだ英語教員Aさんが, ALTに本を返却しながら, 授業づくりについて, 述べています。本文の内容に合うように(①)(②)に適する英語を書きなさい。

A : Thank you for lending me this book.

ALT : Any time. How was it?

A : It was both interesting and informative. I found some important points about foreign language education when reading it. I took useful cues about lessons.

ALT : Could you tell me about them?

A : I learned it is important for teachers to share responsibility with learners to (①) learner involvement. Also I realized that in order to make learners feel that they are really in control, choices should be (②).

ALT : I'm glad to be of your help.

(☆☆☆☆◎◎◎)

【高等学校】

【1】Listen to the dialogues and questions. Choose the most appropriate answer from the three choices, (A), (B), and (C). You will hear the dialogues and questions only once.

Dialogue 1 (M: Mary, T: Tom)

M: Tom, I can't wait for tomorrow's concert!

T: Yeah, me, neither! I'm planning to take the express train to go to the concert hall, which leaves at a quarter to ten. Why don't you come with me?

M: I think the concert will start at 11:00. Even the local train will bring us in time.

T: Let me check the train schedule on the Internet..., is that the one which leaves 17 minutes after the express train?

M: That's right.

T: Then, let's take that train.

Q1. At what time are they going to take a train?

 (A)   (B)   (C)

Dialogue 2　(S: Ms. Sato, T: Tom)

T: Ms. Sato, I seem to have lost my bike key. What should I do?

S: Tom, do you remember where you put it?

T: No. Anyway, I have an appointment with the dentist after school. I can't be late!

S: OK, calm down. Where did you put the key?

T: I think... I put it in the side pocket of my bag, but I couldn't find it.

S: How about in your locker? Some students put their keys in their lockers.

T: There is no way I did that.

S: Check again!

T: Oh... there it is!

Q2.　Where did Tom find his key?

 (A)　In his bag.

 (B)　In his locker.

 (C)　He couldn't find it.

Dialogue 3　(E: Emily, A: Alex)

A: Emily, tell me your idea about the performance. What should our class do to win first prize at the school festival this year?

E: What do you say to singing in chorus as we did last year, Alex?

A: Yeah, that would be great, but I want to try something new!

E: Well, a drama would be fun! I want to show a beautiful costume on the stage.

A: I heard some other classes are planning dramas.

E: Then, how about playing musical instruments? Playing the recorder will be good for a class performance!

A: That's new to me. I haven't seen any classes doing that before.

Q3.　What are they going to do for their class performance?

   (A)　They will deliver a musical performance.

   (B)　They will deliver a short drama.

   (C)　They will deliver a fashion show.

Dialogue 4　(N: Naomi, K: Ken)

K: I didn't know our school color is blue! Naomi, did you know that?

N: Yes, I think each color has its own meaning. Ken, what kind of meaning does blue imply?

K: I have no idea, but it's often said that yellow and orange make us feel happy or excited.

N: Yeah, that's right. Then, what about "blue"?

K: I can say that blue makes us feel "peaceful" and "dependable" .

N: I agree.

K: It is hardly surprising that people view a certain color the same way.

Q4.　What can we learn from their conversation?

   (A)　Different people have different impressions of a certain color.

   (B)　A certain color has a great impact on people's behaviors.

   (C)　People have similar impressions of a certain color.

Dialogue 5　(B: Ben, R: Rachel)

B: Rachel, do you want to go out for dinner or order something to be delivered through the Internet?

R: Well, if we go out, I'd rather go to the new ramen shop near the station.

B: I'm also interested in that shop. A great number of people are always queuing outside.

R: The ramen must be very delicious, but Ben, I am exhausted today. So, I'd rather stay in today.

B: If you say so.

Q5.　What are they most likely to do next?

  (A)　Choose something online for dinner at home.

  (B)　Serve the ramen to many people outside.

  (C)　Go to the newly opened restaurant.

Dialogue 6　(S: Simon, M: Mika)

S: Look, this graph shows how many books students in this school borrowed from the school library.

M: I found it interesting that the number is different in each category.

S: Mika, I want you to look at the difference between this year and the previous year.

M: OK, Simon, what do you want to say with this graph?

S: I found that the number in each category seems to be influenced by what happened in the year. For example, because of the Olympics in 2021, students interested in Japanese Olympians increased.

M: You are right. It appeared to draw students' attention to the books about the real life of Japanese Olympians.

S: I thought Sci-fi books would gain more popularity because the people who are not trained as astronauts travel in space, but it is not as much as I expected.

Q6.　Which graph are they looking at?

(A)

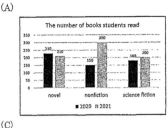

(B)

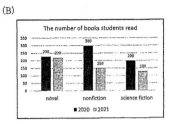

(C)

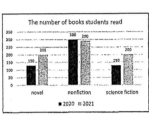

Dialogue 7   (S: Ms. Suzuki, H: Hiroshi)

H: Ms. Suzuki, we have one more thing that is regretful. Quite a few dogs are destroyed in Japan.

S: Yeah, Hiroshi, that's very sad. There is a growing concern about animal rights these days. I heard that a law that protects animal rights will be legislated soon.

H: That's good news, but I think pet owners should also take a responsibility for their action.

Q7.   What is Ms. Suzuki likely to say after this?

    (A)   It is not a serious problem that only a few dogs are killed in Japan.

    (B)   It will take a long time for animals to be protected by the law on animal rights.

    (C)   People who want to have a pet should consider whether they can take care of it.

Dialogue 8   (E: Emi, M: Masao)

E: Masao, I'm thinking about a farewell gift for George.

M: He is going back to the United States next week, right?

E: Yes, a fountain pen would be nice. He likes writing stories.

M: Sounds nice. But that might be beyond the budget.

E: Then, how about a mug which has a picture of us on it because I want him to cherish memories in this school.

M: That's a great idea, but it might be broken on his way back to the United States.

E: You can say that again.

Q8.　At this point, what do they agree about?

   (A)　To give a fountain pen as a gift for their classmate.

   (B)　To make a mug with a picture of students as a token of friendship.

   (C)　To decide not to give a fragile gift to their classmate.

(☆☆☆☆◎◎◎◎)

【2】Listen to the news. To fill in the blanks on each worksheet, choose the most appropriate answer from the three choices, (A), (B), and (C). You will have 20 seconds to prepare before listening to each news announcement. You will hear the passage only once.

Condition

As a high school English teacher, you are looking for some materials so that you can use them in your lessons. You are listening to some news, while taking notes on your worksheet.

News 1

   Is napping always a good thing? Well, not necessarily. Although scientists have discovered that naps can have benefits for both the brain and for the body, naps can be a double-edged sword. Long naps in the afternoon or in the early evening can just take the edge off your sleepiness. It's a little bit like snacking before your main meal.

70

If you are struggling with sleep at night, the best advice is not to nap during the day. Instead, build up healthy sleepiness so that you give yourself the best chance of falling asleep easily and then staying asleep soundly throughout the night.

But if you're not struggling with sleep and you can nap regularly during the day, naps of around 20 minutes taken early in the day can be just fine.

Most people aim to get their recommended seven to nine hours of sleep in one long stretch at night. The technical term for this is monophasic sleep, that is, a single bout of sleep at night. However, we may not have been programmed to sleep in this way.

I'm sure you've experienced a drop in your alertness in the afternoon. Now you may think this afternoon drop in your alertness is because of a big lunch, but there is a preprogrammed drop in your alertness during the afternoon. It happens to most of us between one to four pm. This suggests to us that we may have been designed to sleep in a biphasic pattern, meaning one longer bout of sleep at night and then a short afternoon nap during the day.

(SOURCE: *Are Naps Actually Good for Us?*, Matt Walker, TED TALK, REVISED https://www.ted.com/talks/matt_walker_are_naps_ actually_good_for_us/transcript?language=en)

Worksheet

The Science of Sleep

Advice

・People <u>with</u> sleeping difficulty: [1]

・People <u>without</u> sleeping difficulty: [2]

Sleeping Patterns

・Monophasic sleep: [3]

・Biphasic sleep: [4]

1.

(A) They should stretch their muscles before going to bed.

(B) They should have appropriate naps during the afternoon.

(C) They should avoid napping during the daytime.

2.

 (A) They should exercise for longer than 20 minutes during the daytime.

 (B) They should have a short nap during the afternoon.

 (C) They should have a nutritious lunch.

3.

 (A) To have only one long sleep at night.

 (B) To have relatively short sleep at night.

 (C) To have a drop in our alertness after having lunch.

4.

 (A) To have relatively longer sleep regularly.

 (B) To have short naps several times during the afternoon.

 (C) To have longer sleep at night and shorter sleep during the afternoon.

News 2

 You may not like insects, but all of life on earth needs them to survive.

 Birds, fish and reptiles feed on insects, and if there are no insects, they die from hunger. As they die, predators die, too, which leads to a mass extinction.

 Furthermore, insects pollinate most plants, which means people cannot grow crops without them.

 Insects are very important, so it was a great shock when a report found that the mass of insects fell by 2.5 percent last year. If this continues, there will be 25％ less insects in just 10 years. If that happens, all of life will be in terrible danger.

 There are some answers as to why there are less and less insects. They are probably earth's rising temperatures, the use of chemicals in farming, and so on.

 (SOURCE: *Big Insect Problems*, News in levels, January 17, 2022,

REVISED

https://www.newsinlevels.com/products/big-insect-problem-level-3/)

Worksheet

> Big Insect Problems
>
> The importance of insects
>
> · Insects are important for other animals because
>
> | 1 |
> | --- |
>
> · Insects are necessary for humans in that | 2 |
>
> The concern about insects
>
> · The mass of insects seems to have decreased by
>
> | 3 |
> | --- |
>
> Necessary measures against the problems
>
> · | 4 |

1.

   (A)   insects can play a role to rise earth temperatures.

   (B)   insects can survive even in a poor condition.

   (C)   insects are a crucial part of an ecosystem.

2.

   (A)   insects carry pollen for crops to grow.

   (B)   insects maintain a healthy environment for some creatures.

   (C)   insects greatly help to prevent famine in poor countries.

3.

   (A)   more than 2％ last year.

   (B)   less than 25％ in 10 years.

   (C)   less than 30％ in the past decade.

4.

(A) Though some animals feed on insects, we should regard them as pest to humans.

(B) We should be aware how human activity can lead to an imbalance of ecosystems.

(C) We should regulate the mass of insects to avoid a poor harvest.

News 3

Some hospitals use therapy animals — like Ollie, a six-year-old therapy dog. Ollie is helping children at Rady Children's Hospital to overcome their fear of vaccine shots.

Avery Smith cried over her fear of the vaccine. Then, Ollie came in and sat at the girl's feet. After that, Avery stopped crying and was calm enough to receive the vaccine.

Early in November in 2021, children in the United States aged 5 to 11 were able to get the vaccine. Ever since then, Ollie and 14 other dogs have been helping them get vaccinated at the hospital. They are part of a therapy program paid for by a pet supply company.

Even before the vaccine, therapy dogs were already being used at the children's hospital. Some children at the hospital are fighting cancer or other serious diseases. A hospital programs' director said parents will sometimes hold the dog and seem to feel better, too.

However, some experts say there is a lack of scientific evidence proving that animal therapy improves a patient's medical condition. The researcher also said an animal can distract a patient. Other things such as a favorite toy might have the same effect. Some studies have shown that for short-term pain prevention--interacting with a dog can put your mind at ease by focusing on something else.

(SOURCE: *Can Animal Help Heal People?* VOA, December 6, 2021, REVISED https://learningenglish.voanews.com/a/can-animals-help-heal-people/6333981.html)

Worksheet

Dog Therapy Program

About therapy dogs

   · The dog therapy program in this news is   1

   · The role of the therapy dogs is   2

Views on the therapy dog program

   · The hospital programs' director believes that   3

   · The researcher mentions that   4

1.

  (A)   supported by an American pet supply company.

  (B)   promoted by several psychologists.

  (C)   needed by quite a few hospitals in the U.S.

2.

  (A)   to calm down children, who are afraid of taking medical treatments.

  (B)   to encourage grown-ups to take necessary vaccines.

  (C)   to help children move around the hospital with the help of all 14 therapy dogs.

3.

  (A)   therapy dogs should be trained to find cancer and other serious diseases.

  (B)   therapy dog programs could be improved if more companies fund the hospitals.

  (C)   not only children but also parents can get benefits from therapy animals.

4.

   (A)   medical doctors get distracted by therapy dogs.

   (B)   therapy dogs can be as effective as medicines are.

   (C)   therapy dogs are not the only thing that can support patients.

(☆☆☆☆☆◯◯◯◯)

【3】 You are listening to the lecture about 2018 PISA results in Japan by the supervisor of the BOE (Board of Education). Choose the most appropriate answer from the three choices, (A), (B), and (C). You will have 40 seconds to prepare before listening to the lecture. You will hear the lecture only once.

Thank you for gathering today. I'd like to summarize for you what we learned from PISA's result.

From the most recent OECD PISA 2018 test, the Japanese students' scores in mathematics and science are much higher than those of the OECD average. The OECD analyzed that they have solidly maintained its high level in terms of a long-term trend since the start of the assessment.

In reading literacy, Japan was located in a group of countries that scored better than the OECD average, but the mean score of Japan significantly declined compared to the previous assessment.

Now I'll move on to other features of the result.

The COVID-19 pandemic has led to school closures across the world and forced teachers and students in many countries to adapt quickly to teaching and learning online. But a new OECD PISA report reveals wide disparities both between and within countries in the availability of technology in schools. Regarding the students' use of ICT, the length of time which digital devices are used in school lesson is shorter in Japan. It was the shortest among OECD member countries. The share of students who replied "No time" accounted for about 80％.

As you know, students use ICT for various purposes outside of school. Their use tends to be biased, for example, as you can see in Figure 2, 87.4％

of Japanese students are chatting online and about 48% are playing one-player games. On the other hand, 3% are doing homework on a computer, 6% are browsing the Internet for schoolwork, while OECD average is about 20% respectively.

Look at Figure 3, we can see the relationship between the hours of ICT use and mean scores in one of the three domains: science. In both Japan and the OECD average, mean scores tended to decline for students who use the Internet for 4 hours or more per day outside of school. On the other hand, there was little difference in mean scores in science between Japanese students who use the Internet for 30 minutes or more but less than 4 hours. However, for the OECD average, mean scores tend to be higher for students who use the Internet for a longer time.

According to the results from the survey, we have some suggestions. Now, a measure to accelerate introduction of the ICT environment in schools is the allocation of one computer per learner and the promotion of a high-speed/high-capacity communication network to all classrooms in schools, known as the GIGA School Program.

In addition, we must develop the students' capacity to utilize information. Development of the abilities to acquire information by appropriately using computers, to organize and compare information, to transmit and communicate information, and to save and share data, etc. and the acquisition of basic operational skills are necessary for such activities. We must promote education on information morals concerning appropriate use of smartphones, etc. in collaboration with households and communities.

Thank you for listening.

(SOURCES: *Key Features of OECD Programme for International Student Assessment 2018 (PISA 2018)*,National Institute for Educational Policy Research, Ministry of Education, Culture, Sports, Science and Technology, December 3,2019, REVISED)

Q1.　Which line shows the mean scores of Japan in reading literacy?
(A)　━━▲━━
(B)　━━■━━
(C)　━━●━━

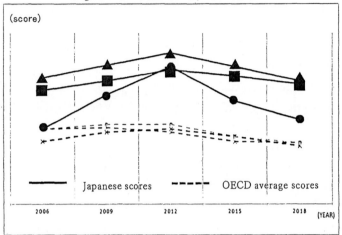

≪Figure 1　CHANGES IN MEAN SCORES≫

Q2.　Which is the most appropriate statement for Japanese students' use of the ICT in schools?

(A)　Students are not forced to adapt to online lessons because of the COVID-19 pandemic.

(B)　Japanese students use digital devices longer than the students in other OECD countries.

(C)　No more than 20 % of Japanese students use digital devices in schools.

Q3.　≪Figure 2≫ shows the percentage of Japanese students who answered "Every day" or "Almost every day". Choose the graph which matches (1) and (2).

(1)　Doing homework

78

(2) Playing online games

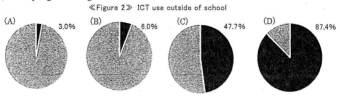

≪Figure 2≫ ICT use outside of school

Q4. According to the lecture, what does ≪Figure 3≫ show?

≪Figure 3≫

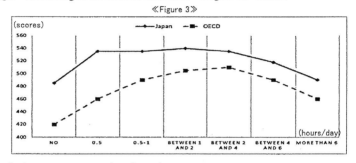

It shows mean scores in science by

(A) ICT use during classroom lessons.

(B) chatting on the Internet during weekdays.

(C) use of the Internet outside of school.

Q5. What is the conclusion of this lecture?

(A) GIGA School Program has already been promoted completely in all high schools.

(B) Students' information morals as well as ICT abilities must be developed.

(C) Introduction of a high-speed network is the best way to get higher scores in PISA assessment.

(SOURCE: https://www.mext.go.jp/kaigisiryo/2019/12/__
icsFiles/afieldfile/2019/12/06/l423070_31.pdf REVISED)

(☆☆☆☆☆◎◎◎◎)

【4】 Hana is a Japanese teacher of English and Eric is an ALT of the school. He is trying to understand Japanese educational systems. They are talking about the new Course of Study for Senior High Schools (Notification 2019). Listen to the dialogue and answer the questions below. You will have 20 seconds to prepare before listening. You will hear the dialogue twice.

Eric:　Well, I heard a new Course of Study has just been enforced this year.

Hana:　That's right. It's for the first-grade this year. For the second and third grades, students are still in the previous curriculums. Every new year from now on, high schools will shift to the new Course of Study.

Eric:　I see.

Hana:　Please look at this figure. This represents the concept of the reformation on the new Course of Study.

Eric:　What does it say?

Hana:　It clearly shows the necessity of setting clear goals; what abilities should be fostered through the curriculum.

Eric:　I'm convinced. Any class should be designed to achieve these goals.

Hana:　Right, those abilities should be evaluated from different viewpoints.

Eric:　I can see three evaluation points on the top of the figure.

Hana:　Exactly. What's more, teachers are expected to give some useful feedback to their students for improvements.

Eric:　Certainly. Good feedback makes good learners.

Hana:　To give good feedback, I think the way of learning in the classroom is important.

Eric:　Hana, could you tell me how students should learn in the classroom? Also, please tell me the reason why.

Hana:　Ok, but we have only a few minutes to the next class. We have to go. I'll answer your question by e-mail later.

Eric:　Thank you. I'm looking forward to it.

(ORIGINAL)

Q1.　According to the dialogue, what are three essential things teachers need to do? Write them down on the answer sheet.

Q2.　If you were Hana, how would you write an e-mail to answer the question Eric asks in the end of the dialogue. Write your idea on the answer sheet. For assistance, you can use the figure below.

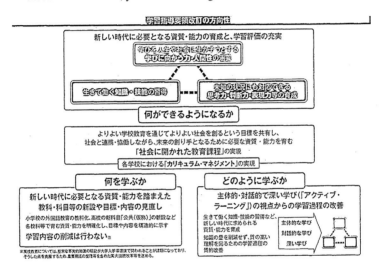

(SOURCE: https://www.mext.go.jp/b_menu/shingi/chukyo/ chukyo3/061/siryo/_icsFiles/afieldfile/2016/07/20/1374453_1.pdf)

Hi, Eric. We didn't have enough time to talk about that interesting topic. So, I'll tell you about it.

(☆☆☆☆☆○○○)

【 5 】 You are a Japanese teacher of English and now are having a lesson about electric vehicles (EV). After reading its history, students are going to explore and read more articles about EV. As a goal activity, they will make a presentation. To show a model, you found an article below, and now you are making a summary in your notebook.

Around the world, governments and automakers are promoting electric vehicles as a key technology to curb oil use and fight climate change. General Motors has said it aims to stop selling new gasoline-powered cars and light trucks by 2035 and will pivot to battery-powered models. This week, Volvo said it would move even faster and introduce an all-electric lineup by 2030.

But as electric cars and trucks go mainstream, they have faced a persistent question: "Are they really as green as advertised?"

While experts broadly agree that plug-in vehicles are a more climate-friendly option than traditional vehicles, they can still have their own environmental impacts, depending on how they're charged up and manufactured. Here's a guide to some of the biggest worries — and how they might be addressed.

Broadly speaking, most electric cars sold today tend to produce significantly fewer planet-warming emissions than most cars fueled with gasoline. But a lot depends on how much coal is being burned to charge up those plug-in vehicles. And electric grids, systems designed to provide electricity, still need to get much cleaner before electric vehicles are truly emissions free.

One way to compare the climate impacts of different vehicle models is with this interactive online tool by researchers at the Massachusetts Institute of Technology, who tried to incorporate all the relevant factors: the emissions involved in manufacturing the cars and in producing gasoline and diesel fuel, how much gasoline conventional cars burn, and where the electricity to charge electric vehicles comes from.

If you assume electric vehicles are drawing their power from the average grid in the United States, which typically includes a mix of fossil fuel and renewable power plants, then they're almost always much greener than conventional cars. Even though electric vehicles are more emissions-intensive to manufacture because of their batteries, their electric motors are more efficient than traditional internal combustion engines that burn fossil fuels.

An all-electric Chevrolet Bolt, for instance, can be expected to produce 189 grams of carbon dioxide for every mile driven over its lifetime, on average. By contrast, a new gasoline-fueled Toyota Camry is estimated to produce 385 grams of carbon dioxide per mile. A new Ford F-150 pickup truck, which is even less fuel-efficient, produces 636 grams of carbon dioxide per mile.

But that's just an average. On the other hand, if the Bolt is charged up on a coal-heavy grid, such as those currently found in the Midwest, it can actually be a bit worse for the climate than a modern hybrid car like the Toyota Prius, which runs on gasoline but uses a battery to bolster its mileage.

"Coal tends to be the critical factor," said Jeremy Michalek, a professor of engineering at Carnegie Mellon University. "If you've got electric cars in Pittsburgh that are being plugged in at night and leading nearby coal plants to burn more coal to charge them, then the climate benefits won't be as great, and you can even get more air pollution."

The good news for electric vehicles is that most countries are now pushing to clean up their electric grids. In the United States, utilities have retired hundreds of coal plants over the last decade and shifted to a mix of lower-emissions natural gas, wind and solar power. As a result, researchers have found, electric vehicles have generally gotten cleaner, too. And they are likely to get cleaner still.

Most of today's electric vehicles use lithium-ion batteries, which can store more energy in the same space than older, more commonly-used lead-acid battery technology. But while 99 percent of lead-acid batteries are recycled in the United States, estimated recycling rates for lithium-ion batteries are about 5 percent.

"The percentage of lithium-ion batteries being recycled is very low, but with time and innovation, that's going to increase," said Radenka Maric, a professor at the University of Connecticut's Department of Chemical and Biomolecular Engineering.

A different, promising approach to tackling used lithium-ion batteries is finding them a second life in storage and other applications. "For cars, when the battery goes below say 80 percent of its capacity, the range is reduced," said Amol Phadke, a senior scientist at the Goldman School of Public Policy at the University of California, Berkeley. "But that's not a constraint for stationary storage."

Various automakers, including Nissan and BMW, have piloted the use of old lithium-ion batteries for grid storage. General Motors has said it designed its battery packs with second-life use in mind. But there are challenges: Reusing lithium-ion batteries requires extensive testing and upgrades to make sure they perform reliably.

(SOURCE: https://www.nytimes.com/2021/03/02/climate/electric-vehicles-environment.html   REVISED)

Your summary notes:

Title:

| (1) |

Advantages:

| (2) |

Disadvantages:

Problems	Solutions
Factors to determine whether electric cars are greener than gasoline-powered cars or not : (3).	→ Shifts from coal-centered plants to creating electricity using natural gas, wind, and the sun.
Ratio of recycling : 　lithium-ion batteries　5% 　lead-acid batteries　　99%	→ time → technology improvement → (4)

Author's position :

| (5) |

Q1.　Choose the most appropriate option for (　1　).

(A)　How eco-friendly are electric vehicles?

(B)　What is the difference between electric cars and gasoline-powered cars?

(C)　What are benefits of electric vehicles?

(D)　How should we reduce the use of traditional vehicles?

Q2.　Choose the most appropriate option for (　2　).

(A)　to use oil to move vehicles and to change climate artificially

(B)　to use oil to move vehicles and to tackle global warming

86

(C) to decrease oil consumption and to make new gasoline-powered cars more efficient

(D) to decrease oil consumption and to tackle global warming

(E) to promote new technology and to change climate artificially

(F) to promote new technology and to make new gasoline-powered cars more efficient

Q3. Choose the option which is <u>NOT</u> appropriate for (3).

(A) the amount of coal burned to create electricity for electric vehicles

(B) the ratio of fossil fuels and renewable energy used to generate electricity

(C) the amount of gasoline traditional cars and plug-in cars need to move

(D) the place where the electricity to charge electric vehicles comes from

Q4. Choose the most appropriate option for (4).

(A) Promises that lithium-ion batteries can be replaced with lead-acid batteries

(B) Hints on how to recycle lead-acid batteries

(C) Use of lithium-ion batteries in different ways

(D) Efficient ways to discard lithium-ion batteries

Q5. Choose the most appropriate option for (5).

(A) The author adheres to the idea that plug-in cars will soon have replaced conventional cars.

(B) The author implies electric vehicles can be saviors for our environment if we can solve some worries.

(C) The author doubts that electric vehicles should be upgraded.

(D) The author suggests people use more and more electric vehicles for the earth right now.

(☆☆☆☆☆◎◎◎◎)

【 6 】 You aim to be a Japanese teacher of English. To understand the current trend of English education, you found the following article. Read the following passage and choose the most appropriate answer to each question.

§1

Feedback on EFL student writing has been shared in various ways. In Japan's current English education, the Ministry of Education, Culture, Sports, Science and Technology has emphasized four skills: speaking, writing, reading, and listening. These are key English communication tools in the 2020 revised Course of Study guidelines for elementary schools, 2021 junior high schools, and 2022 high schools. Traditionally, in English classes in Japan, teachers focused on grammar and vocabulary. Therefore, the Japanese entrance examinations for high school or university were conducted mainly based on reading and listening skills assessments, with multiple-choice tests to measure lexical and syntax knowledge.

Although academic writing has become an important issue in Japanese language education, there has been almost no instruction in English writing in secondary schools (Miyata, 2002). Mainstream English writing in the classroom largely consists in writing single sentences; there is almost no paragraph-length writing practice. Since high school EFL classes in Japan are often grammar-intensive, students have few opportunities to practice free or creative writing exercises and do not learn the process of writing a paragraph. As a result, they lack opportunities to receive writing feedback from classmates or instructors. However, the Ministry's curriculum reform suggests that English education in Japan should become more active, with students using more communication skills to achieve their output abilities, such as speaking and writing in the classroom.

§2

This research proposal focuses on how EFL instructors should approach teaching effective writing skills and provide students the chance to improve their writing and the ways of error corrections from peer feedback.

We address the following research questions: 1. How do Japanese EFL learners give peer feedback on their writing essays? - Do the Japanese EFL learners notice the processes of output products when they receive CF (Corrective Feedback) in the form of either reformulation or error correction in peer feedback? 2. How do Japanese EFL learners organize paragraphs: topic, support, and conclusion? - How do they notice and revise their writing after receiving peer feedback?

This research sought to determine the effects of the interaction in peer feedback and to understand at what points Japanese students focus on feedback correction, addressing the question of how learners show their weakness in correcting peer essay writing, and how these corrections affect their revising processes. Their language features and interaction could illustrate learners' metalanguage or interlanguage skills in the process of second language learning. In addition, how should we as language instructors approach peer or group work in the classroom?

Assuming that psychological barriers affect peer feedback, language instructors should train learners how to assess peer feedback in the classroom. Learners initially hesitate to mark corrections on other students' papers. On the other hand, written feedback or comments could be evidence of the benefits of oral feedback.

§3

In the study conducted by Okugiri, Ijuin and Komori in 2015, the students had 25 minutes to write their essays by hand without the aid of a dictionary or the Internet. The topic of this essay was based on a quote from a study of Japanese student essay writing. Specifically, the students were required to write an essay in response to the statement: *"Currently, people worldwide are able to use the Internet. Some people say that since we can read the news online, there is no need for newspapers or magazines, while others say that newspapers and magazines will still be necessary in the future. Please write your opinion about this issue."* This statement was used because the topic was universal and familiar to everyone.

For our study, during Stage 1, the instructor explained the process of feedback. In Stage 2, the participants wrote their essay for 30 minutes. In Stage 3, they were required to give corrective feedback to their peers. They noted each code, line, or words. The time for the corrective peer feedback was 20 minutes. During the correction time, the students had chances to ask questions about their English grammar or contexts, or discuss the corrections in both Japanese and English. They checked their peers' writing compositions for "lexical features, spelling and form," "syntax, grammatical order, missing words," "context, in appropriate sentences with the theme," and "organizational parts", such as "topic sentence," "supporting sentences," and "conclusion sentences." In Stage 4, the corrective peer feedback was returned to the original writers and they rewrote their revisions for 15 minutes.

§4

In reviewing studies of writing feedback, Storch (2002) discussed equality and mutuality in studies of ESL pair work. To provide effective pair work, the learners should work equal amount and cooperatively. More importantly, the learners will notice their errors and improve their essays by giving each other feedback. Peer feedback activities in ESL tend to lead to more learner-centered class. Izumi (2016) also emphasized that "noticing" in the EFL classroom is an essential factor to effectively focus on form. In pair work, the learners have an audience to raise "audience awareness" about writing. In the process of sharing feedback, they interact with each other, correct errors, and ask questions about the content of their essays. The process brings collaborative learning and scaffolding to EFL classrooms. In the corrective feedback process, each learner might have a different proficiency level.

Learners notice different errors or acquire new language knowledge individually (Hanaoka, 2007). However, it takes time to make Japanese EFL university students feel free to speak and correct errors. They rarely share opinions with one another at the beginning of the term. Wang (2014) found that psychological matters could be seen in peers' rubric evaluation. The learners needed to have an interpersonal relationship to give evaluation rubric points to each other and this affected the usefulness of peer feedback. Therefore, learners need more practice giving feedback in written compositions in EFL classes.

In general, most of the students enter university based on multiple choice type proficiency examinations. During high school, most students learn English more through analytical than experiential learning (Izumi, Shiraku & Okuda, 2011). Therefore, the instructor, who teaches reading and writing courses, should give the learners clear assessment points in the class and train the students to compare sufficient and insufficient essays through reading textbooks or teachers' models as input enhancement (Hanaoka, & Izumi, 2012). It would be difficult or challenging for the learners to give comments to each other without knowing evaluation points established by the teacher. In the curriculum, the teacher is also required to consider the effect of peer or group work. The practice of peer feedback should not only focus on forms of grammar, but also on meaning (Izumi, 2016). The teacher should guide learners how to write their compositions logically, with three main points: topic, supporting paragraphs, and conclusion. Then, the learners would review their writings by themselves and give feedback to others.

(SOURCE: The Features of Japanese EFL Learners' Peer Feedback in Written Compositions 2021/5/20 Hiromi Martin, Komazawa University, Japan Yoko Shirasu, Yokohama College of Commerce, Japan chrome-extension://efaidnbmnnnibpcajpcglclefindmkaj/viewer.html?pdfurl=https%3A%2F%2Fpapers.iafor.org%2Fwp-content%2Fuploads%2Fpapers%2Facl2021%2FACL2021_59496.pdf&clen=235235&chunk=true

REVISED)

Q1.　According to $\boxed{\S\,1}$, what is said to be necessary in order to train the four skills: speaking, writing, reading, and listening? Choose the most appropriate option.

(A)　Instructors encourage students to be more active and communicative in class.

(B)　Instructors emphasize the importance of grammar and sentence structure.

(C)　Instructors measure reading and listening skills with multiple-choice tests.

(D)　Instructors let students practice not paragraph-length writing but single-sentence writing.

Q2.　According to $\boxed{\S\,2}$, what is the aim of the research? Choose the most appropriate option.

(A)　To know why the Ministry has changed Course of study guidelines since 2020.

(B)　To know how instructors can organize paragraphs: topic, support, and conclusion.

(C)　To know why psychological barriers have a positive influence on feedback.

(D)　To know how teachers should let students write better using peer feedback.

Q3.　According to the study mentioned in $\boxed{\S\,3}$, which statement is true? Choose the most appropriate option.

(A)　Students write their essays without knowing what they will do after writing.

(B)　Students don't need to use only English when they are discussing their errors.

(C)　Students don't have to correct grammatical errors during the correction time.

(D)　Students are not given specific topics and write freely without a time limit.

Q4.　What would <u>NOT</u> be the meaning of "<u>scaffolding</u>" in ⎡§4⎤?

(A)　Practical English knowledge.

(B)　A relationship between learners.

(C)　A consideration for the reader.

(D)　Individual evaluation.

Q5.　According to ⎡§4⎤, what do English teachers need in order to improve students' writing skills? Choose the option which is <u>NOT</u> appropriate.

(A)　To have an intimate relationship with students on an individual basis.

(B)　To give students lectures about how to write paragraphs logically.

(C)　To offer equal and mutual peer feedback in the classroom.

(D)　To provide points to evaluate before students read partner's writing.

(☆☆☆☆☆○○○○)

解答・解説

【中学校】

【1】1　ソ　　2　サ　　3　タ　　4　ス　　5　カ　　6　ク　　A　知識及び技能　　B　思考力，判断力，表現力等

〈解説〉今回の改訂で，育成を目指す資質・能力を明確化する方針に沿って，全ての教科等の目標及び内容は「知識及び技能」，「思考力，判断力，表現力等」，「学びに向かう力，人間性等」の3つの柱に基づいて

再整理されている。詳細は中学校学習指導要領解説総則編(平成29年7月)の「第1章　総説　1　改訂の経緯及び基本方針」を参照のこと。A，Bの空所はその柱となる文言を問うている。　A「知識及び技能」の内容は，音声や語彙，表現，文法，言語の働きなどを理解するという「知識」の面と，その知識を「聞くこと」，「読むこと」，「話すこと」及び「書くこと」による実際のコミュニケーションにおいて活用できるという「技能」の面とで構成されている。　B「思考力，判断力，表現力等」を身に付けるためには，外国語によるコミュニケーションを行う目的や場面，状況などに応じて，情報を捉え，それを整理したり吟味したりしながら思考を深めることで，自らの考えを形成したり深化させたり，さらに表現を選択したりして「論理的に表現」することを重視する。

【２】(解答例) When I was a student I used to work part-time at a restaurant. One day, I served the wrong dish to the wrong table. I realized my mistake when a customer pointed it out to me. It was such a shame. Since then, I have always made sure if there is nothing wrong with my work thoroughly, by double-checking or making a check list to be done. What I learned from this experience is that we can improve our behavior to reduce our mistakes if only we determine not to make the same mistake again. (95 words)

〈解説〉「過ちや失敗から学んだこと」を具体的な経験を交えて80語以上で書く。解答例では，学生時代のアルバイトでの失敗談とその後心掛けたことに触れている。最後は，「同じ過ちを繰り返さない」と決心すれば，過ちを減らすために行動を改善できることを学んだとまとめている。

【３】(解答例) This message suggests that if a man learns how to fish, he can catch and eat fishes whenever hungry. That is, teaching a person a useful skill can be more beneficial in the long run than filling a need for him or her temporarily. In terms of education, we can say it's better to teach students how to learn themselves than to just give them some knowledge. This is because once they acquire how to learn themselves, they will be able to continue autonomous learning for a lifetime. (88 words)

〈解説〉ことわざの意味は「ある者に魚を1匹与えれば食べて1日は飢えをしのげるが，魚の捕り方を教えれば一生食いはぐれることはない」。解答例では，「魚を与えること」を「知識を授けること」，「魚の釣り方を教えること」を「学び方を教えることに置き換えて解説している。

【4】1　ウ　　2　②　イ　　③　ア　　3　As the child is running around, the pleats are deforming in both directions either folding together or expanding, and moving in synchrony with the child.　　4　ア

5　(1)　Children aged from four months to three years (can).　　(2)　His background as an (aeronautical) engineer (where he specialized in deployable structures for nanosatellites) (did).　　6　(解答例) Mr. Yasin has developed sustainable children's clothing. Because of his innovative pleat system that expands in multiple directions, a single garment will last much longer from babies through to toddlers. The material can also contract back to its original size ready to be handed down to younger siblings. Extending the life and the use of clothes will help us to reduce water consumption, waste, and CO_2 emissions.

〈解説〉1　「子どもの成長は早く，服が着られなくなるのも早いが…」に続く空所なので，「3歳のモモは『成長に合わせて大きくなる』洋服を着ている」とする。　2　②　空所直後のヤシン氏の「子どもが走り回ると，プリーツが折り重なったり広がったりと両方向に変形し…」から，「モモのような子どもは，常に『動き回って』いるので」とする。on the move「活動的で」。　③　特許出願中のこのデザインがどのように検査されているかを表す副詞を選択する。「『厳密に』検査され，使い続けてもプリーツが落ちないことが証明されている」。イ「不正確に」，ウ「わずかに」，エ「控えめに」などは不適。　3　下線部の文意は「それは最も着心地のよいジャケットである」。プチ・プ

リの特長として直前の文「子どもが走り回ると，プリーツが折り重なったり広がったりと両方向に変形し，子どもとシンクロして動く」を抜き出す。　4　下線部の意味は「近未来的なデザインに驚かれるかもしれないが，ヤシン氏は，いずれあなた方に気に入ってもらえると思っている」。raise a few eyebrows「驚かせる」。grow on～「だんだん～に気に入るようになる」。　5　(1)　設問は「プチ・プリの使用対象者はだれか」。【英文A】の第5段落に「4カ月から3歳までの子どもを対象にデザインされている」とある。　(2)　設問は「ヤシン氏がプチ・プリの服を作るようになったのは，どのような背景が影響しているか」。【英文B】のヤシン氏の1回目の発言参照。「航空エンジニアとして超小型衛星の展開構造を専門に研究していた」とある。　6　スピーチの筆者が最も感銘を受けたのは，ヤシン氏が衣服に関するアイデアを環境保全に役立てたことと書いている。本文の内容に準じ，彼のアイデアがなぜ未来に貢献しているのかについて触れて書く。

【5】1　①　イ　　③　エ　　⑤　ア　　2　②　エ　　④　ウ
3　(1)　They need the freedom to choose.　　(2)　Because it permits learners to see that they are in charge of the learning experience.
(3)　They ask them to choose between given options from a menu, then to make modifications and changes, and finally to select goals and procedures completely on their own.　　4　ウ　　5　①　increase　　②　genuine
〈解説〉1　①　Autonomyという語の説明の一部。イ「それは『自己規制』という分類表示の下でも議論され」が適切。　③　学習者の関与を高める上で重要なことを述べている部分。それは，学習者の学習プロセスについて学習者と責任を共有することである。「学習者は自分たちに起きていることを少なくとも部分的には『コントロールできている』と感じる必要がある」となる。　⑤　生徒は実行すべき完全なプロジェクトを与えられると，必然的に自律的な方法で機能するようになる。すなわち，そのような場では教師は「直接のコミュニケーションネットワークに属さず(教師が介在せず)」，生徒は自分たちをまとめ，目標

達成のための最も適切な行動方針を決定し，その結果をクラスで報告する方法を考案しなければならない，という流れとなる。

2　②　空所を含む文意は「もちろん別の見方をすれば，学習者の自律性を支持する理論的な議論が説得力を持ち，自立して学ぶことができる学習者がより高い能力を『身につける』ことができるという証拠がいくつかあるということだ」。　④　学習者が選択することの大切さと難しさについて述べている段落。空所を含む文意は「このような選択の難しさは，学習者に自分が本当にコントロールできていると感じさせるために学習者が間違った決定を下す可能性があるという点を『酌量し』ながらも，これらの選択が本物でなければならないことである」。allow for the fact that～「～という点を酌量する，くみ取る」。

3　(1)　設問は「自己決定の考え方に基づくと，学習者は動機付けに何が必要か」。第2段落参照。「選択する自由と選択肢を持つことが動機づけの前提条件である」とある。　(2)　設問は「なぜ選択が責任の本質なのか」。第6段落参照。「選択とは学習者が自分自身で学習経験を管理していることを認識させるので，責任の本質である」とある。(3)　設問は「教師はどのように生徒の真の決断の機会を徐々に広げていくのか」。第6段落参照。「まずはメニューから選ぶ，次に修正・変更する，最後に目標や手順を完全に自分で選択するというように生徒の選択力を育てる」とある。　4　第2段落後半より，ウ「グループの内なる成長を通して，学習者の成熟度が増し，学習者は自立に向かう」が正しい。　ア　第7段落より，「本書の著者は，学習者は新しい仲間に伝える方法を見つけることができないと信じている」は誤り。イ　第1段落より，「L2分野をめぐる自律の重要性を論じた人はいない」は誤り。　エ　第2段落前半より，「学習者のモチベーションは誰かの指示によって左右される」は誤り。　5　第5，6段落参照。Aの発言は「学習者の関与を『高める』ためには，教師が学習者と責任を共有することが重要だと分かった。また，学習者に自分が本当にコントロールできていると感じさせるためには，選択は『本物で』あるべきだと実感した」とする。

【高等学校】

【1】Q1　(A)　　Q2　(B)　　Q3　(A)　　Q4　(C)　　Q5　(A)

Q6　(A)　　Q7　(C)　　Q8　(C)

〈解説〉短い対話文を聞いて，内容についての質問に答える選択問題。放送は1回のみ。　Q1　a quarter to ten「9時45分」の特急列車から17 minutes afterの普通列車と言っているので10時2分発となる。

Q2　How about in your locker及びthere it isがポイント。　Q3 Playing the recorder will be good for a class performance及びThat's new to meを聞き取る。　Q4 It is hardly surprising that people view a certain color the same wayを聞き取る。　Q5 I'd rather stay in today及びIf you say soから外出しないことが分かる。　Q6 It appeared to draw students' attention to the books about the real life of Japanese Olympiansがポイント。　Q7 動物の権利を守るべきだとする鈴木夫人の立場を聞き取る。　Q8 You can say that again.「確かにそうだ」の直前に，マグカップは帰国途中に割れてしまうかもしれないと言っている。

【2】News 1　Q1　(C)　　Q2　(B)　　Q3　(A)　　Q4　(C)

News 2　Q1　(C)　　Q2　(A)　　Q3　(A)　　Q4　(B)

News 3　Q1　(A)　　Q2　(A)　　Q3　(C)　　Q4　(C)

〈解説〉ニュースを聞き取り，ワークシートの空所を補充する選択問題。放送は1回のみ。準備に20秒与えられるが，目を通すべき選択肢の英文量が多い。News 1　1　If you are struggling with sleep…以下を読み取る。　2　But if you're not struggling with sleep…以下を読み取る。　3は monophasic sleep「単相性睡眠」の説明，4はbiphasic sleep「二相性睡眠」の説明を読み取る。　News 2　1　第2段落の内容から「昆虫は生態系の重要な一部だ」を正解として選ぶ。　2　第3段落の内容から，「昆虫が花粉を運び，作物が育つ」が正解。　3　第4段落に「去年2.5％減少した」とある。　4　最終段落から，「私たちは人間の活動がいかに生態系のバランスを崩すかを認識する必要がある」が正解。

News 3　1　第3段落から，「アメリカのペット用品メーカーに支援さ

れている」。　2　前半の内容より，「治療を受けることを恐れる子ども
を落ち着かせること」。　3　第3段落から，「子どもだけでなく親もセ
ラピーアニマルから恩恵を受ける場合がある」。　4　最終段落から，
「セラピードッグが患者を支援する唯一のものではない」。

【3】Q1　(C)　　Q2　(C)　　Q3　(1)　(A)　　(2)　(C)　　Q4　(C)
Q5　(B)
〈解説〉長文の講義を聞き取り，内容に関する質問に答える選択問題。放
送は1回のみ。準備に40秒与えられるが，複数のグラフの読み取りが
含まれており，難易度が高い。　Q1　第3段落に「平均スコアが前回
の評価と比較して著しく下落した」とある。　Q2　第5段落から，「日
本の生徒が学校でデジタル機器を使用する割合は20%以下」が正しい。
Q3　第6段落から，(A)が「宿題」，(B)がゲーム。　Q4　第7段落から，
学校外でのインターネット使用を示している。　Q5　最終段落から，
「ICT能力だけでなく，情報モラルを育成する必要がある」。

【4】Q1　・They need to set clear goals.　　・They need to evaluate students
from different viewpoints.　　・They need to give some useful feedback.
Q2　I think students should learn through dialogue or discussion with their
classmates rather than just through reading textbooks or listening to lectures.
We now have a lot of difficulties in our lives such as COVID-I9. We cannot
live without people around us. To solve some problems, we need someone's
help or another idea. Of course, it is important to learn by ourselves, but I
think it is more important for students to cooperate with others in the
classroom. Also, students should have their own thoughts rather than
believing what other people or books say. When we want to know about
something, it is easy for us to find and get the answer through the Internet.
However, I hope students are not satisfied with knowing the answer itself, but
wonder why or want to get more information. (135 words)
〈解説〉記述式問題。対話文の内容に関して英語で答えるものと，学習指

導要領に基づいてALTへの回答を作成するもの。準備時間は20秒。対話文は2度放送される。　Q1　設問は「教師がすべき3つの不可欠なことは何か」。Hanaは「明確な目標を設定すること，多面的に生徒を評価すること，有益なフィードバックをすること」の3つを挙げている。Q2　「生徒は教室でどのように学ぶべきか」とその理由を書いてALTにメールするという設定。解答例では，「学習指導要領改訂の方向性」の図の内容を踏まえて「主体的・対話的で深い学び」を取り上げ，「生徒たちは教科書を読んだり，講義を聞いたりするだけでなく，クラスメートと対話，議論を通して学ぶべきだと思う。COVID-19のように，私たちの生活には様々な困難がある。問題解決のためには，誰かの助けや別のアイディアが必要だ。もちろん，自分で勉強することも大切だが，教室で他の人と協力し合うことがもっと大切だと思う。また，他人や本に書いてあることを鵜呑みにするのではなく，自分の考えを持つことが大切だ。何か知りたいことがあるとき，インターネットを使えば簡単に答えが見つかるが，生徒たちは答えを知ることに満足するのではなく，なぜだろう，もっと知りたいと思ってほしい」と述べている。

【5】Q1　(A)　Q2　(D)　Q3　(C)　Q4　(C)　Q5　(B)
〈解説〉Q1　記事の第2段落に「電気自動車やトラックが主流になるにつれ，『それらは宣伝されているように本当に環境に優しいのか』という根強い疑問に直面するようになった」とあり，以降の段落で電気自動車の利点・欠点，車種による比較などをしている。タイトルとして「電気自動車はどれくらい環境にやさしいのか」が適切である。
Q2　第4段落より，電気自動車の利点としては，(D)「石油消費量を削減することと地球温暖化に取り組むこと」。　Q3　電気自動車がガソリン自動車より環境に優しいかどうかを判断する要素として適切でないものを選ぶ問題。第9段落に「カーネギーメロン大学のジェレミー・ミハレック教授(工学)は『石炭が重要な要素となる傾向がある』と述べている。ピッツバーグにある電気自動車が夜間に充電され，近

くの石炭工場が充電のためにさらに石炭を燃やすとしたら，気候への恩恵はそれほど大きくなく，大気汚染が進む可能性さえある」とあるので，(A)「電気自動車用の電気を作るために燃やされる石炭の量」は要素として適切である。また，第6段落の「もし電気自動車が，化石燃料と再生可能エネルギーの発電所を含む米国の平均的な送電網から電力を得ていると仮定すれば，電気自動車はほとんどの場合従来の自動車よりもはるかに環境に優しいと言える」，第8段落の「(電気自動車の)ボルトが現在中西部にあるような石炭の多い送電網で充電される場合，トヨタ・プリウスのようなガソリンで走るがバッテリーを使用してその燃費を向上させる最新のハイブリッドカーよりも，若干気候に悪い影響を与える可能性がある」から，(B)「発電に使われる化石燃料と再生可能エネルギーの割合」及び(D)「電気自動車を充電するために電気が運ばれてくる場所」は要素として適切である。　Q4　リチウムイオン電池のリサイクル率が低いという問題の解決策は最後から2つ目の段落参照。「使用済みのリチウムイオン電池を蓄電池や他の用途に再利用するという従来とは異なる有望な取り組みがある」からCが正しい。　Q5　筆者の考えは最初か最後に述べられることが多い。最終段落の文意は「日産やBMWを含め，様々な自動車メーカーが，古いリチウムイオン電池をグリッド・ストレージに利用することを試験的に行っている。ゼネラルモーターズは，二次利用を念頭に置いてバッテリーパックを設計しているという。しかし，リチウムイオン電池を再利用するには，信頼性を確保するために大規模なテストとアップグレードが必要であるという課題がある」。これにより，(B)「著者はいくつかの問題を解決すれば，電気自動車は環境の救世主になり得ることを示唆している」が適切。(A)「著者はプラグインカーが近い将来，従来の自動車に取って代わるという考えを支持している」，(C)「筆者は，電気自動車は高性能化されるべきということに懐疑的である」，(D)「筆者は地球のために人々が今すぐにますます多くの電気自動車を使うことを提案している」は誤り。

【6】Q1　(A)　　　Q2　(D)　　　Q3　(B)　　　Q4　(D)　　　Q5　(A)

〈解説〉Q1　設問は「§1によると，スピーキング，ライティング，リーディング，そしてリスニングを訓練するため何が必要だと言われているか」。§1の2段落の最終文参照。(A)「指導者は生徒が授業中にもっと積極的にコミュニケーションをとるよう促す」が適切。

Q2　設問は「§2によると，調査の目的は何か」。§2の第1段落より，(D)「教師が生徒間の相互フィードバックを使って生徒によりよい文章を書かせる方法を知ること」が正しい。　Q3　設問は「§3で述べられている研究によると，どの記述が正しいか」。§3の第2段落参照。訂正を日本語と英語の両方で議論する機会を持ったとあるので，(B)「生徒は誤りを議論しているときに，英語のみ使う必要はない」が正しい。　Q4　設問は「§4において『scaffolding』の意味ではないのは何か」。§4の第1段落参照。「ペアワークでは，ライティングに関する『オーディエンス意識』を高めるため学習者がオーディエンス(読み手)を持つ。ライティングのフィードバックを共有する過程で，学習者はお互いに意見を交わし，誤りを正し，エッセイの内容について質問する。その過程が協働学習とEFL教室にscaffoldingをもたらす」とある。よって，(D)「自己評価」は不適。scaffoldingとは，学習者のレベルに応じて，課題解決に必要な情報や援助を与えることにより学習支援をする指導方法を指す。　Q5　設問は「§4によると，生徒のライティングスキルを上達させるために英語教師は何をする必要があるか。適切でない選択肢を選べ」。§4の第2段落参照。(B)「論理的なパラグラフの書き方についてレクチャーする」，(C)「授業中に平等な生徒間の相互フィードバックを行う」，(D)「生徒が相手の文章を読む前に評価するポイントを提示する」については記述がある。

2022年度　実施問題

【中学校】

【1】次の文は，「中学校学習指導要領(平成29年3月告示)第2章　第9節　外国語　第1　目標」の記述である。(　)に当てはまる語句として適切なものを以下の語群から選びなさい。

> 外国語によるコミュニケーションにおける(　1　)を働かせ，外国語による聞くこと，読むこと，話すこと，書くことの言語活動を通して，簡単な(　2　)などを理解したり表現したり伝え合ったりするコミュニケーションを図る(　3　)を次のとおり育成することを目指す。
>
> (1)　外国語の音声や語彙，表現，文法，言語の働きなどを理解するとともに，これらの(　4　)を，聞くこと，読むこと，話すこと，書くことによる実際のコミュニケーションにおいて活用できる(　5　)を身に付けるようにする。
>
> (2)　コミュニケーションを行う(　6　)などに応じて，日常的な話題や社会的な話題について，外国語で簡単な(　2　)などを理解したり，これらを活用して表現したり伝え合ったりすることができる力を養う。
>
> (3)　外国語の背景にある(　7　)に対する理解を深め，聞き手，読み手，話し手，書き手に(　8　)しながら，(　9　)に外国語を用いてコミュニケーションを図ろうとする(　10　)を養う。

＜語群＞

ア　配慮　　　　　イ　情報や考え　ウ　歴史
エ　技能　　　　　オ　積極的　　　カ　注意
キ　思いや考え　　ク　文化　　　　ケ　態度
コ　相手や内容，場所　サ　知識　　シ　見方・考え方

ス　資質・能力　　　　　セ　主体的　　　　　ソ　思考力・判断力
タ　会話　　　　　　　　チ　目的や場面，状況

(☆☆☆◎◎◎◎)

【2】次のAさんの話した内容に対するあなたの意見を80語以上の英語
(?，.“　”などの記号は語数に含まない)で書きなさい。ただし，以下
に示す「使用する語」を三つ全て使って述べること。
※「使用する語」は，複数形，時制，三人称単数等による語形変化を
してもよい。

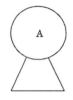

> I've got a nice translating machine!
> I don't have to learn foreign languages any more.

```
使用する語
    ・a translating machine
    ・learn foreign languages
    ・communicate
```

(☆☆☆☆◎◎◎)

【3】主語が三人称単数で現在のことを表す場合の文法事項を扱う単元
で，あなたならどのような言語活動を単元終末に設定しますか。次に
示す内容を合め，80語以上の英語(?，.“　”などの記号は語数に含ま
ない)で具体的に書きなさい。

```
内容
    ・　子供がその言語活動で何を伝えるか。
    ・　子供がその言語活動で誰に伝えるか。
    ・　なぜ，その言語活動を設定したか。
```

(☆☆☆☆◎◎◎)

【4】次の英文は，英語教員Aさんが，英語の授業づくりについて考える
ために，読んだ本の一部である。英文(以下，「本文」という。)を読み，
以下の問いに答えなさい。

During the heyday of the Audiolingual Method(ALM), variations of the
following joke circulated among language teachers:

> FRIEND: Well, how did your trip to Germany go? You're such a
> good German student, you must have had a great time
> talking to Germans!

> GERMAN STUDENT: Well, actually it was kind of tough. [*Pause.*] I
> knew my lines, but the Germans didn't know theirs!

The German student in this joke is commenting on the dialogues that students
learned in ALM classes which gave the false impression that target language
questions had specific answers and that native speakers were standing around
ready to offer those answers. If a question asked where the library was, the
response was always the same, straight ahead, or on the left, or whatever. In
the real world, of course, the library could be anywhere, and the person being
asked about the library might not know where it is or might not want to be
bothered to give directions. Consider these two conversations, the first
representing a 【　①　】 textbook dialogue and the second more similar to a
natural or real-life encounter.

[VOICES FROM THE CLASSROOM]

Conversation 1:

> Visitor: Excuse me. Can you tell me where the mall is?

> Person in the Street: Certainly. It's on the corner of Chestnut and Vine. Just
> go three blocks and turn left. It's right next to the big
> church. You can't miss it!

> Visitor: Thank you!

> Person in the Street: You're welcome.

Conversation 2:

Visitor: Excuse me. Can you tell me where the mall is?

Person in the Street: I don't know. Which mall?　【　②　】

Visitor to Group of People: Excuse me. Can you tell me where the mall is?

Group Person #1: Do you mean Lakeline Mall? I think it's north on Mopac.

Visitor: I think Lakeline Mall. The one with Home Depot. What is Mopac?

Group Person #2: Mopac is Loop 1, but Home Depot is in Gateway on 360.

Visitor: How you get there?

Group Person #1: You turn left at the next light and go about five, maybe ten miles, I'm really not sure, until you get to 183. Just cross 183, and I think it's on your right.

Visitor: Thank you.

Group Person＃1: No problem.

In the first conversation, the visitor's question elicited the exact response the visitor was seeking in a comprehensible form. All the visitor had to do was thank the helpful person in the street, follow the clear directions, and arrive happily at the mall. Unfortunately, real-life conversations are seldom so easy. In Conversation 2, the visitor asked the same well-formed question, but the person in the street needed clarification, "Which mall?" Ultimately, the person in the street could not supply the requested directions and directed the visitor to a group of people. The group of people was more helpful, but even so, several exchanges were necessary before the visitor received the needed information. The second interaction shows how negotiation is necessary to a successful conversational outcome. The visitor did not originally know the name of the mall, and therefore the first set of directions was incorrect. In addition, the directions used a reference, "Mopac" that the visitor was not familiar with. Again, clarification was necessary. In this more normal conversation, 【　③　】 The visitor probably also needed to use extralinguistic information like gestures and facial expressions to facilitate communication. Savignon argues that communicative competence asks learners to use any means of communication possible, not just target language words. Speakers are much more likely to achieve their communicative goals if they supplement their words with appropriate gestures, facial expressions, tone of voice and so on. These actions are examples of communication strategies.

These two conversations illustrate the difference between structured communication activities and authentic communication. Since no one can predict the direction a conversation might take, or the exact structures and vocabulary students will need, true communication is unpredictable. Classroom activities such as role-play activities, problem-solving tasks, and interviews can be used to simulate the natural interactions that students might anticipate in the target language environment. The term structured communication refers to a less authentic form of communication where either the grammatical structure or the content of the response, or both, is dictated in advance by the teacher or the textbook.

Whenever language teachers discuss real communication activities, the question of errors usually arises. Many language teachers fear that asking students to speak spontaneously will cause them to make errors that will be difficult to correct later on; they fear that the errors will become fossilized. Some teachers, especially those who prefer the Audiolingual Method or believe in the Contrastive Analysis Hypothesis, feel that it is necessary for students to master the target language grammar before they are allowed to participate in real communication activities. Importantly, this view has not been supported by research. A number of studies have found that students can develop structured and spontaneous language 【 ④ 】. These studies are consistent with the conversation theories that maintain that spontaneous conversations can actually help students master structured language. The Output Hypothesis and sociocultural theory see errors as a way for learners to test their developing knowledge of the second language.

〔出典：Becoming a Language Teacher: A practical Guide to Second

107

Language Learning and Teaching, Elaine Kolker Horwits, 2008　一部改〕

1　本文のタイトルとして最も適切なものを一つ選び，記号で答えなさい。

　ア　The Developing of Negotiating Ability to Master Structured Communication

　イ　The Importance of True Communication in the Language Classroom

　ウ　A Better Method to Elicit Learners' Communication Strategies

　エ　Differentiating Grammar Teaching and Communicative Competence

2　【　①　】【　④　】に最も適する語句を一つ選び書きなさい。

　①　ア　typical　　　　　　イ　professional
　　　ウ　domestic　　　　　エ　intercultural

　④　ア　asynchoronously　　イ　retroactively
　　　ウ　selectively　　　　エ　simultaneously

3　本文の内容に合うように，【　②　】【　③　】に最も適する英語を一つ選び，記号で答えなさい。

　②　ア　How did you come here?

　　　イ　Thank you for asking me.

　　　ウ　Why don't you ask them?

　③　ア　the visitor had to keep the conversation going by starting a new topic with the group.

　　　イ　the visitor needed to formulate several questions and to offer information that was not anticipated in advance.

　　　ウ　the visitor needed to get some further information about the direction to the place that the visitor had already known well.

4　本文の内容に合うように，次の質問に英語で答えなさい。ただし，7語以上の英語1文とする。

　(1)　Based on Savignon's argument, what does communicative competence ask learners to do?

　(2)　Why is true conversation inconsistent?

　(3)　What are the fossilized errors?

5 本文の内容に最も合っているものを一つ選び、記号で答えなさい。

ア A textbook dialogue is likely to be seen in real communication.

イ Students can learn structured languages through spontaneous conversations.

ウ Structured communication shown in advance by the teacher or textbook is an authentic form of communication.

エ 'Conversations 2' shows that negotiation could be seldom easy, and the visitor should have avoided clarifying information about the mall.

6 本文を読んだ英語教員Aさんが、授業づくりについて同僚のBさんと話している。AさんがBさんに話した _____ の内容を、本文の内容を基に英語で書きなさい。ただし、20語以上の英語とする。英文の数は問わない。

A: I'm planning to have some authentic communication activities for the next class. I'm sure it's important to talk spontaneously in class. I mean, authentic communication that requires the students to spontaneously produce the language.

B: I know. However some students are afraid of making mistakes when they talk in front of other students. Do they need more grammatical practice before they try authentic communication? What do you think?

A:

B: I see. One of the most important things is that the students can think about what they should say and how to say it by themselves.

(☆☆☆☆◎◎◎)

【5】次の英文を読み，以下の問いに答えなさい。

Larry Camerlin knows what desperation sounds like. Each week, his small Massachusetts office answers dozens of frantic phone calls from families of very sick people who hope Larry and his team can help. What they need are flights—to a liver or kidney transplant, to receive ongoing chemotherapy and radiation, or to treat severe burns or other crippling diseases at medical centers far away from home.

As the founder of Angel Flight Northeast, a group that connects patients in need with volunteer pilots who shepherd them, Larry, 68, has ▢_A_▢ turned away a request.

"People come to us at some of the most frightening times of their lives—they're running out of money, out of time, and out of faith," says Larry, who pilots some trips himself while also overseeing scheduling, fund-raising, and other administrative responsibilities. "(①)."

"Larry, a father of four and grand-father of six, has spent his entire career providing hope during trauma. He and his wife, Ruth, built a successful ambulance company, and after they sold the business in 1994, Larry got his pilot's license. Then he read a magazine article about a pilot in California who flew a ten-year-old boy to receive cancer treatment and immediately knew what his next chapter would be. "This enormous emotional wave hit me," Larry says. "(②)."

The first Angel Flight NE trip took to the skies on May 31, 1996. Today, Larry relies on a network of nearly 500 volunteer pilots who donate their own time, planes, and fuel. Larry's crews on the ground, Earth Angels, drive patients to and from the airport. To date, Angel Flight NE has helped 65,000 people. Bonds between patients and pilots can ▢_B_▢ for weeks, months, or longer. One cancer patient took more than 585 trips over ten years. And every single one—for every single patient—is free of charge.

"(③), but being up in the heavens, it's therapeutic to talk to a pilot helping you get better," Larry says. "Mothers, if their children are asleep, may break down about how difficult it is to see their kids so badly hurt." Not every journey, of course, has a storybook ending. Larry had been flying a boy with a life-threatening genetic disorder from Maine to Boston for years.

"He was witty, fun, and insightful—an 11-going-on-40-with-a-PhD-from-Harvard type," says Larry. One day, he got a call from the boy's mother: "Benjamin [name has been changed] is dying, and he would like to see you." Larry flew there the next day.

"Why does God hate me?" Benjamin asked Larry. "I'm only a little boy, and I'm dying. I shouldn't be dying as a little boy." Larry thought for a second. "Look how smart you are, how good you are, how many people you've touched," he said. "God needs you to be one of his special angels. (　④　)".

That flight home from Benjamin's house felt different from usual. "The closer I got to home, the sky became more flushed with yellow and orange," Larry remembers. "The sun dipped below the horizon as I touched down my wheels. Everything was so ethereal. It was like God was telling me everything was going to be OK."

〔Reader's Digest 2016　一部改〕

1　本文中①～④の(　　)に入る最も適切な英語を次のア～エより一つ選び，記号で答えなさい。

　ア　This is what God wants me to do

　イ　We help replace that fear with tremendous healing and hope

　ウ　He loves you so much; that's why he wants you

　エ　Sometimes patients can't talk to their family about their fears

2　本文中の　A　と　B　に入る最も適切な語句をそれぞれ次のア～エより一つ選び，記号で答えなさい。

　A　ア　gradually　　イ　respectively

　　　ウ　often　　　　エ　never

　B　ア　last　　　　イ　end

　　　ウ　graze　　　エ　prevent

3　次の英文は，Larryが現在の活動を始めるまでの経緯についてまと

めたものです。本文の内容に合うようにア〜ウの空欄に英語1語を
入れなさい。

> Larry founded an (　ア　) company, and he and his wife took
> over the business. He got a license to be a (　イ　). Then an article
> in a (　ウ　) about a man who carried a sick boy to get treatment
> made him realize what to do next.

4　本文の内容と合っているものを次のア〜エより一つ選び，記号で
答えなさい。

ア　Benjamin was suffering from a serious disease and he didn't want to
talk to anyone.

イ　The reason why Larry helped a lot of patients was because he had a
disease when he was young.

ウ　Each flight of Angel Flight NE costs very little.

エ　Larry's office receives a lot of phone calls from families with great
urgency every week.

5　本文の内容に合うように，次の質問に3語以上の英語で答えなさい。

ア　What do the volunteer pilots in the network give?

イ　What did Larry think when he saw the sky and the sun on the flight
home from Benjamin's house?

(☆☆☆◯◯◯)

【高等学校】

【 1 】Listen to the dialogues and questions. Choose the most appropriate answer
from the three choices, (A), (B), and (C). You will hear the dialogues and
questions only once.

Dialogue 1

M: I am looking for Mr. Sato. Do you know where he is? One of the students
in his class got injured during P.E. class. The student needs to go to the

hospital.

W: Well, now it is the 3rd period. Look at this schedule. I think he should be in 25HR during this period. (pause) Uh, wait, today the class is exchanged with Mr. Nonaka's class.

M: OK, I will check the timetable and go to the classroom.

Q1.　Which classroom will the man go?

Teachers' Schedule

	1st period	2nd period	3rd period	4th period	5th period
Nonaka	25HR	13HR	23HR		27HR
Ishii		22HR	21HR		MEETING
Aoki	24HR			12HR	11HR
Sato	23HR		25HR	26HR	

(A)　22HR

(B)　23HR

(C)　25HR

Dialogue 2

W: Excuse me. I'd like three tickets for the 5 p.m. showing of the latest movie, please. I prefer seats in the back, if possible.

M: I'm sorry, ma'am, but there is not any availability for three seats next to each other. The theater is nearly full. The film was just released yesterday.

W: No wonder it's so crowded... well, I really want to see it, so I don't mind sitting separately.

M: Let me check again. Oh, three seats together are available in the front row! Someone has just cancelled.

W: OK, I'll take those seats.

Q2.　Where are the woman and her friends most likely to sit?

(A)　　　　　　　　(B)　　　　　　　　(C)

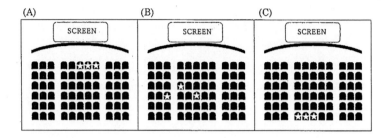

Dialogue 3

M: Are you sure you want to try playing rugby, Christy?

W: Yeah, Dad! It looks so exciting.

M: Mom will be very worried... when you broke your leg while skiing several years ago, she almost fainted you know.

W: You don't need to worry like that. Some of my friends are also into it and I believe it's not as dangerous as you may think.

Q3.　What do we learn about Christy?
- (A)　She wants to try a new sport.
- (B)　She is good at both skiing and rugby.
- (C)　She fainted while practicing skiing.

Dialogue 4

W: Good morning. Can I help you?

M: Yes, I'd like this stain removed. How long will it take?

W: We generally need three full days, but this is a kimono, so it's a little special. I guess we need 1 week or so. Are you in a hurry?

M: Yes, actually I need it on Saturday morning.

W: Then we can do that for an extra $10 and get it ready by tomorrow afternoon.

M: Great! I'll come back sometime tomorrow evening.

114

Q4.   What will the man do?

(A)   Wait and come back on Saturday morning.

(B)   Pay additional charge for faster service.

(C)   Buy a new kimono at this shop.

Dialogue 5

W: Ben? Ben Thompson?

M: Yes, that's me... oh, Cindy, Cindy Williams, right? Long time no see! It's been over ten years!

W: You haven't changed a bit.

M: What are you doing these days? I heard you worked at a hospital.

W: Not anymore. I worked there for a while after college but I always really hoped to teach. So, I went to university again and got a diploma, and now I've worked at our old high school as a science teacher for five years. How about you, Ben? I remember you always said you would like to be a pilot.

M: Actually, I work as a pilot! Now I'm afraid I have to get to the airport. I'll be flying to Tokyo this afternoon. Sorry to run off. Let's stay in touch.

W: Here is my email. Let's catch up when you're back!

M: I'll be sure to contact you.

Q5.   What do we learn from the conversation?

(A)   The man will fly to Tokyo with the woman.

(B)   The woman used to work as a teacher.

(C)   The man will contact with the woman when he is back.

Dialogue 6

M: How was today's demonstration class, Kate?

W: The principal advised me that my explanation about the auxiliary was too long and unclear. Do you agree, John?

M: Yes, also I think you need to improve the length, but students were able to use the grammar well and talk about their futures and dreams.

W: He also told me to choose another specific topic in order to improve students' presentation skills.

Q6.　What point does John agree with the principal?

(A)　Her explanation should be considered for further improvement.

(B)　The grammar point was clear enough for students to understand.

(C)　The topic "future and dream" was obscure for presentation.

Dialogue 7

M: Have you prepared enough for your interview test next week?

W: No, not really. Could you check whether my reason for applying sounds strong enough?

M: OK, then I'll be a professor. Why do you want to study at the Faculty of Pharmacy at this university?

W: I am interested in the diversity of medical services in an aging society, and this university is actively working on the problem of drug overdose in the elderly.

M: Umm, I don't know whether interviewers will regard your reason as good or not.

Q7.　What are they doing?

(A)　They are interviewing.

(B)　They are practicing.

(C)　They are arguing.

Dialogue 8

W: Hello. This is the reception desk. What can I do for you?

M: Hi. I ordered breakfast from room service. I thought I had ordered vegetarian soup for my daughter, but it seems to have meat in it. She can't eat it.

W: I sincerely apologize for the inconvenience, sir. Can I have your room number and your name? I will tell the person in charge to bring a new one.

M: Thanks, but I would appreciate instead if you could just remove the charge from the bill.

Q8.　What does the man want to do?

　(A)　To have new soup.

　(B)　To have the manager apologize.

　(C)　To have the bill corrected.

(☆☆☆○○○)

【2】 Listen to the news and answer the questions. You will have 20 seconds to prepare before listening to each news article. You will hear the passage only once.

> Condition
>
> As a high school English teacher, you are looking for some materials so that you can use them in your lessons. You are listening to some news while taking notes on your worksheet.

News 1

　Ice wine is an expensive sweet wine, often served with dessert. To make it, winemakers leave the grapes to freeze on the vine.

　But German Wine Institute spokesman Ernst Buescher said on March 1, 2020 that none of the country's wine regions were cold enough. Temperatures need to be minus 7 degrees Celsius or lower.

　There have been many warm winters recently, the institute said. In 2017, only seven producers made the wine, and only five in 2013.

　But this seems to be the first time since the first ice wines were made in

1830 that no one has made an ice wine, Buescher said.

(Source: *Germany's warm winter is too hot to make ice wine for the first time since 1830*, the japan times alpha, FRIDAY, MARCH 13,2020, REVISED)

Worksheet

Title [　　　　　　　　　　　W　　　　　　　　　　　]

★Temperature to make ice wine [　　　　　X　　　　　]

★The number of producers that made ice wine

2013	2017	2020
5	7	Y

★This news material can be used

in a unit with an inquiry question "[　　　　Z　　　　]"

Q1.　What is the most appropriate to fill in the blank W as the title for this news article? Choose one from the three choices, (A), (B), and (C).

(A)　Ice winemakers fighting in court for the trademark

(B)　Ice winemakers pulling out of the market

(C)　Ice winemakers suffering from warm winter weather

Q2.　What is the most appropriate to fill in the blank X ? Choose one from the four choices, (A), (B), (C) and (D).

(A)　above seven

(B)　below seven

(C)　above minus seven

(D)　below minus seven

Q3.　What is the most appropriate to fill in the blank Y ? Choose one from the three choices, (A), (B), and (C).

(A)　3

(B)　1

(C)　0

Q4. What is the most appropriate to fill in the blank Z ? Choose one from the three choices, (A), (B), and (C).

(A) Why does the global society view climate change seriously?

(B) How does the agricultural diversity affect our economical attitude?

(C) What drives us to study European history?

News 2

An orangutan named Sandra celebrated her 34th birthday on Valentine's Day at her home in Florida with a special new friend. Sandra made news around the world when she was legally declared a person in 2015.

Sandra was born in a German zoo, but lived for 25 years in Buenos Aires Zoo. She was the only orangutan there, and animal rights groups said her concrete enclosure at the zoo was inadequate.

Then the landmark ruling by an Argentine judge declared that she was legally not an animal but a non-human person. That gave her rights, including the right to live with a sense of her own importance and value.

(Source: *Sandra, the orangutan who is a person, celebrates her 34th birthday on Valentine's Day*, the japan times alpha, FRIDAY, FEBRUARY 28,2020, REVISED)

Worksheet

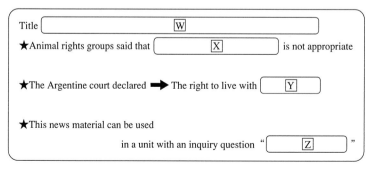

119

Q1.　What is the most appropriate to fill in the blank ⃞W as the title for this news article? Choose one from the three choices, (A), (B), and (C).

(A)　Acceleration of the movement for protecting the ecosystem

(B)　Life as a non-human person

(C)　The secret to the long life of a famous orangutan

Q2.　What is the most appropriate to fill in the blank ⃞X ? Choose one from the three choices, (A), (B), and (C).

(A)　a group of orangutans living with her

(B)　celebration of her birthday

(C)　her living condition

Q3.　What is the most appropriate to fill in the blank ⃞Y ? Choose one from the three choices, (A), (B), and (C).

(A)　dignity

(B)　a partner she loves

(C)　human beings

Q4.　What is the most appropriate to fill in the blank ⃞Z ? Choose one from the three choices, (A), (B), and (C).

(A)　How can we make handling and feeding techniques sustainable?

(B)　What part of animals have an influence on our mental health?

(C)　How are humans and animals different?

News 3

Wasabi is endemic to Japan. The oldest existing mention of wasabi was on a late 7th century wooden plate found at the ruins of Asuka-kyo in Nara Prefecture, and it was already registered as a local specialty and used for medical purposes. Coming from a young country with a history of only about 250 years, this is mind-boggling! Shizuoka Prefecture, which can be reached on a day trip from Tokyo, is said to be the birthplace of wasabi cultivation. Today, the top three places in Japan where wasabi is cultivated are Shizuoka, Iwate and Nagano prefectures.

Wasabi is said to have evolved to be sinus-permeating in order to protect itself from predators like wild boars and deer. We humans must have a sadistic streak within us because we rather enjoy this pungent condiment.

In March 2018, Shizuoka's traditional method of cultivating wasabi was certified as a Globally Important Agriculture Heritage System under the Food and Agriculture Organization of the United Nations.

(Source: *Izu Wasabi mini Museum*, Asahi Weekly, Sunday, July 21, 2019, REVISED)

Worksheet

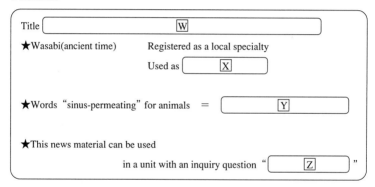

Q1.   What is the most appropriate to fill in the blank W as the title for this news article? Choose one from the three choices, (A), (B), and (C).

(A)   The findings at the ruins in Japan

(B)   Fascinating spot Shizuoka

(C)   The tremendous appeal of Wasabi

Q2.   What is the most appropriate to fill in the blank X ? Choose one from the three choices, (A), (B), and (C).

(A)   cosmetics

(B)   agrochemicals

(C)   remedies

Q3.   What is the most appropriate to fill in the blank Y ? Choose one from the three choices, (A), (B), and (C).

(A)　pleasurable

(B)　irritating

(C)　nutritious

Q4.　What is the most appropriate to fill in the blank $\boxed{Z}$? Choose one from the three choices, (A), (B), and (C).

(A)　What is worth handing down to the next generation?

(B)　How can we find ancient ruins?

(C)　What does the name "wasabi" come from?

(☆☆☆☆○○○)

【３】John and Emi are talking about the ways to motivate their students. Listen to the dialogue and choose the most appropriate answer from the three choices, (A), (B), and (C). You will have 40 seconds to prepare before listening to the dialogue. You will hear the dialogue only once.

W: Adults praise children for outperforming others. They sometimes ask, "who achieved the most?", or "who got the highest score?" Such social comparisons are well intentioned. Adults want to make children feel proud and motivate them to achieve more by winning a game or being the best.

M: Maybe. But social comparisons can backfire. Children might learn to always compare themselves with those around them and become trapped in a cycle of competition.

W: So, you mean children should not compete with each other? I heard that some schools give children participation trophies. "Everybody has won, and all must have prizes." However, such awards may not abolish social comparisons. Despite receiving the same trophy, children are still sensitive to even minor differences in performance between themselves and others. High-performing children who receive the same prizes as low-performing ones may feel unjustly treated.

M: I understand what you mean. So, we have a better approach called "temporal comparisons." Encouraging children to compare themselves with their past self rather than with others, by assessing how much they have learned or improved themselves.

W: Temporal comparisons? Tell me more about it.

M: OK, here is a study of three ways of praising children; social comparisons, temporal comparisons, and no comparison at all.

W: Then, which approach is more suitable to encourage children?

M: The study suggests that all children who compared themselves favorably to others or to their past-self felt proud of themselves. However, children who engaged in social comparison said they wanted to be superior to others. Those who engaged in temporal comparison said they wanted to improve rather than be superior.

W: That is really interesting. I believed that having them compare with others would give them an opportunity to reflect on their own performances and that would make them feel encouraged. Are there any strategies for parents and teachers to encourage children?

M: For one, parents can praise children's improvement over time to let them know they are making progress and heading in the right direction. Also, teachers can create learning contexts that track children's own progress over time, such as report cards that display their changes in learning and performances. By doing so, adults teach children that outperforming oneself is more important than outperforming others and that even small victories may be celebrated.

(Source: *The Problem with Telling Children They're Better Than Others.* SCIENTIFIC AMERICAN MIND, July 2020 REVISED)

Q1.   What did John believe in encouraging children?

(A)   Giving children the same feedback to treat them equally.

(B)　Asking children how much they improved.

(C)　Having children understand how much they outperform others.

Q2.　In the study, the students in the social-comparison condition would write

(A)　"Looking back what I tried this year, I find myself improving little by little."

(B)　"Now that I have that many friends, I feel good and confident."

(C)　"I got a full score on the test, and others couldn't. I find myself really important."

Q3.　According to the dialogue, what is the possible problem when giving "the same trophy"?

(A)　High-performing children may feel their efforts have gone unnoticed.

(B)　Low-performing children would be reluctant to make efforts.

(C)　Teachers may be too sensitive in comparing children.

Q4.　According to the dialogue, which can be used to make children more encouraged and motivated?

(A)　Portfolio in which children accumulate their intellectual properties.

(B)　A pile of papers in which children's good points superior to others are written.

(C)　Lists of the recent tendency in universities' entrance examinations.

Q5.　One of your students says she is not motivated because of the low scores in the writing tests. Based on the dialogue, from the viewpoint of temporal comparison, choose the most appropriate advice.

(A)　"Compare your writing with your classmates' and find some superior points in your own writing skills."

(B)　"Identify in which parts you have improved or not, checking with the rubric."

(C)　"Do not look back at the poor writing last time and just do your best for the next test."

(☆☆☆☆○○○)

【4】 Ken is a first-year-teacher and Eri is his supervisor. Both of them are high school English teachers and they are talking about the questions they will ask students in the English classes. Listen to the dialogue and answer the questions below. You will have 20 seconds to prepare before listening to the passage. You will hear the passage twice.

W: Are your English classes going well?

M: Actually not. Students are so inactive that they sometimes look bored and frustrated. I really want to know how I can improve my lessons.

W: I see. Do you give students sort of questions worth investigating in your classes?

M: Questions worth investigating?

W: Yes, what kinds of questions do you ask in your classes?

M: Well, most of the questions I ask are comprehensive checks; whether students can understand the textbook or not. After reading and listening to English, I have students answer True and False questions.

W: Those questions can be categorized as "factual questions." OK, anything else?

M: Umm...not really. Mostly, as you say, "factual questions." What other kinds of questions could we use?

W: One is the so called "inferential question." Based on what students read and listen to, teachers can have students infer some ideas from the passage to express their own thoughts. Also, related to the topic, we can set some conceptual questions and debatable ones so that students can deepen their understanding about the topic.

M: I understand. But I still believe factual questions are important.

W: It is true that they are important, but that's not enough. If we gave only factual questions, students would not need to express their own ideas.

M: Indeed, it has only one answer, no variation. So, if I have students talk with their partners only for answering such questions, this is just checking answers. Certainly, that does sound boring.

W: Right. The revised Course of Study clearly states that teachers should promote students' proactive, interactive, and deep learning in classes. In order to achieve this, the most important thing is to make good questions worth investigating. If teachers set questions students truly wanted to solve, students could be motivated to be exposed to a wide variety of information, interact with other people, reconstruct their own ideas, and value what they create. Such learning processes will make students more active in classes.

M: A question worth investigating. I have come to understand what is needed to improve my English lessons. By the way, you mentioned the revised Course of Study. It states that it is important to foster students' abilities to think, make judgements, and express what is necessary to solve problems, using acquired knowledge and skills. So, why should teachers foster these abilities in students within high school education?

Q1.　According to the dialogue, what problem does Ken have in his English classes and what advice does Eri give to Ken? Summarize and write them down on the answer sheet.

Q2.　If you were Eri, how would you answer the question Ken asks in the end of the dialogue, "Why should teachers foster these abilities in students within high school education?" Referring how you would foster those abilities in students as a teacher, write your idea on the answer sheet.

(☆☆☆☆☆◎◎◎◎)

【 5 】Read the following passage and answer the questions below.

　Many people are familiar with the popular educational initiative of STEM(Science, Technology, Engineering, and Mathematics), but lately many educators, administrators, and instructional coordinators are favoring a new term: STEAM. The phrase retains the original STEM subjects as tenets, but includes an A which stands for Arts. The shift addresses the focus on creative skills to boost engagement in classrooms. This simple inclusion carries implications that break down common misconceptions about effective pedagogy.

Here are several reasons why STEAM learning should be an integral part of every educational program.

Once instructors explain the basic lessons, students operate largely by themselves or collaborate in small groups for their projects. It's up to the students to examine their and their peers' skills to determine how to best complete a project. In a STEAM curriculum, students work in learning environments which offer minimal risk, and reinforce the idea that making mistakes and failure can be productive. Along the way, learners go at their own pace and skill level; they can spend time with beginning foundations or challenge themselves by working with complex concepts. Students can pursue new tangents of thought, and there is a free-flowing exchange of ideas that isn't bound by intellectual constraints.

A STEAM-centered education is driven by a cross-disciplinary emphasis, exposing learners to multiple, lateral ways of thinking. Subjects such as science and tech aren't valued more than the arts, but all subjects are presented in relationship with one another. It's one thing to write up code for efficient software, (1). Some might think STEAM has always been the basis of most schools and institutions, but true STEAM programs involve subjects taught within the same lesson. With this philosophy, students are able to view the unique advantages of each discipline. It teaches students that they're not limited to one particular subject, or must pick between a technical or artistic topic; their expertise can be formed through a combination of these. The equal representation of subjects promoted by STEAM makes it a truly well-rounded program that appeals to (2)students' evolving curiosity and range of interests.

A central feature of STEAM programs is (3). Learners are working on projects specific to what issues appeal to them. Students decide on a goal and

127

choose which skills to achieve it, allowing them to explore and experiment with various methods. The addition of an artistic component makes complex topics such as math and programming more approachable and less mentally intimidating. Unlike traditional STEM projects, the emphasis isn't on obtaining or analyzing facts or data. Projects are evaluated against a subjective criteria that values creativity, rather than whether the student has concluded a right or wrong answer. This method supports the individual's educational journey and promotes creative expression.

While technical knowledge is a requirement in many industries, creative problem-solving remains one of the most sought-after skills within the job market. Creativity might seem like a skill that comes instinctually to certain individuals, but it's actually one that can be fostered by a proper STEAM education.

Inspiring open-ended, creative exploration serves as a form of productive play and inquiry. The lack of rigidly defined rules to follow encourages learners to demonstrate adaptive critical thinking, think around a given problem, and consider the effects produced by changing different variables. Students ask themselves "(4)" Without having to rely on a fixed procedure, learners hone their ability to assess a large set of details and understand that problem-solving models can be flexible.

STEAM program exposes students to "big picture" concepts seen in the real, physical environment. Projects like building a website or constructing a basic robot enables students to better interact with real-world problems on a smaller scale. This helps them identify and relate to their immediate physical and social environment, such as building software that analyzes statistics or designing architecture that can exist within a major city. (5)This on-going relationship with learning is what makes STEAM stand out as an empowering initiative, and promotes the idea that a concrete education benefits from all academic areas.

(Source: https://blog.kadenze.com/student-life/5-major-benefits-ofintegrating-steam-education/)

Q1. What is the most appropriate to fill in the blank (　1　)?

(A) and the code should be checked and improved repeatedly so that other people can use it

(B) and it is quite another whether other people actually use it efficiently

(C) but it takes strong artistic skills to make sure the product has a user-friendly appeal

(D) but it is another issue whether the code is well-composed or not

Q2. As for the underlined phrase (2), what aspect of STEAM arouses learners' curiosity and interests? Choose the most appropriate one from the four choices, (A), (B), (C), and (D).

(A) Counterintuitive approach

(B) Interdisciplinary approach

(C) Learner-centered approach

(D) Fact-finding approach

Q3. What is the most appropriate to fill in the blank (　3　)?

(A) demonstrative research based on data processing

(B) the cultivation of aesthetic sentiments

(C) the utilization of ICT on learning

(D) hands-on, project-based learning

Q4. What is the most appropriate to fill in the blank (　4　)?

(A) How do I follow the procedure which validity has already been proved and widely-recognized?

(B) How do I customize a solution to best fit the problem?

(C) How can I get much more knowledge and skills to solve the problem?

(D) How can I find a solution only through the scientific methods?

Q5. How can the underlined phrase (5) be explained in other words? Choose the most appropriate one from the four choices, (A), (B), (C), and (D).

(A) Acquiring knowledge fundamental of a phenomenon in real-world.

(B) Fusion of real-world and virtual-world with technology.

(C) Distinction of real-world from virtual-world.

(D) Engagement with real-world applications.

(☆☆☆☆○○○○)

【6】 Read the following passage and answer the questions below.

English education in Japan involves foreign teachers whose presence may reinforce unrealistic expectations of fluency, while access to confident and proficient Japanese speakers of English, perhaps (1) for young Japanese learners, seems comparatively lacking. According to the research by Murphey and Arao, near-peers are "people who might be near to us in several ways: age, ethnicity, gender, interests, past or present experiences, and also in proximity and frequency of social contact", and access to these individuals may influence learners' attitudes and choices. Using an experimental intervention exposing students to successful near-peers, this study investigates changes in self-efficacy beliefs among two groups of 1st-year Japanese university students. This paper summarizes the ongoing study, illustrating the potential value of near-peer role modeling in small group tutorial classes.

Cook argues that pressure on learners to acquire "native-like" language by exposing them to Native-English-Speaking-teachers may deemphasize their development of interlanguage through peer communication and reinforces their perception of learners as "failed native speakers" rather than multicompetent speakers in the process of development. To counteract this, Cook suggests that placing classroom emphasis on successful second-language (L2) users provides a framework wherein learners can recognize their own potential through a sense of shared identity, cultivating beliefs that they are truly using L2 to communicate rather than attempting imitations of native speakers. Bandura's finding that "seeing or visualizing people similar to oneself perform successfully raises efficacy beliefs in observers that they possess the capabilities to master comparable activities" speaks to the idea that learners in need of greater self-confidence may benefit from exposure to successful learners with whom they readily identify and favors Cook's recommendation that learners be provided opportunities to observe their peers communicating successfully in L2.

This study was informed by Murphey's findings in its use of prerecorded video to expose learners to Near Peer Role Modelings (NPRMs). In Murphey's research, NPRMs address viewers directly, making unambiguous and positive statements about language learning. The intervention employed in the present study took a more indirect approach, exposing students to examples of authentic English communication between slightly older and more advanced students from the same university. Two 2nd-year students were recruited to perform in a series of these videos and were compensated for their time. In each 5-minute video, the pair engages in extemporaneous discussion about a familiar topic (e.g., food, travel, and the like) while demonstrating the course's target Communication Strategies (CSs) to repair communication breakdowns. To promote authenticity, the NPRMs were given no advance notice regarding topics and received no prompting. The NPRM videos were viewed biweekly by all members of the intervention group (Group A). After viewing these videos as homework, participants completed a reflection assignment which included awareness-raising items that required participants to identify the NPRMs' use of CSs, to notice and report on aspects of the conversation, and to relate their impressions of the videos to their development. Topics for classroom pair discussion were coordinated to match each video. Although members of Group B also discussed these topics, they did not carry out the video activities or reflective practice.

Murphey and Arao suggested that learners reporting dissatisfaction with their L2 development may benefit more from NPRMs than more confident learners. An examination of several data sources from this project appears to validate this inference. Initial survey results revealed that focus students Takayuki, Juri, and Ai possessed low confidence in their English ability when compared to Mayuko and Yukari. This was later corroborated by their interview responses and instructors' field notes. A review of these students' reflections and interview comments indicate that the low-confidence group found the NPRM activities more helpful and enjoyable.

Although the less confident students identified NPRM activities as valuable, Yukari and Mayuko believed that other classroom activities were more effective; furthermore, they were more likely to criticize the NPRMs for errors. The NPRM video activities were described as an opportunity to watch and listen to CS usage in authentic conversation; beyond this, the concept of NPRMing was not explained. Yukari and Mayuko appear to have assumed that the NPRM videos featured Japanese learners rather than so-called native speakers to illustrate difficulties experienced by Japanese speakers of English.

Survey data was revisited after discovering that learners with lower confidence may be more likely to respond positively to NPRM activities. This finding raised the question of whether a positive response to the intervention may lead to improved classroom performance. A large number of anonymous respondents in both groups precluded a full comparison of performance scores (based on teacher assessment, attendance, and homework completion). Fortunately, the top and bottom five performers in both Groups A and B had chosen to self-identify, allowing changes in these individuals' questionnaire responses to be examined directly. Figure 1 provides a visual review of differences in learner self-efficacy beliefs reported by the most successful and least successful students in both Group A and B. High performing students' agreement with statements such as "I have language learning aptitude" remained relatively consistent, as did the reported beliefs of low performers in Group B.

The low performers in the intervention group, however, displayed an average increase of 1.6 points (on a five-point Likert scale) in agreement with these statements following 10 weeks of NPRM activities. This indication that the self-efficacy beliefs of low performers may be positively influenced by NPRMing adds a new dimension to Murphey and Arao's finding that exposure to NPRMs may be more successful in increasing self-efficacy beliefs in learners dissatisfied with previous language learning experiences. (SOURCE: Walters, J. R. (2020). *Senpai: Learner responses to near-peer role modeling intervention.* JALT Postconference Publication Issue 2019. 1; August 2020 REVISED)

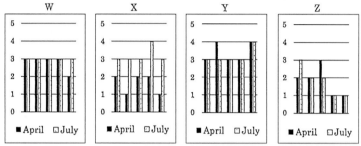

Figure 1. Top and bottom five performing participants' agreement with high self-efficacy statements in April and July.

Q1.　What is the most appropriate to fill in the blank (　1　)?

(A)　people in higher status

(B)　just the objects of envy

(C)　more effective exemplars

(D)　the capable ones beyond the reach

Q2.　Bandura's study shows that

(A)　the presence of native speakers is imperative to improve learners' capabilities.

(B)　observing peers' performances affect observers' self-efficacy positively.

(C)　the errors learners make affect their language learning negatively.

(D)　Japanese university students are confident in communicating successfully in pair activities.

Q3.　In the study the author conducted, learners of the intervention group

(A)　made their own videos to show their performances.

(B)　checked their peers' language errors when watching video as an assignment.

(C)　watched their near peer's performances on videos and wrote the reflections.

(D)　were given some positive words which are clear and easy to understand.

Q4.　The figure representing the low performers in intervention group is

(A)　W

(B)　X

(C)　Y

(D)　Z

Q5.　Based on the perspective of the author's study, what can JTEs do to increase the self-efficacy of lower performers? Choose the most appropriate one from the four choices, (A), (B), (C), and (D).

(A)　To introduce a variety of language activities.

(B)　To enhance the authenticity using the materials such as CNN or TED Talk.

(C)　To show as many good examples of selected students as possible.

(D)　To make clear the goal of the English classes and show it in the beginning of the unit.

(☆☆☆☆○○○)

解答・解説

【中学校】

【1】1　シ　　2　イ　　3　ス　　4　サ　　5　エ　　6　チ　　7　ク　　8　ア　　9　セ　　10　ケ

〈解説〉外国語科の目標について基本的な語句の選択問題である。キーワードは選択肢がなくても解答できるようにしておきたい。小中高の連携なども視野に，小学校の外国語活動，外国語などの目標や言語材料

などにも時間があれば目を通しておきたい。

【2】(解答例)　I think it's true that a translating machine is useful as an aid when we try to communicate. However, the aim to learn foreign languages is not only to convey what we want to say or just information but to interact with people who have various backgrounds and understand their cultures and their ways of thinking. We'll have more chances to meet them at the workplace or in our local community. I'm sure it would enrich our life. That's why I think we need to learn foreign languages. (88 words)

〈解説〉「翻訳機を手に入れたので，外国語を学ぶ必要がない」と言うA に対する意見を書く。80語であれば4～5文程度を目安にまとめられる。解答例では，英語を学ぶ目的を「言いたいことや情報の伝達」ではなく，「様々なバックグラウンドを持つ人との交流や文化・考え方を理解すること」としてまとめている。

【3】(解答例)　I will assign my students to write an essay about a favorite person and talk about him or her to their classmates. In their speeches, the students should explain what the person is like and the things that the person does that makes him or her so special to them. In this activity, it's necessary for the students to use the third person singular forms. That's why I think it's a perfect activity at this stage as a summary of this grammar point. (83 words)

〈解説〉解答例では，三人称単数現在形を扱う単元のまとめとして，お気に入りの人についてエッセイを書いて発表する活動を取り上げている。三人称を学ぶことで表現の幅が大いに広がる。まずは身近で興味のあるトピックを取り上げることが大切である。

【4】1　イ　　2　①　ア　　④　エ　　3　②　ウ　　③　イ
4　(解答例)　(1)　It asks them to use any means of communication possible. (10 words)　　(2)　It's because no one can predict the direction a conversation might take, or the exact structures and vocabulary speakers will

need. (21 words)　　(3)　They're errors that are difficult to correct later on. (9 words)　　5　イ　　6　(解答例)　Learning structured languages and spontaneous conversations are compatible. I think testing developing grammatical knowledge in actual language-use situations is important for them. (22 words)

〈解説〉1　本文では，構造化されたコミュニケーション(活動)と本物のコミュニケーションを比較し，授業では，後者に近づけることが大切だとしている。よって，イ「言語教室における真のコミュニケーションの大切さ」が適切。　2　①　空所の下の[VOICES FROM THE CLASSROOM]の項のConversation 1参照。質問者が求めている返答が即座にかえってきている。typical textbook dialogue「典型的な教科書の対話」と言える。　④　直後に「多くの研究が，自然発生的な会話は生徒が構造化された言語をマスターするのを実際には助けていると主張する会話の理論と一致する」とあることから，空所にはエ「同時に」を入れて，「多くの研究が生徒は構造的言語と自然発生的言語を同時に身に付けることができると示している」とする。　3　②　空所後，別の人たちに同じ質問をしていることから，「彼らに尋ねたらどうですか」が適切。　③　教科書の対話とは異なるという内容が入る。「通常の会話では，訪問者はいくつかの質問をし，そして前もって予測できない情報を与える必要がある」が適切。　4　(1)　「Savignonの議論に基づくと，コミュニカティブコンピテンスは学習者に何をするよう求めているか」。最後から3つ目の段落の後半参照。「あらゆる可能なコミュニケーションの手段を使うことを求めている」。

(2)　「本物の会話はなぜ一貫性がないのか」。最後から2つ目の段落の前半参照。「誰も会話が向かう方向，生徒が必要とする的確な構造や語彙も予測できないから」。　(3)　「化石化した間違いとは何か」。最終段落の2文目参照。「後に訂正するのが難しい間違い」。　5　最終段落の後半参照。「多くの研究が，自然発生的な会話は，生徒が構造化された言語をマスターするのを実際には助けていると主張する会話理論と一致する」とある。よって，イ「生徒は自然発生的な会話を通し

て構造化された言語を学ぶことができる」が正しい。　6　本文の内容に準じ，本物のコミュニケーションを通して構造的な言語獲得が可能であることに触れる。

【5】1　①　イ　　②　ア　　③　エ　　④　ウ　　2　A　エ
B　ア　　3　ア　ambulance　　イ　pilot　　ウ　magazine　　4　エ
5　(解答例)　ア　They give their own time, planes, and fuel. (8 words)
イ　He thought God was telling him everything was going to be OK. (12 words)
〈解説〉1　①　「人々(患者)は人生で最も恐ろしい時に私たち(Angel Flight NE)のところに来る―彼らにはお金，時間，そして信仰もない」に続くLarryのせりふとして，イ「私たちはそのような恐れを格別の癒しと希望に替える手伝いをする」が適切。　②　第4段落はLarryが現在の活動を始めるきっかけになったことがらが書かれている。「この大きな感情の高まりが私を襲った」に続く文として，ア「これは神が私にしてほしいと思っていることだ」が適切。　③　空所後に「しかし，天空にいると，元気になるよう手伝ってくれるパイロットと話すことは癒しである」と続くことから，エ「時に患者は恐ろしさについて家族に話すことができない」が適切。　④　自分は神に嫌われていると言うBenjaminという少年にLarryがかけた言葉として，ウ「神様は君をとても愛している。だから神様は君を欲しているんだ」が適切。　2　A　「Angel Flight Northeast，困っている患者と彼らに尽力するボランティアパイロットをつなぐグループの創設者として，68歳のLarryは一度も依頼を断ったことがない」となる。turn away「(申し出などを)拒否する」。　B　「患者とパイロットの絆は数週間，数カ月，もっと長く続くことがある」となる。　3　Larryが現在の活動を始めるまでの経緯については第4段落参照。ア「Larryは救急車の会社をつくった」，イ「彼はパイロットになるための免許をとった」，ウ「治療を受けるため，病気の少年を運んだ男性についての雑誌の記事を見て，彼は次に何をすべきか気づいた」となる。　4　第1段落2文目より，エ

137

「Larryのオフィスは毎週，急を要する家族からの電話を非常にたくさん受けている」が正しい。　5　ア　質問は「ネットワークにいるボランティアパイロットは何を提供するのか」。第5段落の2文目より，「彼らは自身の時間，飛行機，そして燃料を提供する」。　イ　質問は「LarryはBenjaminの家から帰りの飛行で空と太陽を見た時，何を思ったか」。最終段落の最終文より，「神が全てうまくいくと自分に言っていると思った」。

【高等学校】

【1】Q1　(B)　　Q2　(A)　　Q3　(A)　　Q4　(B)　　Q5　(C)
Q6　(A)　　Q7　(B)　　Q8　(C)

〈解説〉対話文と質問を聞いて，答えとして適切なものを3択で答える問題。対話文は一人3回程度，計6回程度のやりとりである。英文量としては，長いもので150語程度の英語で日常会話が中心。選択肢も問題用紙に示されており，英文自体も易しい。さほど手こずることはないだろう。英文は1回のみ放送される。

【2】News 1　Q1　(C)　　Q2　(D)　　Q3　(C)　　Q4　(A)
News 2　Q1　(B)　　Q2　(C)　　Q3　(A)　　Q4　(C)
News 3　Q1　(C)　　Q2　(C)　　Q3　(B)　　Q4　(A)

〈解説〉100語～150語程度のニュースを聞いて，問題用紙に印刷されている空所を補充し，ワークシートを完成させる問題。表や選択肢なども含めると英文量が多く，難易度が高い。20秒与えられる準備の時間に，問題用紙に印刷されている表や選択肢にどれだけ目を通すことができるかがポイントである。英文は1回のみ放送される。

【3】Q1　(B)　　Q2　(C)　　Q3　(A)　　Q4　(A)　　Q5　(B)

〈解説〉聞き取りのスクリプトとしてはやや長めの350語以上からなる対話文を聞いて，問題用紙に印刷されている質問に選択肢で答える問題。準備の時間が40秒しかないので，質問文だけでも目を通して，聞き取

るべき必要な情報を絞ることが大切。英文は1回のみ放送される。

【4】Q1　Ken wants his students to be more motivated and interactive in his English classes. However, Ken asks the students only factual questions. So, students just check if their answers match what is described in the textbook. Also, they don't have a lot of opportunities to express their own ideas, nor deepen their understanding about the topic.

Eri advises him to give students other types of question worth investigating. Those questions will stimulate the students to be exposed to a wide variety of information, interact with others, reconstruct their own ideas, and value what they create. Thus, teachers can promote students' proactive, interactive, and deep learning in the classes.

Q2　The reason why students' abilities to think, make judgements, and express themselves in a manner to solve problems using acquired knowledge and skills should be fostered lies in the reflection of the upcoming age, known as Society 5.0. AI has dramatically been advancing and global society has rapidly grown up. In these circumstances, the younger generation will face some unpredictable problems which are difficult to find clear answers. In order to solve them and achieve a sustainable society, those abilities are essential.

In the process of students' proactive, interactive, and deep learning, we can encourage students to set their inquiry questions, cooperate with diverse people, look for relatively optimal or convincing answers, and create something valuable, making full use of acquired knowledge and skills.

〈解説〉対話文を聞いて，英語で要約文を完成させる問題と，対話文の最後に男性が提起している質問「なぜ高校教育において教師はこれらの能力(問題解決に必要な思考力，判断力，表現力)を育成するべきなのか」に英語で答える問題。英文は2回放送される。語数指定はないが，100語〜150語程度を目安にするとよい。

【5】Q1　(C)　　Q2　(B)　　Q3　(D)　　Q4　(B)　　Q5　(D)

〈解説〉Q1　空所前は，STEAM教育において，「科学や技術」が「芸術」より尊重されるのではなく，全ての教科が互いに関わりあっているという内容なので，科学や技術だけでなく芸術も大事だという文脈になるようにする。効率的なソフトウェアにコードを書くことは大切だが，(C)「できあがったものが使い勝手がよいと思われるか確認するためには，かなりの芸術的スキルが必要である」とする。　Q2　問いは「下線部(2)に関して，STEAMのどんな側面が学習者の好奇心や興味を呼び起こすのか」。同段落の1文目参照。STEAM中心の教育の特徴として領域横断を重視するとある。よって，(B)「複数の分野にまたがるアプローチ」が正解。　Q3　STEAMプログラムの特徴を表すものを選ぶ。空所の後に「学習者は自分たちが興味のある問題に関するプロジェクトに取り組む」と続くことから，(D)「実践的なプロジェクトに基づく学習」が適切。　Q4　STEAM教育において，生徒がどのように問題解決をするのかが書かれている段落である。「想像を掻き立てるような終わりのない探求」，「順応可能なクリティカルシンキング」，「様々に変化するものによってもたらされる影響を考える」などの表現から，生徒のせりふとして，(B)「どのようにすれば私は問題に合わせて解決策をカスタマイズできるか」が適切。　Q5　下線部を含む文意は「学習との継続的な関わりは，力強い新たな取り組みとしてSTEAMを際立たせているものである」。学習との継続的な関わりとは，STEAMプログラムのことを指す。同段落では，ウェブサイトや基礎的なロボットをつくるプロジェクトが実社会では統計資料を分析するソフトウェアをつくったり，建築物をデザインしたりするのに役立つとしている。よって下線部を言い換えるものとして，(D)「実世界の応用へ関わること」が正しい。

【6】Q1　(C)　　Q2　(B)　　Q3　(C)　　Q4　(B)　　Q5　(C)

〈解説〉Q1　空所を含む文意は「日本の英語教育は外国人教師を必要としており，流暢に話すことを過度に期待される一方，英語を話すこと

に自信があり堪能な日本人は比較的不足しているようだ」という内容。「英語を話すことに自信があり堪能な日本人」を，(C)「日本の若い学習者にとって効果的なお手本」と言い換えている。　Q2　Banduraの研究については，第2段落後半参照。「自分自身と類似している人が上手くやっているのを見る，即ち視覚化することは，見る者に自身も同等の活動を極める能力があるという効力感を起こさせる」とある。よって，(B)「仲間のパフォーマンスを見ることは，見る者の自己効力感に肯定的な影響を与える」が正しい。　Q3　筆者が行った研究において，介入群の学習者が行ったことについては，第3段落4文目以降参照。介入群の学習者は，隔週でビデオを視聴し，振り返りの課題を行ったとある。よって，(C)「同輩のパフォーマンスを見て，振り返りを書いた」が正しい。　Q4　介入群でパフォーマンスが低い者を表している図を選ぶ。パフォーマンスの低い者の結果については，最終段落参照。リッカート尺度で1.6ポイント上昇したとある。図1の4月と7月を比較して，Xでは合計で8ポイント，平均で1.6ポイント上昇している。

Q5　問いは「筆者の研究の見方に基づくと，パフォーマンスの低い者の自己効力感を増すためにJTEは何ができるか」。最終段落のまとめの文参照。「パフォーマンスの低い者の自己効力感は，NPRMingによって肯定的な影響を受ける」とある。同輩の模範を示すこと，即ち，(C)「選定された生徒のよい例をできるだけたくさん見せること」が適切。

【中学校】

【1】次の文は，「中学校学習指導要領(平成29年3月告示)　第2章　第9節　外国語　第1　目標」の記述である。(　　)に当てはまる語句を正しく書きなさい。

> 　外国語によるコミュニケーションにおける(　1　)を働かせ，外国語による聞くこと，読むこと，話すこと，書くことの(　2　)を通して，簡単な情報や考えなどを理解したり表現したり伝え合ったりする(　3　)資質・能力を次のとおり育成することを目指す。

(☆☆☆○○○)

【2】次の文は，「中学校学習指導要領(平成29年3月告示)　第2章　第9節　外国語　第2　各言語の目標及び内容等」に示されている，言語活動に関する事項における「ウ　読むこと」「エ　話すこと[やり取り]」「オ　話すこと[発表]」の言語活動例である。「ウ　読むこと」「エ　話すこと[やり取り]」「オ　話すこと[発表]」それぞれの領域にあてはまる言語活動例を(あ)〜(か)からすべて選び，記号で答えなさい。ただし，(あ)〜(か)の記号はすべて使用し，同じ記号は2回以上使用しないこととする。

> (あ)　社会的な話題に関して聞いたり読んだりしたことから把握した内容に基づき，読み取ったことや感じたこと，考えたことなどを伝えた上で，相手からの質問に対して適切に応答したり自ら質問し返したりする活動。
>
> (い)　日常的な話題について，簡単な表現が用いられている広告やパンフレット，予定表，手紙，電子メール，短い文章など

から，自分が必要とする情報を読み取る活動。

(う) 社会的な話題に関して聞いたり読んだりしたことから把握した内容に基づき，自分で作成したメモなどを活用しながら口頭で要約したり，自分の考えや気持ちなどを話したりする活動。

(え) 関心のある事柄について，相手からの質問に対し，その場で適切に応答したり，関連する質問をしたりして，互いに会話を継続する活動。

(お) 日常的な話題について，事実や自分の考え，気持ちなどをまとめ，簡単なスピーチをする活動。

(か) 簡単な語句や文で書かれた社会的な話題に関する説明などを読んで，イラストや写真，図表なども参考にしながら，要点を把握する活動。また，その内容に対する賛否や自分の考えを述べる活動。

(☆☆☆◎◎◎)

【3】A中学校では，総合的な学習の時間で「自分たちの住む地域を活性化しよう。」というテーマ学習を行っている。それに関連して，3年生の英語の授業において，「わたしたちの住んでいる地域社会を住み続けられる町にするために何かできるか？(What can we do to make our community to be a sustainable one?)」というテーマで意見交換することを言語活動に設定した。生徒がテーマに興味を持てるようにするために，あなたならどのようなことをするか。40語以上60語以内の英語で書きなさい。

(☆☆☆◎◎◎)

【4】以下の意見について，最初に賛成・反対どちらかの立場を明確にして，あなたの考えを書きなさい。その際，理由を二つ以上挙げ，40語以上60語以内の英語で書きなさい。

> Teachers have to give their students homework every day.

(☆☆☆○○○)

【5】「中学校学習指導要領(平成29年3月告示)　第2章　第9節　外国語　第2　各言語の目標及び内容等　英語　1　目標　(5)　書くこと」の目標の一つである。

> イ　日常的な話題について，事実や自分の考え，気持ちなどを整理し，簡単な語句や文を用いてまとまりのある文章を書くことができるようにする。

　また，「中学校学習指導要領(平成29年3月告示)解説　外国語編　第2章　第2節　1　目標　(5)　書くこと　イ」には，「メールや手紙，日記，レポート，スピーチ原稿などの形式により，事実を伝えたり，出来事を描写したり，考えを述べたり，気持ちを伝えたりすることができるようになることを目指す。」とある。

　この目標及び解説の内容を踏まえて，あなたなら，どのような活動を設定するか。以下に示す内容を含め，60語以上80語以内の英語で書きなさい。

　・言語活動の内容
　・その言語活動を設定した理由

(☆☆☆○○○)

【6】次の英文を読み，あとの問いに答えなさい。

　When is the last time you tried something new? Anything－from switching to a new toothpaste to playing a new sport? You'd be surprised at how much it can affect your life, even just for the moment.

　How can a new toothpaste possibly affect you that much? By trying a new product, you're opening up to change, keeping contemporary, adapting and learning. Also that new product may have a new ingredient, such as a

144

polishing agent, that may actually do what it promises and make your teeth shinier than they were before.

Let's look at something bigger—trying a new sport can be an exhilarating experience, but it can be quite humbling, too. Take veteran snow skiers, for example. Accomplished on the hills, they feel confident attempting a black diamond run, the toughest on the slopes. Now that same person decides to try snowboarding and can (　①　) make it from the rental hut to the bottom of the lift! These two winter sports are very different, requiring different forms of muscle control, stance and balance. And knowing how to do one definitely does not make you nowledgeable on the other.

Consider the effect of trying something new in your workplace. Going beyond your own job description to cover for someone or pitch in gives you insight into your colleagues'skills and daily demands, plus a new perspective of your own.

A friend of mine is in sales. The other day he was asked to be on a panel discussing the more technical aspects of his company. Nervous at first, he opted to take on the challenge. He studied up on the parts of the company he didn't know in detail, and asked around how panel discussions usually work. After the event, he felt he had not only learned more about his company, but he had gained pride in taking on a challenge and succeeding. His confidence increased, along with his self-esteem.

When a baby is first born, he or she (　②　) — no likes or dislikes, no experiences. It's up to that child's parents to introduce new things all the time—from the most basic concepts such as colours, to all the available varieties of fruits and vegetables. Without trying new things, that baby won't even know that they exist.

When we try something new, we learn a little bit more about ourselves: our likes and dislikes; our areas of expertise and those that challenge us; our strengths and weaknesses. If we try it and we don't like it, we don't have to continue using the product, or playing the sport or eating the food. We can always go back to what we know. But if we do like what we've tried, we can learn from it and incorporate it into our world, making our lives fuller and richer.

〔出典: *Metro* [Ottawa City], November 7, 2006　一部改〕

1　(　①　),　(　②　)に入る最も適切なものを選択肢ア～エより一つ選び，記号で答えなさい。

①　ア　alternately
　　イ　acutely
　　ウ　likely
　　エ　barely

②　ア　takes over the role in the family
　　イ　differentiates emotional expressions
　　ウ　arrives with a clean slate
　　エ　has a concept of favorites

2　英文のタイトルとして適するものを選択肢ア～エより一つ選び，記号で答えなさい。

ア　New experiences improve our lives.
イ　Challenging something new affects our physical health.
ウ　The key to success is persisting with old favorites.
エ　Pursuing one thing can change your life.

(☆☆☆◎◎◎)

【7】次の英文を読み，あとの問いに答えなさい。

It did not take long for me to recognize the therapeutic potential of Max, the hypoallergenic 5-month-old Havanese puppy I adopted in March 2014. He neither barked nor growled and seemed to like everyone, especially the many children that come up and down our block. When I asked if a crying child passing by would like to pet a puppy, the tears nearly always stopped as fluffy little Max approached, ready to be caressed. So I signed us up for therapy dog training with the Good Dog Foundation, which met conveniently in my neighborhood. If we passed the six-week course, we would be certified to visit patients in hospitals and nursing homes, children in schools, and people in other venues that recognize the therapeutic potential of well-behaved animals.

Training involves a joint effort of dog and owner, usually in groups of four to eight pairs. The dog can be any size, any breed, but must be housebroken; nonaggressive; not fearful of strangers, loud or strange noises, wheelchairs or elevators, and able to learn basic commands like sit, lie down and leave it. Good temperament is critical; a dog that barks incessantly, nips or jumps on people uninvited would hardly be therapeutic.

During our first visit to patients at my local hospital, a woman who said she'd had a "terrible morning" invited Max onto her bed, showered him with affection and, crying with pleasure, thanked me profusely or bringing him around to cheer her up.

Moments later, on the pediatrics ward, a preverbal toddler hospitalized with croup spotted Max and came charging down the hall squealing with delight. The two met eye-to-eye; Max even appeared to smile, and she giggled as she patted his head.

I don't know about Max, but I was hooked. I agreed to bring him for monthly patient visits, with a promise to do more if my schedule permitted, and I was able to do the required pre-visit bath.

A therapy dog need not be small and fluffy. A neighbor with a "mush" of a 90-pound American pit bull named Pootie has had similar experiences at the Veterans Affairs New York Harbor Healthcare System's Brooklyn campus. During the first visit, one patient told him repeatedly, "You made my day."

But while a hospital's voluntary pet therapy program is designed to aid patients, in my experience the chronically stressed hospital staff benefits as much if not more from pet visits. "Can I pick him up?" is the typical request from hospital personnel I encounter, and some don't even wait for me to say yes.

Therapy pets differ from service animals like those that guide the blind, detect impending health crises for people with epilepsy or diabetes, or stimulate learning for children with autism or cerebral palsy.

Studies have shown that after just 20 minutes with a therapy dog, patients'levels of stress hormones drop and levels of pain-reducing endorphins rise. Endorphins are the brain's natural narcotic, the substance responsible for the runner's high that helps injured athletes ignore pain.

In elderly patients with dementia, depression declines after they interact with a therapy animal. And researchers at the University of Southern Maine showed that therapy dog visits can calm agitation in patients with severe dementia.

In a controlled study of therapy dog visits among patients with heart disease, researchers at the University of California, Los Angeles, found (A) reduction in anxiety levels and blood pressure in the heart and lungs in those who spent 12 minutes with a visiting animal, but no such effect occurred among comparable patients not visited by a dog.

Therapy dogs are often described as better than any medicine. They know (B) when someone needs loving attention. Last winter, when I was felled by the flu (despite my annual shot), 1-year-old Max lay at the foot of my bed for hours on end, making none of his usual demands for attention and play.

In an intriguing pet therapy program, sometimes called pets behind bars, benefits accrue to both the animals and the humans with whom they interact. Shelter dogs considered, unadoptable and living on "death row" are assigned to be cared for and trained by selected prison inmates, including convicted killers and rapists, many of whom have serious anger issues.

The inmates work to socialize the dogs, teaching them to trust people, behave appropriately and obey simple commands. In turn, violence and depression among the inmates is lessened; they learn compassionate behavior, gain a sense of purpose, and experience unconditional love from the dogs in their care.

At the completion of training, rehabilitated dogs are offered to people who want to give a shelter animal a permanent home. Through the Safe Harbor Prison Dog Program at Lansing Correctional Facility in Lansing, Kan., for example, some 1,200 dogs have been adopted as pets.

〔出典：New York Times February 29, 2016　一部改〕

1　(　A 　), (　B 　)に適した語をア～エから選び, 記号で答えなさい。

A　ア　an ignoble
　　イ　a general
　　ウ　a conventional
　　エ　a significant
B　ア　intricately
　　イ　instinctively
　　ウ　accidentally
　　エ　respectably

2　下線部の理由を, 本文中の英語10語で抜き出しなさい。

3　本文の内容に合うよう, 次の質問に英語で答えなさい。

How does training shelter dogs influence prison inmates?

4　本文の内容と異なるものを選択肢ア～エより一つ選び, 記号で答えなさい。

ア　A pet therapy program called pets behind bars is beneficial for both the animals and the humans with whom they interact.

イ　Interacting with therapy dogs raises patients' level of pain-reducing endorphins.

ウ　Max was registered for therapy dog training because he is a small, fluffy and disobedient dog.

エ　Therapy pets are different from service animals like those that guide blind people, detect impending health crises for people with epilepsy or diabetes, or stimulate learning for children with autism or cerebral palsy.

(☆☆☆◎◎)

【8】次の英文を読み，あとの問いに答えなさい。

As intermediate teachers, one of our major concerns is motivating our students. How can we engage our students in meaningful learning experiences and, at the same time, create a lifelong love for learning?

A Brockville public school is attempting to address this growing problem by giving their students the opportunity to become totally engaged in their learning experiences.

For example, a main part of the school's instructional strategy is an independent research project. At the beginning of each term, students explore a theme-based topic that interests them. They are required to develop a process portfolio that shows their planning, research notes, and rough drafts of their written report. The finished product involves three key components: local, national, and international contacts; a written report; and a multimedia presentation－a two-day symposium in which students present to the class and members of their community.

In the course of their independent studies, students were asked to make contacts with people working in their area of research. One student studying global warming established a partnership with an environmental organization. In addition to providing key information, his contact invited him to attend a United Nations-sponsored international conference in Montreal. Hearing this, the school worked with their administrators so that a few of their students could attend. The students took photographs and made videotapes, and made a presentation to their peers on their return.

This experience went way beyond the school's expectations. It exposed their students to an international perspective on global issues. They became very impassioned about such environmental issues as the Kyoto Protocol, nuclear waste, endangered species, and pollution. The knowledge they gained was much deeper and richer than the teachers could ever have provided using a traditional approach to teaching.

As the students developed a passion for the environment, they quickly realized that because of their knowledge and understanding, they now had a "voice" to share with others, and that they, as individuals, could make a difference. They began to comprehend the power of knowledge, and soon they were writing editorials and letters to people in power. The teachers couldn't stop smiling as they heard the students suggesting ways of reducing greenhouse gases and slowing down global warming.

The energy and momentum this approach to learning created further reinforced their belief in it. Passion for learning cannot be taught; it is something each student must experience. Authentic experiences give students the opportunity to explore their passions, which in turn "hooks" them into becoming lifelong learners.

The teachers there had never been so challenged, yet so fulfilled. The energy created by the students motivated them to continue to build this program, and to provide enriched experiences for all.

Some teachers may find this approach difficult because the learning experiences and challenges do not necessarily follow the sequential flow of a textbook. There is often an element of the "unknown" because of the variety of student interests, abilities, and learning styles. Flexibility and teamwork are essential ingredients in teacher planning when working with the experiential model.

(①) is another consideration. Experiential education can be very difficult to evaluate conventionally. The (①) and evaluation strategies of the teachers from the Brockville public school include the use of achievement chart targets from ministry documents, qualitative analysis, process portfolios, and exhibitions. One of their challenges is to match the learning taking place with the curriculum expectations because students take part in such a wide variety of learning activities and situations often involving team and partner collaboration. The teachers use multiple intelligences ("M.I.") to encourage students to show their understanding of content in ways that are comfortable for them by reflecting on their "M.I." strengths and learning styles. They also encourage them to explore other areas of their "M.I." as ways to strengthen those skills.

Finally, it is important that all people involved believe in the benefits of this approach to learning and the continued support of administration is also a vital component to its success.

If we encourage our students to take risks, then we, as educators, must be willing to do so as well. All students want to know how school relates to the real world. If we are to help students become lifelong learners, it is our responsibility (　②　).

〔出典：Voice：Spring 2006　一部改〕

1　(　①　), (　②　)に入る適切なものを選択肢ア～エより一つ選び，記号で答えなさい。

①　ア　Assignment / assignment
　　イ　Expense / expense
　　ウ　Assessment / assessment
　　エ　Plagiarism / plagiarism

②　ア　to supply them with opportunities to experience working in a real world setting.
　　イ　to provide a meaningful context where they can make that connection.
　　ウ　to show them a clear goal and every step they can take to achieve it.
　　エ　to provide them with examples so they can connect their in-class learning to the real world.

2　本文の内容に合うよう，次の質問に英語で答えなさい。

(1)　What did the Brockville public school students who became enthusiastic about the environment notice?

(2)　Why can some teachers feel that the initiative of the Brockville public school would be challenging to implement?

3　次の指示に従って，本文の内容に合うよう，適する答えを英語で

書きなさい。

(1)　List the three major things that form a completed independent research project at the Brockville public school.

(2)　Give an example of a Brockville public school student making contacts with professionals working in the field of their research topic.

(3)　Give an example of how the teachers at the Brockville public school use multiple intelligences to assist the students' learning.

(☆☆☆◎◎)

【高等学校】

【 1 】 Listen to the short sentences and choose the most suitable response from the three choices, (A), (B), and (C). You will hear the sentences only once.

Q1．Is that the fridge you bought yesterday?

　(A)　Yes. That's from my mother.

　(B)　Yes. What do you think about it?

　(C)　Yes. I use it for sleeping.

Q2．Where did you get this cute stuffed animal?

　(A)　I don't like the shopping mall.

　(B)　Tom and I are crazy about teddy bears.

　(C)　Tom gave it to me as my birthday present.

Q3．Every time I chat with her, I turn red and get clumsy.

　(A)　You should take a deep breath before you speak.

　(B)　Why don't you make it yourself?

　(C)　You should change your clothing to her favorite taste.

Q4．It's nice to finally meet you in person.

　(A)　I think I'm going to meet you at last.

 (B) You must be the last person to see this movie.

 (C) I'm afraid you are speaking to the wrong person.

Q5．There used to be a cafe on this corner.

 (A) Here's my corner.

 (B) OK. This way, please.

 (C) This picture brings back memories.

(☆☆○○○○)

【2】Listen to the dialogues and questions. Choose the most appropriate answer from the three choices, (A), (B), and (C). You will hear the dialogues and questions only once.

Dialogue 1

M: Did you check the email from Prof. Yamada? The next history class will be cancelled again. I've been preparing for the presentation with my group members!

W: I know, and he called off the presentation day without telling us a new date.

M: I'm wondering if he's OK.

W: I'm not sure, but I haven't seen him since last Wednesday. I just hope he's feeling alright.

Q1. What does the woman imply about Prof. Yamada?

 (A) She is relieved to hear that his class was cancelled.

 (B) She shows her concern about his illness.

 (C) She wants him to give more time for presentations.

Dialogue 2

M: Hi, Emily. I'm feeling sick since this morning, but I have to pick up Mr.

154

Masuda from the Fujiyama Company at the station this afternoon. I am wondering if you can go to the station instead of me.

W: Sorry, John. I have an important conference at that time. My department is so busy these days. I don't want to bother my manager. Why don't you ask Sam? He was very kind enough to help me find a new apartment.

M: I see. But I cannot trust him, because when I ask him to do something, he sometimes forgets.

W: I think he is the only person you can ask.

M: Well, I will think about it.

Q2. What does Emily think of Sam?

(A) He is not helpful.

(B) He is considerate.

(C) He should pick up their manager instead.

Dialogue 3

M: Mom, I'm home! Guess what I found on my way home?

W: Oh my goodness, a puppy! He's probably lost.

M: Well, he looks hungry. Let's give him something to eat and... mom, can we keep him? Please?

W: No, Bob. We are not allowed to have pets in the apartment. Also, he's wearing a collar so we should try to find his owner, right?

M: (sigh) OK, I see... anyway let's get him some milk.

W: Then, let's take his picture and upload it to Twitter.

M: That's a great idea!

Q3. What does the woman suggest to her son?

(A) To try to find the owner using SNS.

(B) To keep the dog in their apartment.

(C) To buy the dog a new collar.

Dialogue 4

M: Excuse me. Could you move your car, please? It's in front of my office, and I have a customer coming soon. He needs to park there.

W: I'm sorry. I was just picking up some things from the shop next door. I'll be out of your way soon.

M: Thank you. Could you use the parking lot for the customers of this shopping street across the road next time?

W: I didn't know they had a parking lot over there. I'll be sure to do that.

Q4.　Why is the man complaining?

   (A)　Because the parking lot by his shop is closed.

   (B)　Because the woman left her belongings in his office.

   (C)　Because the woman's car is in the way of his customer.

Dialogue 5

M: Jessica, have you got a gift for Lisa's baby?

W: Yes, a set of nice blue baby clothes. But now I'm worried Lisa may not like the color.

M: Why? I'm sure she will like it.

W: What if it's a baby girl? I can't give blue clothes to a baby girl.

M: Jessica, no one worries about those kinds of stereotypes anymore, do they? It's the twenty-first century!

W: You'd be surprised how often people still hang on to tradition.

M: Then, how about keeping the receipt so that Lisa can exchange it if necessary?

W: Good idea.

Q5.　Why is Jessica worried?

   (A)　Because Lisa already has blue baby clothes.

(B)　Because the gift Jessica bought may be unsuitable.

(C)　Because Jessica cannot find the receipt for the gift.

(☆☆☆◎◎◎)

【3】 Listen to the dialogue about "Math Anxiety" and choose the most appropriate phrase from the three choices, (A), (B), and (C). You will have 20 seconds to prepare before listening to the passage. You will hear the passage twice.

M: Hello, doctor. Could you explain your research on the relationship between children's insecure attachment to their mothers and mathematical achievement?

W: Well, the aim of our work was to further reveal the origins of math anxiety; those are the feelings of tension and anxiety that interfere with the solving of mathematical problems. We know from many studies that this anxiety has a negative impact on performance, even on very simple tasks such as single-digit calculation.

M: Interesting. Then, what makes some individuals more exposed to developing this anxiety than others?

W: In a research, we show that insecure attachments lead to higher levels of math anxiety, which in turn leads to poorer mathematical performance. This was the case for both untimed and timed measures of mathematical achievement. Also, these associations were independent of children's sex and IQ.

M: In that case, what can teachers do for the students with math anxiety?

W: Math anxiety might be addressed through involvements relating to the child's attachment security. Teacher-child relations can soften the negative effects of insecure attachment and, consequently, math anxiety. Specifically, improving teachers'skills to sensitively respond to these problems might reduce math anxiety and improve math performance, at least in the context of insecurely attached children. Also, negative effects such as aggressive behavior resulting from children's insecure attachment to their mothers can be weakened by a higher quality relationship between the children and their teachers.

(SOURCE: Sarah Watters (2015)　*"Study links insecure maternal attachment to math anxiety in children"*, REVISED)

Q1.　According to the research, math anxiety is (　　).
　(A)　one of the obstacles in solving math problems
　(B)　a disability every child needs to overcome
　(C)　a statement given by the students who are not good at math

Q2.　Insecure attachment (　　).
　(A)　interrupts poorer mathematical performance
　(B)　encourages students to do single-digit calculation
　(C)　negatively affects children's mathematical performance

Q3.　Characteristics of math anxiety are seen among (　　).
　(A)　children who show aggressive behavior very often
　(B)　children regardless of the gender and intelligence
　(C)　even adults who have higher levels of competence

Q4.　According to the research, which is <u>NOT</u> effective as a solution?
　(A)　Having the appropriate support of well-trained teachers.
　(B)　Helping mothers feel more secure attachment.
　(C)　Making a good child-teacher relationship.

(☆☆☆◎◎◎)

【4】Listen to the passage about "Water Footprint" and choose the most appropriate phrase for each question. You will have 20 seconds to prepare before listening to the passage. You will hear the passage twice.

The water footprint is an indicator of freshwater resources appropriation which brings valuable insight about the environmental impact of consuming some products. It consists of three components: the blue, green and grey water footprint. The blue water footprint is the volume of freshwater evaporated from surface water and groundwater, to produce crops. The green water footprint is the volume of water stored in the soil as soil moisture. The grey water footprint is the volume of polluted water that associates with the production of all crops.

In Argentina, potatoes are irrigated using groundwater while, at the same time, both fertilizers and agrochemicals are applied. In order to assess the virtual water content of potato production, the green, blue and grey components of the water footprint were calculated by considering the different volumes of water involved in the crop production arising from evaporation, rainfall, irrigation, and fertilizer pollution.

The water footprint of potato in this region was 323,99 m³/t. The total amount of the blue water and green water was 56.4%. The proportion of blue water is about a quarter, which showed the significant role of irrigation on this crop. The fraction of grey water was the greatest, indicating the importance of nitrogen fertilizers and the consequent risk of groundwater pollution.

Several strategies and recommendations emerged from this study aimed at reducing the water footprint and achieving the sustainability of potato production, such as improvements on the irrigation and fertilization efficiencies, technical advice for farmers, and legal and tax regulations on groundwater use.

(SOURCE:http://www.sciencedirect.com/science/article/pii/ S0959652614012827, REVISED)

Q1. According to the passage, what are the three components of the water footprint? Choose the suitable description for each blank from the list.

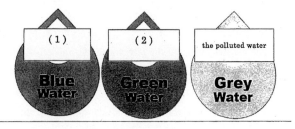

(A)　the water available from the soil

(B)　the amount of fresh water consumed by cattle

(C)　the water from rivers, lakes, or wetland

Q2.　According to the passage, what percentage is each water footprint? Choose the correct answers from the list.

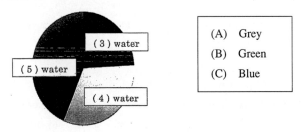

(A)　Grey

(B)　Green

(C)　Blue

Q3.　According to the passage, what is the aim of the research? Choose the most appropriate answer.

(A)　Finding effective water use and sustainable crop production.

(B)　Finding reasonable water appropriation for people in the studied region.

(C)　Finding a much safer way in water consumption.

(☆☆☆☆○○○)

【5】Listen to the passage on education for the next generation in Japan and complete the summary below by filling in the underlined parts with 6 words or less for each part. You will have 20 seconds to prepare before listening to the passage. You will hear the passage twice.

Japan's Ministry of Education, Culture, Sports, Science and Technology is now carefully considering how to adjust the education system to meet the needs and values of Society 5.0, from primary school to university level. In 2017, the ministry set up a committee on the issue, which included specialists in cutting-edge areas like AI.

In the era of AI and IoT, people no longer need to memorize every single fact. Many tasks today are best carried out by computers. Therefore, the emphasis must be on human skills such as communication, leadership and endurance, as well as curiosity, reading skills and comprehension.

To make this happen, Japan is considering two radical changes that could be critical. If successful, the shifts would be relevant to traditional education systems worldwide and position Japan as a role model for teaching, in the age of high technology.

The first change is to make grade progression more flexible. This would mean that instead of either totally failing or totally passing each year, more support classes would be provided to ensure there are no gaps in understanding. For example, if a student passes fifth grade but didn't do well in math, he or she could retake the fifth-grade course, subject until the skills are fully learned and understood. It's around fifth, sixth and seventh grade that basic skills are supposed to be perfected. These are the foundations for everything. If you don't have the reading skills and if you try to learn history, physics or chemistry, you won't understand definitions and you will get lost.

Removing the barriers between subjects and disciplines is the other adjustment that must be made for the next generation to be prepared for the super-smart future, according to the former minister.

Today in Japan, as in many countries across the world, students taking university entrance exams are divided into two groups: those who study humanities and social sciences, and those who study hard science and math.

The choice is one or the other. Yet in a world where technology is integrated into nearly every part of society, that approach will no longer be practical.

If you are studying biology as a major, you should also study humanities so that when you are faced with a philosophical or ethical issue in your future career, such as the concept of designer babies, you can combine your scientific knowledge with ethics.

(SOURCE: https://foreignpolicy.com/sponsored/how-japan-is-preparing-its-students-for-society-5-0/ REVISED)

To be successful in Society 5.0, students should develop (a)——————. There are two initiatives to realize this.

One is related to progression of grades. Students should be allowed to retake (b)——————. The other is related to the barriers between subjects. Students should study (c)——————.

(☆☆☆☆◎◎◎◎)

【6】 Read the following speech script from TED and answer the questions below.

At graduate school I studied positive psychology to learn what truly makes people happy. But what I discovered there changed my life. The data showed that chasing happiness can make people unhappy. And what really struck me was this: the suicide rate has been rising around the world, and it recently reached a 30-year high in America. Even though life is getting objectively better by nearly every conceivable standard, more people feel hopeless, depressed and alone. There's an emptiness gnawing away at people, and you don't have to be clinically depressed to feel it. Sooner or later, I think we all wonder: Is this all there is? And according to the research, what predicts this despair is not a lack of happiness. It's a lack of something else, a lack of having meaning in life.

But that raised, some questions for me. Is there more to life than being happy? And what's the difference between being happy and having meaning in life? Many psychologists define happiness as a state of comfort and ease, feeling good in the moment. Meaning, though, is deeper. Our culture is obsessed with happiness, but I came to see that seeking meaning is the more fulfilling path. And the studies show that, people who have meaning in life, they're more resilient, they do better in school and at work, and they even live longer.

So <u>this</u> all made me wonder: How can we each live more meaningfully? To find out, I spent five years interviewing hundreds of people and reading through thousands of pages of psychology, neuroscience and philosophy. Bringing it all together, I found that there are what I call four pillars of a meaningful life. And we can each create lives of meaning by building some or all of these pillars in our lives.

The first pillar is belonging. Belonging comes from being in relationships where you're valued for who you are intrinsically and where you value others as well. But some groups and relationships deliver a cheap form of belonging; you're valued for what you believe, for who you hate, not for who you are. True belonging springs from love. It lives in moments among individuals, and it's a choice -- you can choose to cultivate belonging with others.

Sometimes we reject people in small ways without realizing it. I do, I'll walk by someone I know and barely acknowledge them, I'll check my phone when someone's talking to me. These acts devalue others. They (1). But when you (2), you (3).

For many people, belonging is the most essential source of meaning: those bonds to family and friends. For others, the key to meaning is the second pillar: purpose. Now, finding your purpose is not the same thing as finding the job that makes you happy. Purpose is less about what you want than about what you give. A hospital custodian told me her purpose is healing sick people. Many parents tell me, "My purpose is raising my children." The key to purpose is using your (4). Of course, for many of us, that happens

163

through work. That's how we contribute and feel needed. But that also means the issues like disengagement at work, unemployment, low labor force participation. Without something worthwhile to do, people flounder. Of course, you don't have to find purpose at work, but purpose gives you something to live for, some "why" that drives you forward.

The third pillar of meaning is also about stepping beyond yourself, but in a completely different way: transcendence. Transcendent states are those rare moments when you're lifted above the hustle and bustle of daily life, your sense of self fades away, and you feel connected to a higher reality. For one person I talked to, transcendence came from seeing art. For another person, it was at church. For me, I'm a writer, and it happens through writing. Sometimes I get so in the zone that I lose all sense of time and place. These transcendent experiences can change you. One study had students look up at 200-feet-tall eucalyptus trees for one minute. Afterwards they felt less self-centered, and they even behaved more generously when given the chance to help someone.

Belonging, purpose, transcendence. Now, the fourth pillar of meaning, I've found, tends to surprise people. The fourth pillar is storytelling, the story you tell yourself about yourself. Creating a narrative from the events of your life brings clarity. It helps you understand how you became you. But we don't always realize that we're the authors of our stories and can change the way we're telling them. Your life isn't just a list of events. You can edit, interpret and retell your story, even as you're constrained by the facts.

I met a young man named Emeka, who'd been paralyzed playing football. After his injury, Emeka told himself, "My life was great playing football, but now look at me." People who tell stories like this — "My life was good. Now it's bad." -- tend to be more anxious and depressed. And that was Emeka for a while. But with time, he started to weave a different story. His new story was, "Before my injury, my life was purposeless. I partied a lot and was a pretty selfish guy. But my injury made me realize I could be a better man." That edit to his story changed Emeka's life. After telling the new story to himself, Emeka started mentoring kids, and he discovered what his purpose was: serving others. The psychologist Dan McAdams calls this a "redemptive story," where the bad is redeemed by the good. People leading meaningful lives, he's found, tend to tell stories about their lives defined by redemption, growth and love.

(SOURCE: Smith, E. E. (2017). *There's more to life than being happy.* (Speech Script from TED) REVISED)

Q1. What does the underlined "this" refer to?

(A) Seeking meanings in our lives can be defined as a state of deeper comfort.

(B) Results of the studies make it clear that resilient people often live longer.

(C) Feeling happiness has become an obsession for everyone in our culture.

(D) Having meanings in our lives is more fulfilling than feeling happy.

Q2. Put the sentences in the correct order to fill in the blank (1), (2), and (3).

(A) lead with love

(B) make them feel invisible and unworthy

(C) create a bond that lifts each of you up

Q3. Choose the most appropriate phrase to fill in the blank (4).

(A) insight to achieve your own goal

(B) insight to engage yourself in work

(C) strengths to cooperate in your family

(D) strengths to serve others

Q4. According to the script, which statement is <u>NOT</u> true? Choose one.

(A) Whether or not belonging is formed with others depends on our behavior towards them.

(B) Purposes are not just found in the workplace, and how they contribute

165

to others has important implications.

(C)　Enhancing self-centeredness and originality consequently makes our life meaningful.

(D)　Interpreting and retelling our own story can help us discover new aspects of our life.

Q5.　By using the concept of "storytelling", how can you edit this story? Imagine the situation and make your own story following the sentences below in 10－15 words.

> I couldn't pass the entrance exam. So I had to enter the university I didn't want to.

(☆☆☆◎◎◎)

【7】 Read the following passage and answer the questions below.

Children from the poorer strata of society begin life not only with material disadvantages but with cognitive ones. Decades of research have confirmed this, including a famous 1995 finding by psychologists Betty Hart and Todd Risley: By age four children reared in poverty have heard 30 million fewer words, on average, than their peers from wealthier families. That gap has, been linked to shakier language skills at the start of school, which, in turn, predicts weaker academic performance.

But the sheer quantity of words a toddler hears is not the most significant influence on language acquisition. Growing evidence has led researchers to conclude quality matters more than quantity, and the most valuable quality seems to be back-and-forth communication—what researchers variously call conversational turns, duets or contingent talk.

A paper published in February in *Psychological Science* brings a new dimension of support to this idea, offering the first evidence these exchanges play a vital role in the development of Broca's area, the brain region most closely associated with producing speech. 'Further, the amount of conversational turns a child experiences daily outweighs socio-economic status in predicting both activity in Broca's area and the child's language skills.

The study, from the lab of neuroscientist John Gabrieli of Massachusetts Institute of Technology, involved 36 children, ages four to six, from a range of socio-economic backgrounds. It had three components: First, researchers used standardized tests to evaluate each child's verbal ability and derive a composite score. Second, the brain of each child was scanned using functional magnetic resonance imaging (fMRI) while the child listened to very short (15-second) stories. Lastly, adult-child communication at home was evaluated for two days using a state-of-the-art recording and analysis system called LENA (Language Environment Analysis) to measure adult speech, the child's utterances and their conversational turns—paired exchanges separated by no more than five seconds.

The researchers confirmed the classic 1995 finding that, overall, kids from wealthier families hear more words. And although their sample was small, they even confirmed the 30-million-word gap between the poorest and richest children. But what correlated most closely with a child's verbal score was not the number of words he or she heard but the number of conversational turns. And these exchanges were the only aspect of language measured by LENA that correlated with the intensity of activity seen in Broca's area during the fMRI story session. "We found that by far the biggest driver for brain development was not the number of words spoken but the conversations," Gabrieli says. And although on average parents with greater income ane education have more of these verbal exchanges with their youg children, "there's pretty good diversity," he notes. In other words, some low-income parents engaged in a lot of conversation with their child and some wealthier parents conversed relatively little.

The researchers calculated that a child's verbal ability score increased by one point for every additional 11 conversational exchanges per hour.

How exactly exposure to these exchanges alters Broca's area is a question Gabrieli's team is exploring in subsequent research. "We know that greater activation in Broca's area was associated with better verbal abilities overall, so it seems like greater activation is good," he says. One possibility is back-and-forth communication promotes more connections between brain cells in that region.

The study is a "very, very important" addition to a growing body of work, says developmental psychologist Kathryn Hirsh-Pasek, director of the Infant Language Laboratory at Temple University, who was not involved in the work. "We have known for quite a while that conversational turns—or what in my work we call conversational duets—are very important for building a foundation for language and maybe for learning generally. What hadn't been done is to link it where we knew it had to be linked—to changes in the brain."

Verbal exchanges have two components that, children must master: temporal contingency and semantic contingency—essentially, understanding the timing of human conversation and how to respond meaningfully. Research, including Hirsh-Pasek's, has shown ☐ .

Contingent language begins in infancy—well before words emerge—when parents begin cooing and gooing at their babies, who respond in kind. Socio-economic differences in this behavior arise during the first year of life, according to a 2017 study of 141 11-month-olds by Michelle McGillion of the University of Sheffield in England and colleagues.

Research in this area has big implications for parents and caregivers. The search is on for interventions that will increase adult-child conversation and boost early language skills, especially for families living in poverty. McGillion's study, for instance, showed language learning took off for babies in low-income settings when caregivers were given instructions to spend 15 minutes a day engaging their infant by commenting on whatever the baby looked at. Unfortunately, the improvements did not persist at age two with this low-intensity intervention.

Encouraging conversation seems particularly necessary in an era when both children and adults are spending more time with devices and less in face-to-face communication. "The exchanges are not only about words but about feelings, about paying attention to someone else," Gabrieli observes. Hearing language from television or Alexa, he says, "does very little compared to these exchanges."

(SOURCE: Claudia Wallis (2018), *Talking with - Not just to - Kids Powers How They Learn Language*", SCIENTIFIC AMERICAN, Revised)

Q1. According to the passage, what is the most important factor to develop children's language abilities?

(A) Socio-economic status

(B) Academic performance

(C) Conversational turns

(D) The number of words spoken

Q2. According to the passage, what did the lab of John Gabrieli examine in the research?

(A) It examined how long adult-child talks continued using data processing device.

(B) It examined how adult-child communication at home affected children's character building.

(C) It examined the correlation between the verbal interactions and the activation of children's brains.

(D) It examined the correlation between the parents' social status and their children's academic achievements.

Q3. According to the passage, what did the lab of John Gabrieli find out in the research?

(A) The number of words children hear has the greatest impact on children's language development.

(B) There is no correlation between conversational exchanges and brain

169

development.

(C)　Overall language skills including conversational duets affect children's academic achievements.

(D)　There is a gap in the quantity of verbal exchanges even among families with higher income.

Q4.　According to the passage, which statement is the most appropriate for the blank 　　 ?

(A)　children cannot learn this from watching television, although they can learn it via video-chat technology such as Apple's FaceTime

(B)　there is a possibility that children can learn this from watching television if their parents are beside them

(C)　new technologies such as video-chat and Apple's FaceTime need to be developed so that children can control them

(D)　this can be learned if watching television is strictly restricted and using the new technologies is promoted

Q5. According to the passage, what did Michelle McGillion and her colleagues find out in the research?

(A)　The rate of adult-child conversational exchanges is decreasing because of the advances of devices.

(B)　Socio-economic differences have nothing to do with learning contingent language.

(C)　Babies start learning the timing of human conversation and how to respond meaningfully.

(D)　Giving some comments about what an infant looks at for fifteen minutes a day is effective regardless of his or her age.

(☆☆☆☆○○○○)

【8】In the unit "The Power of Anime" in Communication English I, you are supposed to set the object as students can understand the value of Japanese animations and share it with people overseas.

In this school, each student has his or her own pen pal in Hawaii. As the goal activity of this lesson, they are making cards to introduce their favorite Japanese animations to their friends.

Below is one of their works and this is the first draft the student has submitted. As an English teacher, write your feedback to the student, including two good points and one suggestion to improve.

Dear John,

I will tell you about my favorite anime. I like "Tonari no Totoro".
I think Totoro is cute animal. It is kind and help Mei. I think Totoro is very popular all over the world. It is simple story and beautiful picture. When we see this movie, we feel same feeling like home. It give me power when we are sad. We can understand that family is important and this is same all over the world. I think this movie is more better than other Ghibli anime.

From Ken (Shizuoka)

(☆☆☆○○○)

【9】 Frey & Osborne say in their paper titled, *The future of employment*, that in the future about 47 % of all U.S jobs are vulnerable to computerization. In such a situation, what should the role of high school English teachers be? Write your idea on the answer sheet. For assistance, you can use the keywords below.

keywords

[facilitate / scaffold / coach]
[communication / collaboration / creativity / critical thinking]

(☆☆☆☆○○○○)

解答・解説

【中学校】

【1】1　見方・考え方　　2　言語活動　　3　コミュニケーションを図る

〈解説〉外国語科の目標は，「簡単な情報や考えなどを理解したり表現したり伝え合ったりするコミュニケーションを図る資質・能力」を育成することである。このためには，出題箇所に続く(1)〜(3)に示された「知識及び技能」，「思考力，判断，表現力等」，「学びに向かう力，人間性等」それぞれに関わる外国語特有の資質・能力を育成する必要があり，その際，外国語教育の特質に応じて，生徒が物事を捉え，思考する「外国語によるコミュニケーションにおける見方・考え方」を働かせることが重要である。学習指導要領および同解説を熟読のうえ，目標については文言を正確に記憶しておきたい。

【2】ウ　読むこと…い，か　　エ　話すこと[やり取り]…あ，え
　　　オ　話すこと[発表]…う，お

〈解説〉今回の改訂により，従来1つの領域とされていた「話すこと」が，「話すこと[やり取り]」と「話すこと[発表]」の2つの領域に分けられた。中学校においては，従来の「聞くこと」，「読むこと」，「書くこと」の3つの領域と併せて，これら5つの領域の言語活動を通してコミュニケーションを図る資質・能力を育成することが目標として示されている。本問の場合は，例えば，あ「適切に応答したり自ら質問し返したりする」，え「互いに会話を継続する」などから，「話すこと[やり取り]」と容易に判断できると思われるが，学習指導要領および同解説を参照し，個々の領域の目標，内容，配慮事項，言語活動例について一歩踏み込んだ理解が必要である。

【3】First of all, I'll introduce the students the idea of "The 17 Sustainable Development Goals" set by the United Nations General Assembly so that they can have an image of "sustainable" and apply its idea to their own community. Then I'll make some groups and give each group a chance to talk about their plan to make a presentation. (59 words)

〈解説〉指定語数が40〜60語以内と少ないので，できるだけ簡潔にまとめる。解答例では，国連の「持続可能な開発のための17の目標」を紹介して生徒に具体的なイメージを持たせ，それらの考え方を自分たちの地域社会に当てはめて，グループごとに計画を話し合い発表させるという流れを提案している。取り組みがすでに始まっている自治体の例などを紹介することも，生徒にとって参考になるだろう。

【4】I agree with this opinion. I have two reasons. First, giving homework will help expose the students to English every day. It's important for them especially at an early learning stage. Second, it'll also help teachers understand what level our students are on and give each of them an appropriate feedback. (51 words)

〈解説〉解答例では，宿題を毎日出せば生徒は毎日英語に触れることができるし，教師は生徒の学習レベルを把握し適切なフィードバックを返すことができるとして，賛成の立場で書かれている。なお，学習者の自律を促すという観点から解答することもできる。その際には教師としてどのような働きかけをするかを述べる必要がある。

【5】Writing fan letters in English is one of the good class activities. I think that having fun in writing English is the most effective way for students. They write to their favorite actors, singers or sport players overseas. That can motivate the students. When they want to use words and expressions they haven't learned, they're willing to look up appropriate ones in the dictionaries and learn by themselves. That can also give them authentic learning opportunities. (76 words)

173

〈解説〉書く活動においては，読み手を意識して書くことが大切であるので，その設定を明確にしておくことが必要である。解答例では，生徒が好きな海外の俳優や歌手やスポーツ選手にファンレターを書く活動を挙げている。自分の伝えたいことを，辞書を調べてでも英語で書きたいという意欲が期待できる。

【6】1　①　エ　　②　ウ　　2　ア

〈解説〉1　①　空所を含む文は，ベテランのスキーヤーがスノーボードに挑戦したらどうなるかについて書かれている。空所の次の文以降では，この2つのスポーツが姿勢もバランスも全く異なっており，片方の知識はもう片方の役に立たないと述べているので，「どうにかこうにかレンタル小屋からリフトの下まで行くことができるくらいだ」とするのが適切。barely ～「辛うじて～する」。　②　赤ちゃんは好きも嫌いも，何の経験もなく生まれてくるという文脈であるから，arrives with a clean slate「白紙の状態でやってくる」が適切。　2　筆者の主張は最初，または最後の段落に書かれていることが多い。最終段落の最終文「試したことが気に入れば，それから学ぶことができるし，それを自分の世界に取り入れ，自分の人生をより充実し豊かなものにできる」から，ア「新しい経験は私たちの人生を向上させる」が適切。

【7】1　A　エ　　B　イ　　2　He neither barked nor growled and seemed to like everyone　　3　Prison inmates learn compassionate behavior, gain a sense of purpose, and experience unconditional love by training shelter dogs.　4　ウ

〈解説〉1　A　第11段落には，心臓病の患者がセラピードッグと一緒に過ごす場合とそうではない場合の対照研究結果が書かれている。「患者の不安レベル，血圧がかなり低くなった」とするのが適切。significant「著しい」。　B　第12段落では，筆者がインフルエンザで倒れたとき，マックスがじっとベッドの足元に横たわっていたとある。「セラピードッグは，人がいつ優しい心遣いを必要としているか本能

的に知っている」とするのが適切。instinctively「本能的に」。　2　下線部の意味は「マックスが癒す力を持っているかもしれないと私はすぐに気づいた」。直後の文の前半から解答する。「彼は吠えることもうなることもなく，誰のことも好きなようだった」。　3　設問は「シェルタードッグを訓練することは刑務所の囚人にどのように影響するか」。囚人による訓練内容と囚人に見られる変化は，第14段落に記されている。　4　ウ「マックスは小さく，毛がフワフワして，反抗的だったのでセラピードッグ訓練のため登録された」。第1段落の2〜4文目参照。「反抗的だった」という箇所が誤り。

【8】1　①　ウ　　②　イ　　2　(1)　They realized that now they had a "voice" to share with others, and they could make a difference.　　(2)　It's because the learning experiences and challenges do not necessarily follow the sequential flow of textbook and there is often an element of the "unknown".　3　(1)　local, national, and international contacts; a written report; and a multimedia presentation.　　(2)　One student studying global warming established a partnership with an environmental organization and his contact invited him to attend a United Nations-sponsored international conference in Montreal.　　(3)　The teachers use "M.I." to encourage students to show their understanding of content in ways that are comfortable for them by reflecting on their "M.I." strengths and learning styles and to explore other areas of their "M.I." as ways to strengthen those skills.

〈解説〉1　①　第10段落2文目で「経験的な教育は，従来の方法では評価することがかなり難しい」と述べていることから，1つ目の空所を含む文は「アセスメントは，また別の考慮すべき事柄である」，2つ目の空所を含む文は「ブロックビルパブリックスクールの教師たちのアセスメントと評価の方法は…」とするのが適切である。　②　空所を含む文は，生徒たちが生涯学習者となるための教師の責任について述べている。「生徒たちが(実社会との)関係を作ることができるような意義ある状況を与えること」が教師の責任である。　2　(1)　質問は「環

境について夢中になったブロックビルパブリックスクールの生徒たち
は何に気づいたか」。第6段落の1文目に着目し解答する。

(2)　質問は「なぜ，ブロックビルパブリックスクールの新たな取り組
みは実行するには骨が折れる，と感じる教師がいるのか」。第9段落の
1，2文目参照。　3　(1)　質問は「ブロックビルパブリックスクール
で，完成した自主的リサーチプロジェクトを構成する主要な3つのも
のを挙げよ」。第3段落の最後の文から解答する。　(2)　質問は「彼ら
のリサーチトピックの分野で研究する専門家とコンタクトをとってい
る，ブロックビルパブリックスクールの生徒の一例を示せ」。第4段落
の2，3文目に着目し解答する。　(3)　質問は「ブロックビルパブリッ
クスクールの教師たちは，生徒の学びを援助するためどのようにM.I.
を使うか一例を示せ」。第10段落の最後の2文参照。

【高等学校】

【1】Q1　(B)　　Q2　(C)　　Q3　(A)　　Q4　(C)　　Q5　(C)
〈解説〉単文を聞いて，その英文の応答として適切なものを3択で答える
　問題。Q1を例にとると，「あれはあなたが昨日買った冷蔵庫ですか」
　に対してYes. What do you think about it?「はい。それをどう思いますか」
　を選択する。いずれも英文自体は易しい。英文は1回のみ放送される。

【2】Q1　(B)　　Q2　(B)　　Q3　(A)　　Q4　(C)　　Q5　(B)
〈解説〉対話文と質問を聞いて，答えとして適切なものを3択で答える問
　題。対話文は一人3回程度，計6回程度のやりとりである。Q1を例にと
　ると，「女性はヤマダ教授についてどのようなことをほのめかしてい
　ますか」に対して「彼女は彼の病気を気にかけている」を選択する。
　英文と質問は1回のみ放送される。

【3】Q1　(A)　　Q2　(C)　　Q3　(B)　　Q4　(B)
〈解説〉250語程度からなる対話文(数学の成績と不安定型愛着との関係に
　ついて)を聞いて，内容に一致する文や語句を3択で答える問題。選択

肢の表現はスクリプトとは異なり，微妙に言い換えられているので，やや難易度が高い。20秒与えられる準備の時間に，問題用紙に印刷されている選択肢や設問に目を通し，聞き取りのポイントを把握しよう。英文は2回放送される。

【4】Q1 (1) (C)　　(2) (A)　　Q2 (1) (C)　　(2) (B)
(3) (A)　　Q3 (A)
〈解説〉300語程度の英文を聞いて，質問に選択肢で答える問題。20秒間，質問，選択肢，図に目を通す時間が与えられる。英文は2回放送されるが，Q2を例にとると，The total amount of the blue water and green water was 56.5%. The proportion of blue water is about a quarter …から答えを導き出さなければならず，難易度が高いと言える。メモを適切に取りながら聞き進めていくことが必要である。

【5】(a) human skills / communication, leadership, and endurance / curiosity, reading skills, and comprehension　　(b) the subjects they aren't good at / the subjects they failed /the subjects not fully learned / the subjects to be perfect　　(c) (both) humanities and science / subjects (those) from two groups / social and hard sciences
〈解説〉英文を聞いて，問題用紙に印刷されている要約文の空所を補充し，要約文を完成させる問題。英文は400語程度で，聞き取りのスクリプトとしては長い。また，(b)を例にとると，if a student passes fifth grade but didn't do well in math, he or she could retake the fifth grade course subject until the skills are fully learned and understood…から答えを導き出さなければならない。「6語以内で」という制限つきなので，解答するのにさらに工夫が求められ，難易度の高い問題である。

【6】Q1 (D)　　Q2 (1) (B)　　(2) (A)　　(3) (C)　　Q3 (D)
Q4 (C)　　Q5 However, I met a professor who understands me. I found the purpose of my future. (16 words)

〈解説〉Q1　第2段落で，筆者は「幸せであること」と「生きがいを持つこと」の違いについて考察し，(D)「生きがいを見出すことが，より充実した生き方だ」とわかったと述べている。第3段落で，このことがさらに「『どのようにしたら有意義な人生を送れるのか』という疑問を生んだ」という話の流れになっている。　Q2　「これらの行為(知り合いに挨拶をしない，話しかけられているときにスマホをチェックする)は他人を軽んじている」に続く文として，(B)「その行為は彼らに，自分は無視され価値がないと感じさせるだろう」→(A)「しかし愛情を持って導けば」→(C)「お互いを高める絆ができる」と続く。

Q3　第6段落は，2つ目の柱である「目的」について述べている段落である。4文目に「あなたが与えるもの」に多く関わるとある。よって，「目的」の鍵となるのは，(D)「他人の役に立つため力を発揮すること」である。　Q4　第7段落の最後の文参照。3つ目の柱「超越」の経験をした後に，被験者が自己中心的でなくなる研究結果から，(C)「自己中心と独創性を高めた結果，人生は有意義になる」が誤り。　Q5　最終段落の最後の2文参照。4つ目の柱の「ストーリーテリング」では「悪いことは良いことで埋め合わせをする」。有意義な人生を送っている人はそのような話をするとある。よって逆境(望んでいなかった大学に入学した)に対して，肯定的な意味づけとなる英文を解答とする。

【7】Q1　(C)　　Q2　(C)　　Q3　(D)　　Q4　(A)　　Q5　(C)

〈解説〉Q1　問いは「子どもの言語能力を発達させる最も大切な要因は何か」。第2段落参照。「会話のやり取り」の意味を表すものとして，back-and forth communication, conversational turns, duets, contingent talkなど様々な名称が挙げられている。　Q2　問いは「ジョン・ガブリエリの研究室は調査で何を調べたか」。第4段落参照。子どもの言語能力，子どもの脳，親子のコミュニケーションの3つの項目が挙げられているので，(C)「言語のやり取りと子どもの脳の活性化」が適切。　Q3　問いは「ジョン・ガブリエリの研究室は調査で何を発見したか」。第5段落の最後の2文参照。概して高収入・高学歴の親は子どもたちと

の会話のやり取りが多いが，かなりの差異があり，低収入でも会話の多い親や，裕福でも会話の少ない親もいると述べている。したがって，(D)「高収入の家族間でも言語によるやり取りの量に差異がある」が適切。　Q4　第9段落で，言語によるやり取りをすることで，子どもたちは時間的偶発性(会話の間)や意味上の偶発性(意味のある返答)を身につけるとある。よって，(A)「子どもたちは，アップルのフェイスタイムのようなビデオチャット技術でそれらを身につけることができるが，テレビを見ることでは身につけられない」が適切。　Q5　問いは「ミシェル・マクギリオンと同僚は調査で何を発見したか」。この調査については第10段落参照。1文目に，偶発的な言語は幼児期に始まると述べられているので，(C)「赤ちゃんは人間の会話の間や意味のある返答をする方法を学び始める」が適切。

【8】 You made a nice card to introduce a Japanese anime. I have some comments on your card. You have written some reasons why this anime should be introduced to the world. And your ideas are based on your personal experiences or sympathy for others. Also, you may not know the word "nostalgia", but you tried to use other English words to express your feeling. This is important to improve your writing skills. To improve your card, you can use some words such as "so", moreover", "however", and "thus" to make the flow of your idea much clearer. Anyway, your message will reach your friend in Hawaii.

〈解説〉生徒の英文原稿(自分の好きな日本のアニメを海外の友達に紹介)にフィードバックをするという設問。解答例では，この映画が世界の人に紹介されるべきと考える複数の理由を述べていること，自身の経験や他人への思いやりに基づいて考えを述べていること，知っている単語を使って何とか自分の考えを伝えようとしていることを良い点として挙げている。また，接続詞等を入れて流れが明確になるようアドバイスをしている。実際の現場でも，生徒の原稿を生かしながら改善方法を具体的に示すことが大切である。

【9】The role of the English teacher, regardless of advances in technology, will remain the same, to cultivate communicative ability in a second language, as well as to encourage students to be self-supporting and contribute to national welfare. Artificial Intelligence (AI) can do many things people can do. However, some experts in this field point out that it requires people to control its system, because it doesn't make ethical judgements. It is in the process of the collaboration and communication that we can foster moral sentiments. When I studied in Canada, I got some ideas from different points of view of my friends. I realized that we need to have a lot of discussions to be matured as a person. In such situations, not only better language skills but also humanity is indispensable. As an English teacher, we should show our students what humanity is and how to build good relationship with other people. No matter how fast information technology evolves, I believe teacher's role on this point will never change.

〈解説〉将来，多くの仕事がコンピューター化の影響を受けると言われている中で，高校の英語教師の役割はどうあるべきかを問うている。語数指定はされていないが，150語〜200語程度を目安にしたい。生徒との人間関係や信頼関係の上に教育は成り立っている。このような人間的な側面を解答に盛り込むとよい。

2020年度　実施問題

【中学校】

【1】【放送問題】

Listen to the description and choose the most suitable word from (A) to (D) below. The description will be read only once.

1　(A)　chocolate

　　(B)　hamburger

　　(C)　cake

　　(D)　gratin

2　(A)　traffic jam

　　(B)　crossroad

　　(C)　sidewalk

　　(D)　pedestrian bridge

(☆☆○○○○)

【2】【放送問題】

Alisa is a new ALT from Canada. Listen to the conversation between Alisa and a Japanese teacher of English, Mr. Tanaka. Choose the correct answer for the following questions. The conversation, the questions and the choices will be read only once.

1　(A)

　　(B)

　　(C)

　　(D)

2　(A)

　　(B)

　　(C)

(D)

(☆☆☆◎◎◎)

【３】【放送問題】

Listen to the following passage of an essay written by a Frenchman, Paul, who has lived in Japan for a year. Then, answer the following questions. The passage and questions will be read only once.

1　He was interested in _____.

2　_____.

3　_____.

4

(☆☆☆☆◎◎◎)

【４】【英作文】

　A中学校では，2年生の学年だよりのコラムで，いろいろな職業について紹介をしています。1月号では，「中学校の英語教師」を取り上げることになり，英語科のB先生が担当することになりました。英語教師を目指した理由と英語の授業を通して生徒に伝えたいことを含めた内容を英語で書くことにしました。あなたが，B先生ならどのような内容を書きますか。英単語60語以上80語以下で書きなさい。

(☆☆☆☆◎◎◎◎)

【５】【英作文】

　次の意見について，理由を含め，あなたの考えを書きなさい。理由

を二つ以上挙げ，英単語40語以上60語以下で書きなさい。

> Japan will be a cashless society in the near future.

(☆☆☆○○○)

【 6 】【英作文】

　次は，「中学校学習指導要領(平成29年3月告示)第2章　第9節　外国語」の読むことの目標の一つです。

> イ　日常的な話題について，簡単な語句や文で書かれた短い文章の概要を捉えることができるようにする。

　この目標をねらいとして，あなたは授業でどのような活動を設定しますか。また，その際の留意点を二つ挙げ，英単語60語以上80語以下で書きなさい。

(☆☆☆○○○)

【 7 】次の英文を読み，あとの問いに答えなさい。

　Recently, as a British man took a train from London to Manchester, he found himself becoming steadily enraged. A woman had picked up her phone and begun a loud conversation, which would last an unbelievable hour. Furious, (　①　)

　When the train arrived at its destination, the man bolted. He'd had enough of the woman's rudeness. But the press were now waiting for her on the platform. And when they gleefully showed her his messages, she used just one word to describe his actions:rude.

　The man's tale is something of a microcosm of our age of (　②　), fueled by social media (and, often, politics). What can we do to fix this?

　Studies have shown that rudeness spreads quickly and virally, almost like the common cold. Just witnessing rudeness makes it far more likely that we, in turn, will be rude later on. Once infected, we are more aggressive, less creative and worse at our jobs. The only way to end this chain of rudeness is to make a conscious decision to do so. We must have the guts to call it out, face to face. We must say, "Just stop." For that man, that would have meant approaching the woman, telling her that her conversation was frustrating other passengers and politely asking her to speak more quietly or make the call at another time.

The rage and injustice we feel at the rude behavior of a stranger can drive us to do odd things. In my own research, surveying 2,000 adults, I discovered that the acts of revenge people had taken ranged from the ridiculous ("I rubbed fries on their windshield") to the disturbing ("I sabotaged them at work"). That man did shine a spotlight on the woman's behavior—but from after, in a way that shamed her.

We must instead combat rudeness (③). When we see it occur in a store, we must step up and say something. If it happens to a colleague, we must point it out. We must defend strangers in the same way we'd defend our best friends. But we can do it with grace, by handling it without a trace of aggression and without being rude ourselves. Because once rude people can see their actions through the eyes of others, they are far more likely to end that the chain of themselves. As this tide of rudeness rises, civilization needs civility.

〔出典：Time：February16, 2018　一部改〕

1　(①)～(③)に入る最も適切なものを選択肢ア～エより一つ選び，記号で答えなさい。

①　ア　the man asked the conductor to discipline her.
　　イ　the man approached her, complaining about her rudeness.
　　ウ　the man began to tweet about the woman. He took a picture of her and sent it to his more than 40,000 followers.
　　エ　the man angrily rose from his seat and stormed out to the next car so he could get away from her voice.

②　ア　crimes of intimidation

イ　increasing rudeness

ウ　media policy

エ　sophisticated methods of complaining

③　ア　head on

イ　maliciously

ウ　in a roundabout way

エ　with hesitation

2　英文の内容と適するものを選択肢ア～エより一つ選び，記号で答えなさい。

ア　The moment the man tried to escape from the woman's rudeness, he was surrounded and questioned by the press.

イ　Witnessing other people being rude makes people less inclined to spread rudeness because it makes them more aggressive and worse at their job.

ウ　From the author's survey, he noticed that people who become enraged because of rudeness do stupid things or cause commotions.

エ　Rudeness spreads constantly in a society of highly advanced information technology.

3　英文が最も伝えたいことは何か，選択肢ア～エより一つ選び，記号で答えなさい。

ア　People resent anger towards insane attitudes and cause irrational behavior from their own anger.

イ　These days, there are many problems in confronting someone's rudeness.

ウ　There is a low possibility that even a rude person can change his or her behavior by objectively considering how it is viewed by others.

エ　We should politely respond to the person face to face to prevent the cycle of rude behavior.

(☆☆☆◎◎)

【8】次の英文を読み，あとの問いに答えなさい。

While the debate regarding how much screen time is appropriate for children rages on among educators, psychologists, and parents, it's another emerging technology in the form of artificial intelligence and machine learning that is beginning to alter education tools and institutions and changing what the future might look like in education. It is expected that artificial intelligence in U.S. education will grow by 47.5% from 2017-2021 according to the Artificial Intelligence Market in the US Education Sector report. Even though most experts believe the critical presence of teachers is irreplaceable, there will be many changes to a teacher's job and to educational best practices.

AI has already been applied to education primarily in some tools, that help develop skills and testing systems. As AI educational solutions continue to mature, the hope is that AI can help fill needs gaps in learning and teaching and allow schools and teachers to do more than ever before. AI can drive efficiency, personalization and streamline admin tasks to allow teachers the time and freedom to provide understanding and adaptability — uniquely human capabilities where machines would struggle. By leveraging the best attributes of machines and teachers, the vision for AI in education is one where they work together for the best outcome for students. Since the students of today will need to work in a future where AI is the reality, it's important that our educational institutions expose students to and use the technology.

Adjusting learning based on an individual student's particular needs has been a priority for educators for years, but AI will allow a level of differentiation that's impossible for teachers who have to manage 30 students in each class. There are several companies such as Content Technologies and Carnegie Learning currently developing intelligent instruction design and digital platforms that use AI to provide learning, testing and feedback to students from pre-K to college level that gives them the challenges they are ready for, identifies gaps in knowledge and redirects to new topics when

186

appropriate. As AI gets more sophisticated, it might be possible for a machine to read the expression that passes on a student's face that indicates they are struggling to grasp a subject and will modify a lesson to respond to that. The idea of customizing curriculum for every student's needs is not viable today, but it will be for AI-powered machines.

Artificial intelligence tools can help make global classrooms available to all including those who speak different languages or who might have visual or hearing impairments. Presentation Translator is a free plug-in for PowerPoint that creates subtitles in real time for what the teacher is saying. This also opens up possibilities for students who might not be able to attend school due to illness or who require learning at a different level or on a particular subject that isn't available in their own school. AI can help break down silos between schools and between traditional grade levels.

An educator spends a tremendous amount of time grading homework and tests. AI can step in and make quick work out of these tasks while at the same time offering recommendations for how to close the gaps in learning. Although machines can already grade multiple-choice tests, they are very close to being able to assess written responses as well. As AI steps in to automate admin tasks, it opens up more time for teachers to spend with each student. There is much potential for AI to create more efficient enrollment and admissions processes.

Ask any parent who has struggled to help their teenager with algebra, and they will be very excited about the potential of AI to support their children when they are struggling at home with homework or test preparations. Tutoring and studying programs are becoming more advanced thanks to artificial intelligence, and soon they will be more available and able to respond to a range of learning styles.

There are many more AI applications for education that are being developed including AI mentors for learners, further development of smart content and a new method of personal development for educators through virtual global conferences. Education might be a bit slower to the adoption of artificial intelligence and machine learning, but the changes are beginning and will continue.

〔出典：Forbes：July25, 2018　一部改〕

1　"a priority for educators for years" とはどのようなものだと書かれているか，日本語で答えなさい。

2　下線部Artificial intelligence toolsは，具体的にどのような生徒に対して役立つことが予想されると書かれているか，日本語で四つ挙げなさい。

3　教師が，子どもと過ごす時間を確保できるよう，AIはどのようなことができる可能性があるか，また，保護者のためにはどのようなことができるか，それぞれ一つずつ具体的に日本語で書きなさい。

4　次の質問に英語で答えなさい。

(1)　Why do our educational institutions need to let students experience AI?

(2)　The more advanced AI gets, what might a machine be able to do to make a lesson more suitable for students?

(☆☆☆◎◎◎)

【高等学校】

【1】Listen to the short sentences and choose the most suitable response from the three choices, ア, イ, ウ. You will listen to the short sentences only once.

Q1.　Do you know when the conversation class will start?

ア　Not until October.

イ　You need to sign up for a membership.

ウ　That sounds interesting.

Q2.　I am wondering if I should try some volunteer activity.

ア　You should! Money counts!

イ　You should! You would regret it!

ウ　You should! It is so rewarding!

Q3. How come you are avoiding me?

   ア   You probably think so.

   イ   What makes you think so?

   ウ   I just wanted to know why.

Q4. I am so stupid to lock myself out.

   ア   All right. That depends.

   イ   All right. I can help you.

   ウ   All right. It's up to you.

Q5. Did you see Taro's photo on Twitter? He took a picture of his car between his thumb and his index finger.

   ア   Yes, where should I park his car?

   イ   Yes, I want to buy the same one.

   ウ   Yes, the car looked like a toy.

(☆☆○○○○)

【2】 Listen to the dialogues and the questions. Choose the correct answer from the three choices, ア, イ, ウ. You will listen to the dialogues and questions only once.

Dialogue 1

   W: Where shall we go for our next trip? What do you think of Thailand?

   M: I'm not really interested in swimming or shopping, but I'd like to visit the Buddhist temples and elephant camps.

   W: Me too. I've always wanted to go elephant trekking and enjoy the scenery of the tropical jungle.

   M: That's funny. I've had the same dream.

   Q: What do they like about Thailand?

     ア   Swimming and shopping.

     イ   Its culture and nature.

     ウ   Camping in the jungle.

Dialogue 2

M: Thanks for watching me practice my speech, Mrs. Wilson.

W: No problem. I was quite impressed with your gestures.

M: You don't think they were too exaggerated?

W: No, they made your points clear.

M: I was concerned I'd overacted.

W: You should articulate your words carefully, though. Be more precise with your pronunciation.

M: Okay.

Q: What does Mrs. Wilson suggest the student do?

　ア　He should speak slowly.

　イ　He should stop gesturing.

　ウ　He should pronounce clearly.

Dialogue 3

W: Lastly, could you sign here? OK, you are all set to experience driving an electric car.

M: Oh, it's going to be so exciting. I didn't think I could rent an electric car.

W: You're lucky. We only have one here, and it hasn't been rented out today. You're going to enjoy driving it. It's very quiet and comfortable.

M: Wonderful! And I'm fully covered for all day today.

W: Yes, you are. Including damage to windows and tires, as well as loss of the key.

Q: What is the woman explaining?

　ア　The cost of possible repairs.

　イ　The good and bad points of the car.

ウ　Features of the car and its insurance.

Dialogue 4

M: Good morning, Mrs. Millington. What can I do for you?

W: I'd like to ask you about the studio apartment my son and I took a look at the other day.

M: Oh, did you decide to rent it for your son?

W: Umm... He really liked it, but to be honest, it seems rather expensive. I think it's too spacious for a single college student and it's located a bit far from his school.

M: Well, if you're willing to sign the rental contract now, I'm sure the owner would lower the rent.

W: OK. Since my son is up for it, I guess I'll go along with it, but only if the owner lowers the rent.

M: I'll talk to him right now.

Q: What does Mrs. Millington decide to do?

ア　Ask the owner about the discount directly.

イ　Rent the studio apartment if the owner reduces the price.

ウ　Look for a studio apartment that is closer to the college.

Dialogue 5

W: Mr. Robins, there's something I'd like to talk to you about. Do you have a moment?

M: Sure. What's going on?

W: Uh... Actually I've made up my mind to quit high school. I can't afford it because my mother is having many financial troubles. So I'm thinking about working at a nursing home.

M: I'm sorry to hear that, but I believe there are still ways to finish high school. How about applying for a correspondence high school?

W: What's that?

M: It's a school where you can do the assignments and acquire credits while working.

W: Really? Sounds interesting. What should I do to get more details?

M: How about sending a request for a brochure to the school?

W: Ok. I will.

Q:　What will the student probably do?

　ア　She will continue working.

　イ　She will drop out of school.

　ウ　She will ask for further information.

(☆☆☆○○○)

【3】Listen to the passage about "Aging and Driving", and choose the most appropriate phrase from the three choices, ア, イ, ウ. You will have 20 seconds to prepare before listening to the passage. You will listen to the passage two times.

　Everyone ages differently, so there is no official cutoff as to when someone should stop driving. However, older adults are more likely to violate traffic regulations and get into accidents than younger drivers. What causes this increase? As we age, factors such as decreased vision, impaired hearing, slowed motor reflexes, and worsening health conditions can become a problem.

　Aging also tends to result in a reduction of strength, coordination, and flexibility, which can impact your ability to safely control a car. The following are typical symptoms elderly drivers suffer. First, neck pain or stiffness can make it hard to look over their shoulders. Second, leg pain can make it difficult to move their feet from the gas pedal to the brake pedal, and diminished arm strength can make it hard to turn the steering wheel quickly and effectively. Third, their reaction times can slow down with age and also they can lose the ability to effectively divide their attention between multiple activities.

They may have driven their entire life and take great pride in their safety record, but as they age, it is critical that they realize their driving ability can change. They may feel shocked or overwhelmed at the prospect of losing some of their independence, but by keeping their mind open to new possibilities, they can still maintain an active, vibrant, and rewarding lifestyle without a car.

(SOURCE :

https://www.helpguide.org/articles/alzheimers-dementia-aging/how-aging-affects-driving.htm　REVISED)

Q1.　When elderly people, drive cars, (　　).
　ア　they consider their ages and refrain from driving by themselves
　イ　they tend to be in traffic accidents more often than the young
　ウ　they have a choice to return their license to get some reward

Q2.　Elderly drivers cause traffic accidents because (　　).
　ア　their body functions become degraded
　イ　their mental statuses become unstable
　ウ　they tend to become too careful

Q3.　According to the author, after giving up driving, elderly people should (　　).
　ア　try to be positive towards a new lifestyle
　イ　keep pride in their safety record
　ウ　be dependent on the public transportations

Q4.　Elderly people should give up driving when (　　).

ア　they start having regular health checkups and doing exercises
イ　they lose some of their independence
ウ　they become aware that their competency weakens

(☆☆☆○○○)

【4】Listen to the passage about "Organ Transport" and choose the most appropriate phrase for each question. You will have 20 seconds to prepare before listening to the passage. You will listen to the passage two times.

Now, India may join a growing list of countries that use unmanned aerial vehicles for transporting medical materials. Officials are looking into using drones to beat traffic and get organs to transplant patients faster than ever.

Although the plan is still in its early stages, Jayant Sinha, a junior aviation minister, said that one possible use of the technology is "drone corridors" between drone ports built on the roofs of hospitals. Sinha said, "One of the applications for drones that has come forward is for transporting organs, so that is something that we have discussed with a large hospital company transporting organs right now and has found it to be very difficult, given how crowded Indian streets are."

Because of the time-sensitive nature of organ transport, Indian authorities sometimes organize "green corridors" that part traffic to allow vehicles carrying donor organs to reach their destination in good time, but drones offer a better alternative. It just goes in the sky and nobody is impacted. Organ transport happens very efficiently and in a very safe way.

Dr. Joseph Scalea of the University of Maryland School of Medicine has carried out successful trials of organ-transporting drones in the United States. He made a number of test flights carrying a human kidney. His institution once paid $80,000 to transport one liver on a charter flight, and he believes that drones could cut costs while revolutionizing the use of transplant organs.

Barriers to wider adoption of civilian drone flights fall into three broad categories. The first is concerned with the effect on the doctor-patient relationship if organs are transported by drone; the second is technology, which covers worries about speed, range and safety in a sphere that is in continuous development; and the third concerns the rules and regulations covering drone flights, about which authorities have been careful.

"Organ transport is an ideal initial use for civilian drone flights," Scalea said, explaining that a small number of time-sensitive flights would be easier for authorities to control than other potential applications such as grocery deliveries, which would involve a far larger number of drones and flights.

(SOURCE : CNN December 22, 2018

https://edition.cnn.com/2018/12/21/health/medical-transport-drones-scli-intl/index.html　REVISED)

Q1.　Which phrase is the most proper to fill in the brackets 1 & 2 of the following chart?

	Difficulties in carrying organs	→	What is or has been done
India	Streets are always crowded	→	(　　1　　)
The US	(　　2　　)	→	A number of test flights by drones

ア　Fighting with authorities

イ　High cost of charter flights

ウ　Parted traffic for the vehicles to pass

エ　Accidents like falling into a pond

オ　Waiting for a long time for an organ transplant

カ　Receiving grocery deliveries

Q2.　Choose three words from ア to カ which show possible difficulties about civilian drone flights.

ア　human relationship　　イ　hospitals　　ウ　technology

エ　regulations　　オ　cost　　カ　traffic

195

Q3.　Which statement is true?

ア　The project to use drones for organ transportation has just started.

イ　Authorities have finally started making standards for drone flights.

ウ　The speed of drones is fast enough but they are not stable enough to carry organs safely.

(☆☆☆☆◎◎)

【5】Listen to the passage on CAN-DO Statements and complete the summary below by filling in the underlined parts. You will have 20 seconds to prepare before listening to the passage. You'll listen to it two times.

　　The Can-Do Statements are self-assessment checklists used by language learners to assess what they "can do" with language in the Interactive, Receptive, and Productive modes of communication.

　　Ultimately, the goal for all language learners is to develop a functional use of another language for one's personal contexts and purposes.

　　The Can-Do Statements serve two purposes to advance this goal: for teaching programs, the statements provide learning targets for curriculum and unit design, serving as progress indicators; for language learners, the statements provide a way to chart their progress through incremental steps.

　　The more learners are engaged in their own learning process, the more intrinsically motivated they become. Research shows that the ability of language learners to set goals is linked to increased student motivation, language achievement, and growth in proficiency.

　　How can teachers use the Can-Do Statements for teaching language? First, use the Can-Do Statements to set long-term learning goals.

　　Choose specific Can-Do Statements or customize your own to establish learning targets for themed units and lessons. These targets can help drive your instruction to be more performance-oriented and provide more opportunities for your learners to produce language.

Also, share with your students the Can-Do Statements you are targeting for each day's lesson and show them how those targets relate to the unit goals. Encourage learners to set their own goals and provide the guidance and class time for self-assessment and reflection. When developing performance assessments, use wording from the Can-Do Statements in the rubrics, so that your learners know exactly what you expect of them.

Finally, help learners to understand how what they write or say actually demonstrates if they have met the goal of the Can-Do Statements. In this way you can help them become more independent learners, who are able to set their own goals and provide evidence. Learning that is guided by Can-Do Statements enables one to become an autonomous and life-long learner.

(SOURCE : NCSSFL(National Council of State Supervisors Council) - ACTFL(American Council on the Teaching of Foreign Languages) Can-Do Statements - *Progress Indicators for Language Learners*. REVISED)

- ・ CAN-DO statements are the lists which assess ①_____ ____ with language.
- ・ By using CAN-DO statements, teachers can set long-term learning targets and make ②_____.
- ・ By using CAN-DO statements, learners can assess their writing or speaking and ③_____.

(☆☆☆☆☆◎◎◎)

【6】 Read the following passage and answer the questions below.

Norman Garmezy, a developmental psychologist and clinician at the University of Minnesota, met thousands of children in his four decades of research. But one boy in particular stuck with him. He was nine years old, with an alcoholic mother and an absent father. Each day, he would arrive at school, with the exact same sandwich: two slices of bread with nothing in between. At home, there was no other food available, and no one to make any. Even so, Garmezy would later recall, the boy wanted to make sure that "no one would feel pity for him and no one would know the ineptitude of his mother." Each day, without fail, he would walk in with a smile on his face and a "bread sandwich" tucked into his bag.

The boy with the bread sandwich was part of a special group of children. He belonged to a cohort of kids—the first of many—whom Garmezy would go on to identify as succeeding, even excelling, despite incredibly difficult circumstances. These were the children who exhibited a trait Garmezy would later identify as "resilience." Over many years, Garmezy would visit schools across the country, focussing on those in economically depressed areas, and follow a standard protocol. He would set up meetings with the principal, along with a school social worker or nurse, and pose the same question: Were there any children whose backgrounds had initially raised red flags—kids who seemed likely to become problem kids—who had instead become, surprisingly, a source of pride? "What I was saying was, 'Can you identify (1) in your school?'" Garmezy said, in a 1999 interview. "There would be a long pause after my inquiry before the answer came. If I had said, 'Do you have kids in this school who seem to be troubled?,' there wouldn't have been a moment's delay. But to be asked about children who were adaptive and good citizens in the school and making it even though they had come out of very disturbed backgrounds—that was a new sort of inquiry. That's the way we began."

Resilience presents (2) for psychologists. Whether you can be said to have it or not largely depends not on any particular psychological test but on the way your life unfolds. If you are lucky enough to never experience any sort of adversity, we won't know how resilient you are. It's only when you're faced with obstacles, stress, and, other environmental threats that resilience, or the lack of it, emerges: Do you succumb or do you surmount?

Environmental threats can come in various guises. Some are the result of low socioeconomic status and challenging home conditions. (Those are the threats studied in Garmezy's work.) Often, such threats—parents with psychological or other problems; exposure to violence or poor treatment; being a child of problematic divorce—are chronic. Other threats are acute: experiencing or witnessing a traumatic violent encounter, for example, or being in an accident. What matters is the intensity and the duration of the stressor. In the case of acute stressors, the intensity is usually high. The stress resulting from chronic adversity, Garmezy wrote, might be lower—but it "exerts repeated and cumulative impact on resources and adaptation and persists for many months and typically considerably longer."

In 1989 a developmental psychologist named Emmy Werner published the results of a thirty-two-year longitudinal project. She had followed a group of six hundred and ninety-eight children, in Kauai, Hawaii, from before birth through their third decade of life. Along the way, she'd monitored them for any exposure to stress: maternal stress in utero, poverty, problems in the family, and so on. Two-thirds of the children came from backgrounds that were, essentially, stable, successful, and happy; the other third qualified as "at risk." Like Garmezy, she soon discovered that not all of the at-risk children reacted to stress in the same way. Two-thirds of them "developed serious learning or behavior problems by the age of ten, or had delinquency records, mental health problems, or teen-age pregnancies by the age of eighteen." But the remaining third developed into "competent, confident, and caring young adults." They had attained academic, domestic, and social success—and they were always ready to capitalize on new opportunities that arose.

What was it that set the resilient children apart? Because the individuals in her sample had been followed and tested consistently for three decades, Werner had a trove of data at her disposal. She found that several elements predicted resilience. Some elements had to do with luck: a resilient child might have a strong bond with a supportive caregiver, parent, teacher, or other mentor-like figure. But another, quite large set of elements was psychological, and had to do with how the children responded to the environment. From a young age, resilient children tended to "meet the world on their own terms." They were autonomous and independent, would seek out new experiences, and had a "positive social orientation." "Though not especially gifted, these children used whatever skills they had effectively," Werner wrote. Perhaps most importantly, the resilient children had what psychologists call an "internal locus of control" : they believed that they, and not their circumstances, affected their achievements. The resilient children saw themselves as the orchestrators of their own fates. In fact, on a scale that measured locus of control, they scored more than two standard deviations away from the standardization group.

Werner also discovered that resilience could change over time. Some resilient children were especially unlucky: they experienced multiple strong stressors at vulnerable points and their resilience evaporated. Resilience, she explained, is like a constant calculation: Which side of the equation weighs more, the resilience or the stressors? The stressors can become so intense that resilience is overwhelmed. Most people, in short, have a breaking point. On the flip side, some people who weren't resilient, when they were little somehow learned the skills of resilience. They were able to overcome adversity later in life and went on to flourish as much as those who'd been resilient the whole way through. This, of course, raises the question of how resilience might be learned.

(SOURCE : THE NEW YORKER February 11, 2016)

Q1.　According to the passage, which statement is most appropriate?
　ア　If you are raised in economically depressed areas, you'll have resilience.
　イ　Resilience emerges only when facing extreme and sudden stress.
　ウ　If you never face any adversity, you have no resilience.

エ　Resilience emerges when you are exposed to adversity.

Q2.　Choose the most appropriate phrase to fill in the blank (　1　).

ア　stressed children we could possibly help recover from trauma

イ　stressed children who have been brought up by troubled parents

ウ　stressed children who are making it here

エ　stressed children who are from stable and successful backgrounds

Q3.　Choose the most appropriate phrase to fill in the blank (　2　).

ア　an evidence

イ　a challenge

ウ　an opportunity

エ　a role

Q4.　According to Emmy Werner, which statement is true about resilience?

ア　How resilient you are may change as the circumstances change.

イ　Resilient children don't believe they can influence their own futures.

ウ　The more adverse experiences we have, the more skills of resilience we acquire.

エ　Researchers are continuously trying to figure out how to measure one's resilience.

Q5.　According to Emmy Werner, the most important element to predict resilience is "internal locus of control". Based on this concept, give advice to a student facing a difficult situation. Write in 10-15 words.

(☆☆☆☆☆○○○)

【7】　Read the following passage and answer the questions below.

Article 1

The Sustainable Development Goals are a call for action by all countries ―

poor, rich and middle-income － to promote prosperity while protecting the planet. They recognize that ending poverty must go hand-in-hand with strategies that build economic growth and address a range of social needs including education, health, social protection, and job opportunities, while tackling climate change and environmental protection.

Article 2

A couple of months ago during the OECD's Global Forum on Responsible Business Conduct, I heard a new term: SDG washing. After green washing and blue washing－using a UN logo to signpost sustainability without doing much－the term SDG washing points to businesses that use the Sustainable Development Goals to market their positive contribution to some SDGs while ignoring their negative impact on others. For example, a car company may market their electric cars as stopping global warming (SDG ① ↑). Yet, the cobalt in their batteries may be mined by five-year old kids in Congo (SDG ② ↓).

It is clear that the world will never reach the SDGs without businesses. While businesses can make positive contributions, such as creating jobs, finding innovative solutions for climate challenges, or contributing to human capital development, they can also cause or contribute to negative impacts, such as exploiting labor in supply chains, damaging the environment, or engaging in corrupt practices. Businesses should pay due attention to ensure that they avoid undermining the SDGs by causing or contributing to negative impacts.

Civil society organizations have asserted that "business responsibility for respecting human rights is too often viewed only as a matter of compliance and risk management, which underestimates the hugely positive development impacts that will be achieved through improved treatment of the millions of workers and communities affected by business activities around the world." Indeed, I have seen companies use the following excuse: We may have forced labor in our supply chain, but we have a great scholarship program for girls. (1)That is a no go. People have criticized companies for cherry picking — basically highlighting certain positive effects on a particular SDG and ignoring any negative impacts. Companies cannot compensate for doing harm on one SDG by doing well on another SDG. How, then, should companies proceed?

On the one hand, risk-based research processes grounded in the UN Guiding Principles for Business and Human Rights and the OECD Guidelines for Multinational Enterprises can help define expectations. Companies should prioritize their efforts on where their negative impacts on the SDGs are most severe.

On the other hand, profiling positive contributions to certain SDGs is fine and good, and where business can make a lot of money. (2)In other words, in doing well by doing good, business can deliver significant value to the SDGs. It is reported: "Achieving the Global Goals opens up US$12 trillion of market opportunities in the four economic systems examined by the Commission. These are food and agriculture, cities, energy and materials, and health and well-being. They represent around 60% of the real economy and are critical to delivering the Global Goals. To capture these opportunities in full, businesses need to pursue social and environmental sustainability as avidly as they pursue market share and shareholder value. If a large enough number of companies joins us in doing this now, together we will become an unstoppable force. If they don't, the costs and uncertainty of unsustainable development could swell until there is no viable world in which to do business."

Ultimately, companies should do their research on all SDGs to avoid undermining these goals. This is the essential baseline. Just think about what not having child labor in the supply chains would mean for the SDGs. A focus on managing the negative impacts on the SDGs is most urgent. This approach, taken together with the focus and positive impacts on certain SDGs, is a recipe for businesses to maximize their contribution to the SDGs.

(SOURCE : Article 1: Nieuwenkamp, R. (2017). Ever heard of SDG washing? The urgency of SDG Due Diligence REVISED

Article 2: https://www.un.org/sustainabledevelopment/)

Q1. What is SDG washing?

ア SDG washing means that companies use the SDGs to advertise their products and gain their reputation without considering bad influences.

イ SDG washing means that companies are making efforts to wash the poverty away from each country under the name of SDGs.

ウ SDG washing means that companies announce that SDGs will not leave anyone behind in order to guarantee the society.

エ SDG washing means that companies sell the products related to SDGs as one of their business strategies and use the profit for themselves.

Q2. (SDG ① ↑) and (SDG ② ↓) in the passage respectively shows one of the SDGs in the figure on the previous page. Which combination is the most appropriate? The arrow " ↑ " means "positive" effect and " ↓ " means "negative" effect.

ア ① : 15 Life on Land

    ② : 9 Industry, Innovation and Infrastructure

イ ① : 13 Climate Action

    ② : 8 Decent Work and Economic Growth

ウ ① : 2 Zero Hunger

    ② : 11 Sustainable Cities and Communities

エ ① : 4 Quality Education

    ② : 16 Peace, Justice and Strong Institutions

Q3. What does the underlined part (1) refer to in this context?

  ア It is impossible for companies to use the excuse for cherry picking.

  イ It is impossible to have forced labor and a great scholarship program for girls.

  ウ It is inconsistent to criticize companies for doing harm on one SDG.

  エ It is inconsistent to highlight positive effects and ignore negative ones.

Q4. What does the underlined part (2) imply? Choose the most appropriate phrase for the blank in the sentence below.

> In other words, companies are (   ) by contributing to societies, and business can deliver significant value to the SDGs.

  ア guiding social sustainability

  イ starting competitive business

  ウ earning large profit

  エ prioritizing negative impacts

Q5. What we learn from this passage is that

  ア by taking risks to prioritize profits, companies will achieve great popularity and hide the negative effects on the sustainability.

  イ by doing the research on negative impacts on SDGs, companies will return more profits to shareholders and achieve more popularity.

ウ by taking the negative impacts on SDGs into consideration, companies will eventually contribute to the sustainable development of society.

エ by following the concept of the SDGs, companies will be troubled when making a balance and sacrifice their contribution to society.

(☆☆☆☆☆◎◎◎)

【8】Put the words in the correct order and complete the sentences. Write the letter from (a) to (g) that fits in the blanks from (1) to (10).

Q1.

A: Are we all ready to take off for our trip?

B: Well, before we get going, ( ) ( ) (1) ( ) ( ) (2) ( ).

(a) see   (b) are   (c) me   (d) locked

(e) let   (f) all the doors   (g) if

Q2.

A: How was the party you went to with John last night?

B: It was great and I guess John also had a good time. I saw him talking to ( ) ( ) (3) ( ) ( ) (4) ( ).

(a) usually   (b) does   (c) he   (d) than

(e) there   (f) more   (g) the guests

Q3.

A: Are you sure you want to be an astronaut? You'll have to compete with so many people from all over the world.

B: I know that. Still, I'm ready to ( ) (5) ( ) (6) ( ) ( ) ( ).

(a) takes   (b) my dream   (c) it   (d) realize

(e) do   (f) to   (g) whatever

Q4.

A: The heat is severe and we have had very little rain this summer.

B: Exactly. That's why the usage of water is becoming a major political and economic issue in our prefecture, (   ) (7) (   ) (   ) (   ) (8) (   ) areas.

(a) its   (b) in   (c) many   (d) due

(e) populated   (f) to   (g) scarcity

Q5.

A: I've heard that Jim has earned a fortune by selling and buying stocks online. I'm wondering if I should give it a try.

B: You must be kidding. You hardly know anything about the stock market. Can't you (   ) (   ) (9) (   ) (10) (   ) (   )?

(a) with   (b) lose   (c) imagine   (d) could

(e) how much   (f) just one click (g) you

(☆☆☆☆○○○○)

【9】In your English Expression I class, students have just learned the description of cities and towns. As a goal activity, they will write a brief report on the most attractive city in Shizuoka. Students will be evaluated by their classmates.

Write the instructions you will give at the beginning of the class. You have to include the following 4 points and write more than 6 lines.

① Content: what information should be included

② Post-writing activity: what kind of task they will do

③ Evaluation: how the students will be evaluated

④ After class: how the reports will be used

```
Hello, everyone. Today you will write a report on the most attractive city in Shizuoka.




                                                              【6行目】


```

(☆☆☆☆◎◎◎◎)

【10】 Read the following instructions and answer the questions in English.

Q1.　What is the advantage of the ICT tools in your classroom? How do you help your students to learn by using them? Choose one or more tools from the box below and write down your idea in one paragraph. Pay attention to the paragraph structure and write in about 8 lines.

The tools currently available in the classroom are

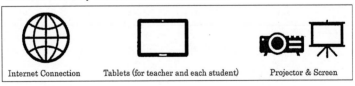

Internet Connection　　　Tablets (for teacher and each student)　　　Projector & Screen

Q2.　Now, you are teaching Lesson 2, "Save the Ocean" in Communication English I class. In order to develop students' communication ability, you have to make the goal activity. What activity do you want to do? What is the aim of it? Describe the activity in about 5 lines, You need to use the tool(s) you chose in Question 1. The following is the summary of Lesson 2.

Scientists believe that the amount of garbage thrown into the ocean is increasing, much of which is single-use plastic, or plastic used only once before throwing away. The garbage seriously damages oceans and sea creatures there.

(☆☆☆☆☆◎◎◎◎)

解答・解説

【中学校】

【1】1 (C) 2 (D)

〈解説〉スクリプトが公表されていないが，何かの説明を聞いて，正しい単語を選ぶ問題である。音声は1度しか流れない。 1 選択肢は食べ物である。(D)は「グラタン」という意味。 2 選択肢は交通関連のもので，(A)が「交通渋滞」，(B)が「交差点」，(C)が「歩道」，(D)が「歩道橋」という意味。

【2】1 (C) 2 (A)

〈解説〉スクリプトが公表されていないが，ALTと日本人英語教員の会話を聞いて，質問に対する正しい答えを選ぶ問題である。音声は1度しか流れない。選択肢は印刷されていないため，問題文と選択肢の全てを聞き取って答える必要がある。

【3】解答略。本年は問題・解答とも公表されていない。

〈解説〉スクリプトが公表されていないが，1年間日本に住んでいるフランス人のポールという人が書いたエッセイを聞いて英語で答える記述式問題である。音声は1度しか流れない。聞きながらメモを取り，書

いた英文を後から見直すとよいだろう。4問あるが，1問目だけは問題
用紙に，聞き取りのヒントとなる冒頭部分が，He was interested inと印
刷されている。確実に聞き取りたい。

【4】 I learned English from a wonderful English teacher in junior high school.
Thanks to him, I enjoyed studying English very much and wanted to share the
pleasure of learning English with others. So, I wanted to become an English
teacher. By the way, I also like listening to English songs. I will show you
simple songs. By listening them, I want to introduce native English and
different cultures in other countries to you. The world is interesting because
we are different. Let's enjoy studying English! (85words)
〈解説〉学年だよりにおいて，中学校の英語教師を目指した理由と，英語
の授業を通して生徒に伝えたいことを書く問題である。語数は60語以
上80語以下である。読み手が1月頃の中学2年生であることを考え，中
学2年生が理解できそうな文構造や表現を用いて書く必要がある。

【5】 I do not agree with the idea. Firstly, cashless payments cannot be available
if electricity supply stops. Japan was affected by natural disasters, which
caused serious power outages. Secondly, I am concerned about cyber security
risks. Our personal information can be stolen by hackers without noticing it.
Therefore, I do not think Japan will become a completely cashless society.
(59words)
〈解説〉日本が近い将来現金を使わないキャッシュレスな社会になるとい
うことについて，二つ以上の理由とともに自分の意見を書く問題であ
る。語数は40語以上60語以下と多くないため，自分の立場を明確にし，
論理的な理由を書くようにする。

【6】 In my class, I will encourage students to grasp the main idea of a short
passage by reading aloud. Then, I will ask only one question what the passage
is about. I will let students express their opinion with a brief phrase. Teachers

should not focus on details in this activity. The passages should be written in plain English, so that students can follow easily. Also, topics should be about students' everyday life to attract their interest and help them presume the overview of the passage. (86words)

〈解説〉学習指導要領の目標に基づいた活動とその留意点二つを60語以上80語以下で書く問題である。解答例ではまず生徒に音読させ，それを基に簡単な語句を用いて内容に対する意見を述べられるようにする活動を挙げている。なお，設問は「読むこと」の目標のひとつであるが，学習指導要領の「2　内容〔思考力，判断力，表現力等〕」を見ると，「(2)　情報を整理しながら考えなどを形成し，英語で表現したり，伝え合ったりすることに関する事項」「イ　日常的な話題や社会的な話題について，英語を聞いたり読んだりして得られた情報や表現を，選択したり抽出したりするなどして活用し，話したり書いたりして事実や自分の考え，気持ちなどを表現すること」と示されている。このことから，一歩踏み込んだ活動を設定したものである。

【7】1　①　ウ　　②　イ　　③　ア　　2　ウ　　3　エ
〈解説〉他者の失礼なふるまいについて，どのように対処するのかについて書かれた英文を読んで答える問題である。　1　①　第2段落の3文目に，プラットフォームで報道記者が待っていたという記述があること，そして第5段落の最終文に，男性は女性の行為にスポットライトを当てた，という記述があることから，急激にその女性に多くの注目が集まることを男性がしたことがわかる。　②　第3段落の最終文で"What can we do to fix this?"と書かれているが，thisが指す内容の一部を答える問題である。第2段落の最後の単語がrudeであり，rudenessという単語が第4段落で繰り返し出てきていることからイが正答であるとわかる。　③　最終段落の1文目にinsteadという単語が入っていることから，その前までに書かれていることの反対の内容が空欄に入ることが予測できる。第5段落では失礼な振る舞いについて復讐をするという内容が書かれているため，それとは異なる内容を入れる。head on

は「正面」という意味。　2　第5段落の1文目において，「他者の失礼なふるまいに対しての怒りや正義感から，私たちは変なことをしてしまう」と書かれているため，ウが適切。アは選択肢中のheが誤り。sheでないと本文と一致しない。イは選択肢中のlessが誤り。怒りは大きくなる。エの選択肢はconstantlyが誤りである。第4段落の1文目にquickly and virallyと書かれている。　3　エは，第6段落4文目の「親友を守るのと同様に他者のことも守らなければならない」と一致する。また，最後から2文目においても"to end that the chain of themselves"とあるが，これはエの"to prevent the cycle of rude behavior"の類似表現である。

【8】1　個々の生徒の特定のニーズに基づいて学習を調整すること。
2　・異なる言語を話す生徒　　・視覚，聴覚障害をもつ生徒
・病気で学校に通うことができない生徒　　・自分の学校で受けられない特別な教科を受けたい生徒　3　AIが教師の代わりに宿題やテストの採点をすることで，教師は子供と過ごす時間を増やすことができる。またAIは，家で宿題やテスト対策に困っている子供たちのために，家庭教師の役割を果たすことができる。　4　(1)　Today students need to work in a future where AI is the reality, it's important that our educational institutions expose students to and use the technology.

(2)　Machines can read the expression that passes on a student's face that indicates they are struggling to grasp a subject and will modify a lesson to respond to that.

〈解説〉AIが教育に果たす役割について書かれた英文を読んで答える問題である。　1　a priority for educators for yearsは第3段落の1文目にある。この文の主語は"adjusting learning based on an individual student's particular needs"であるので，この部分を訳せばよい。　2　下線部は第4段落の冒頭にある。この段落中に"those who"や"who"で始まる説明が4種類の生徒について書かれている。　3　第5段落にAIは宿題やテストの採点ができること，そして第6段落に家で宿題やテスト対策

に困っている子供を助けることができると書かれている。

4 (1) 質問の内容は「なぜ教育組織は生徒にAIを体験させる必要があるのだろうか」である。第2段落の最終文の部分が解答に該当する箇所である。 (2) 質問の内容は「AIがさらに進歩すると，機械は授業をより生徒に合うようにするために何ができるだろうか」というものである。第3段落の下から2文目が該当箇所であるため，該当する部分の表現を用いて書くとよい。

【高等学校】

【1】Q1 ア Q2 ウ Q3 イ Q4 イ Q5 ウ
〈解説〉短文を聞いて適する応答を答える問題である。音声は1度しか流れない。 Q1 「いつ会話のクラスが始まるか知っていますか？」という質問である。時期を尋ねている。 Q2 「何かボランティア活動をすべきかどうか考えている」と言っているのでウの「そうすべきだ。そうする価値がある」が適している。 Q3 "How come〜?"で「なぜ〜?」という意味。 Q4 "lock oneself out"で「〜を締め出す」という意味。 Q5 "index finger"は「人差し指」のこと。「親指と人差し指の間で車を挟んでいる写真を撮った」と言っているため，車が小さく見えることを含意している。

【2】Q1 イ Q2 ウ Q3 ウ Q4 イ Q5 ウ
〈解説〉男女の会話を聞いて質問に答える問題である。音声は1度しか流れない。 Q1 男性が「仏教寺院と象園に行きたい」と言っており，それに対して女性が賛同している。 Q2 女性は最後に「もっと正確に発音しましょう」とアドバイスしている。 Q3 女性の2回目の発言で車のことを「とても静かで快適である」と説明し，それに対して男性が「今日一日中，完全に保険でカバーされているのか」を尋ねている。それに対して女性は「窓やタイヤの破損や，鍵の紛失までカバーしている」と説明している。 Q4 女性の最後の発言で「賃料が安くなる場合のみ，そのワンルームマンションを借りる」と述べている。

"only if"「そうである場合のみ」という意味。　　Q5　男性の最後の発言で「学校にパンフレット送付の依頼をしてはどうか」と提案しており，それに対して女性が賛同している。

【3】Q1　イ　　　Q2　ア　　　Q3　ア　　　Q4　ウ

〈解説〉加齢と車の運転についての英文を聞いて答える問題である。音声を聞くまでに20秒の猶予があり，2回聞くことができる。　　Q1　第1段落の2文目において「年配のドライバーは若いドライバーよりも交通違反をおかしやすく，事故に遭いやすい」と述べている。　　Q2　第1段落の最終文において，視界の問題や聴覚の問題，反射の問題が現れることが述べられている。　　Q3　第3段落の最終文において，「新しい可能性に目を向けて，車がなくても積極的に，そして活気に満ちた価値のある生活を維持できる」と述べている。　　Q4　第3段落の1文目において「歳を取るにつれて運転能力が変わることに気づくことが重要である」と述べている。

【4】Q1　(1)　ウ　　　(2)　イ　　　Q2　ア，ウ，エ　　　Q3　ア

〈解説〉臓器をドローンで移送することに関しての英文を聞いて答える問題である。音声を聞くまでに20秒の猶予があり，2回聞くことができる。　　Q1　(1)　第2段落の最終文でインドの道路が大変混雑していることを述べている。それを解決するために，第3段落の1文目において，臓器を運ぶ車の交通を分けると述べている。　　(2)　第4段落からアメリカの状況の説明が始まっている。第4段落の3文目において，以前は飛行機をチャーターして臓器を運んでいたため8万ドルかかっていたが，ドローンはそのコストを抑えることができると述べている。Q2　第5段落に3つのカテゴリーを挙げている。その3つとはdoctor-patient relationship, technology, the rules and regulationsであるため，それぞれ対応する選択肢を選んで解答する。　　Q3　第2段落の1文目において，its early stagesと述べているため，ドローンを使って臓器を移送することはまだ始まったばかりであることがわかる。イについては，最

終段落において「様々なルールができてドローンの飛行を管理できるようになることが望ましい」ことを述べているため，まだルールはできていないので誤り。ウは第3段落の3文目でスピードも安全性も確保されていると述べているため誤りである。

【5】① what (language) learners can do　② their teaching more performance-oriented / more chances (for the learners) to produce language　③ become more independent (learner) / become a(n) (autonomous and) life-long learner

〈解説〉CAN-DO statementについての説明を聞いて答える問題である。音声を聞くまでに20秒の猶予があり，2回聞くことができる。

① CAN-DO statementがどんなことを評価するためのリストかを尋ねている。第1段落において "to assess what they "can do" with language" と述べている。　② CAN-DO statementを使うことによって，教員は長期的な学習目標を立ててどんなことを作ることができるかということを尋ねている。第6段落の2文目から解答する。　③ CAN-DO statementを使うことによって，学習者は自分自身のライティングやスピーキングを評価することができ，どうなるかという問題である。最終段落の2文目から解答する。

【6】Q1 エ　Q2 ウ　Q3 イ　Q4 ア　Q5 You have the power to change your situation. Keep going! / It is only you who can overcome your difficulties. Never give in! / Only you can control your future. Believe in yourself and you can succeed.

〈解説〉逆境に遭遇した子供の中にはそれを跳ね返していく子がいるという英文である。　Q1 第3段落の3文目において「もし何も逆境を経験していていなければ，あなたがどれくらい逆境を跳ね返すのかがわからない」と書かれている。つまり，逆境にさらされたときに跳ね返す人なのかどうかがわかる。　Q2 第2段落の後ろから2文目で，"making it even though they had come out of very disturbed backgrounds" と

書かれているため，このmake itを活用する。　Q3　心理学者にとって
ある子供がどれくらい逆境を跳ね返す子なのかを知るためには，何か
特定の心理テストなどでは測定できないと書かれている。つまり，こ
れはとても測りにくい特性であるため，a challenge「課題，(難しいが)
やりがいのある仕事」が入る。　Q4　第5段落からEmmy Wernerが登
場しており，第6段落の5文目において，「子供が環境にどのように反
応するのかが関係する」と書かれている。したがって，環境が変わる
と反応の仕方も変わると考えられる。　Q5　下線部の直後において，
「環境ではなくあなた自身が，何かを達成できるかどうかに影響する」
と書かれている。そのため，この考えに基づいて，逆境に直面した生
徒へのアドバイスを書く。

【7】Q1　ア　　Q2　イ　　Q3　エ　　Q4　ウ　　Q5　ウ
〈解説〉持続可能な目標(SDG)についての英文を読んで答える問題である。
Q1　Article 2の第1段落にSDG washingの定義が書かれている。2文目に，
SDGのポジティブな貢献を利用しつつ，他のネガティブな影響を無視
するビジネスのことを指すと述べている。　Q2　Article 2の第2段落に
ポジティブなものとネガティブなものが並べられている。ポジティブ
なものの中には仕事の創造，天候の変化に関する革新的な解決の発見，
人的資本の発展に関する寄与がある。ネガティブなものには供給の連
鎖における労働力の搾取，環境破壊，悪弊への携わりがある。これら
をヒントにして当てはまるものを選ぶ。　Q3　下線部(1)のthatは直前
の文の内容を指している。直前の文は，「我々は供給連鎖で労働力を
搾取しているかもしれないが，女児のための素晴らしい奨学金プログ
ラムがある」という内容であるが，下線部(1)はこれを認めることはで
きないという内容である。下線部(1)の後に「ネガティブな影響を無視
してポジティブな影響だけに焦点を当てることはできない」と書かれ
ている。　Q4　下線部(2)はIn other wordsで始められているため，直前
の文を言い換えているということがわかる。直前の文では，「企業は
多くのお金を稼ぐことができる」と書かれており，これがウのearning

large profitに当てはまる。 Q5 最終段落の4文目と5文目に着目する。ここには「ネガティブな影響に焦点を当てることでSDGへの貢献を最大にすることができる」と書かれている。

【8】Q1 1 (a) 2 (b) Q2 3 (f) 4 (a) Q3 5 (g)
6 (a) Q4 7 (f) 8 (c) Q5 9 (g) 10 (b)
〈解説〉Q1 整序後は, "let me see if all the doors are locked"となる。ここでのifは「〜かどうか」。 Q2 "the guest there more than he usually does"となる。ここでのdoesはtalksの代わりに使われている。 Q3 "do whatever it takes to realize my dream"となる。whatever it takesで「何が何でも」。 Q4 "due to its scarcity in many populated"となる。due toは「〜のために, 〜のせいで」。 Q5 "imagine how much you could lose with just one click"となる。「1回クリックしただけでどれくらいのお金を失う可能性があるのかを想像してみなさい」という意味である。

【9】You have to include why you have chosen the city and what's attractive about it. After writing, in a group of four people, swap reports and read. Then you'll vote and decide on the best report in your group. In the next class, with the best reports from all the groups, we'll make a Shizuoka Sightseeing Brochure. OK? （別解1） In your report, please write the name of the city and the reasons why you've chosen it. After you all finish writing your report, you will get into small groups and edit it to make a group poster. All the posters will be put on the wall of the corridor and anyone can read and put a Post-it with some message on their favorite one. （別解2） Please write the name of the city you've chosen and the reasons why you've chosen it. After you all finish writing your report, you'll get into small groups with the classmates who've chosen the same city. Exchange your reports and decide on the best report describing the city. Then, the chosen reports from each city group will be exhibited in the 1st graders' "We Love Shizuoka" Exhibition Room during the school festival.

〈解説〉英語表現Iのクラスにおいて，静岡県で最も魅力的な都市についての短いレポートを書く際の指示を英語で書く問題である。①どんな情報が含まれなければならないか，②書いた後にどんなタスクをするのか，③どのように評価されるのか，④そのレポートをどのように使うのか，という4点を含めて解答用紙に6行以上で書く。この4点を含めて書く以外には特に大きな制限はないため，自分だったらどのようにするのかを考えて自分自身のアイディアを入れて書く必要がある。

【10】1　One of the advantages of using ICT tools is to attract student's attention and interest in the topic. By using the projector and screen, we can show the pictures and movies. Students can look up at the screen, not to the textbook on the desk. Also with the pictures and movies, they can have the clear image about the topic and raise interests. Like these, ICT tools will encourage students to study harder.　（別解）　One of the advantages of the ICT tools is that the students can check and improve their own performances. Their performances can be recorded on tablets when they make speeches or play skits. Then they'll see their own performances. They can analyze and revise their performances themselves. In addition, teachers can check the recorded performances to grade the students. In this way, ICT tools will greatly improve English classes.　Q2　I would like to have students make a PR movie on a tablet to stop ocean pollution. Then students will show it on a screen. They will explain how serious the present situation is. By doing this, they can express their opinions more clearly.　（別解）　Students can have presentations about people's efforts on water pollution in Japan. During the presentations, they can show photos, figures and graphs, using tablets and a projector. The aim of this activity is to make use of the language they have learned through the lesson and explain the situations clearly.

〈解説〉Q1　インターネット接続，タブレット，プロジェクターとスクリーンという3つの中から1つ選んで，どのようにこれらを活用するのかを書く問題である。奇抜な答えを書く必要は無く，普段これらの

ICTを使って英語の授業や模擬授業においてしていることを書けばよい。　Q2 "Save the Ocean"というユニットにおける最後の活動でどのようなことをするのかを書く活動である。Q1で選んだICTを組み込んで書かなければならないことに注意する。その活動と目的を書くようにする。ユニットの最後の活動であるため，スピーキング活動やライティング活動を念頭に置くと考えやすいであろう。

2019年度　実施問題

【中学校】

【 1 】【放送問題】

Listen to the description and choose the most suitable word from A to D. The description and choices will be read only once.

1　(A)

　　(B)

　　(C)

　　(D)

2　(A)

　　(B)

　　(C)

　　(D)

(☆☆☆○○○○)

【 2 】【放送問題】

Tom is a new ALT and Ms. Yamamoto is a Japanese teacher of English working at the same school. They are now in the teachers' room. Listen to the conversation. Choose the correct answer for the following questions. The conversation and the questions will be read once.

1　(A)

　　(B)

　　(C)

　　(D)

2　(A)

　　(B)

　　(C)

　　(D)

(☆☆☆○○○○)

【3】【放送問題】

Listen to the following passage of the essay written by a Canadian, Daniel, who lives in Japan. Answer the questions. The passage and questions will be read twice.

1

At (　：　)　　※算用数字で書きなさい。

2 ＿＿＿＿＿＿＿＿＿＿＿＿＿＿＿＿＿＿＿＿＿＿＿＿＿＿＿＿.

3 (A)

(B)

(C)

(D)

4

（☆☆☆○○○）

【4】次の英文は，ある中学3年生の生徒が『My Dream』というテーマで書いたものです。この生徒の英作文に対して，あなたはどのようなコメントを書きますか。生徒の英語学習への意欲を高めることができるように，英単語30語以上40語以下で書きなさい。

My dream is to be a professional tennis player.

I like to play tennis very much.

I want to play at Wimbledon like Kei Nishikori.

He plays tennis very well. His Air-K is cool.

Now I'm practicing tennis very hard for the next game every day.

I get tired after practice, but I'll never give up!

（☆☆☆○○○）

【5】以下の主題について，あなたは賛成ですか。それとも反対ですか。賛成か反対か，あなたの立場を明らかにし，その理由を二つ挙げ，英単語40語以上50語以下で書きなさい。

> Junior high school students should not have their own cell phones.

(☆☆○○○)

【6】「中学校学習指導要領解説　外国語編　（平成20年9月）　第2章　第9節　外国語　第2　各言語の目標及び内容等　英語　2　内容　(1)　言語活動」には，以下のように示されています。

> イ　話すこと
> （ウ）　聞いたり読んだりしたことなどについて，問答したり意見を述べ合ったりなどすること。

　この指導事項を踏まえて，あなたはどのような英語の授業を行いますか。授業の中で行う活動をあげ，その活動を設定した理由を示しながら，英単語50語以上70語以下で書きなさい。

(☆☆☆☆○○○○)

【7】次の英文を読み，あとの問いに答えなさい。

　Common knowledge is not that common. What's obvious at home may be unknown abroad. It can be frustrating when foreign people don't understand what we take for granted. Let me illustrate this with a story.

　Several years ago, I flew to Atlanta, Georgia, to attend an international conference. I was jet-lagged after my long flight from Japan, but eager to register for the event. Luckily, the conference center was near my hotel, so (①). I figured that would allow me to stretch my legs and see the city. On the way there, a funny incident occurred.

　There was a broad avenue from my hotel to the center. Off in the distance, across the street, I saw a figure coming toward me. It was a tall guy, a local resident of Atlanta. Suddenly, he started waving in my direction, even though we were on opposite sides of the road.

"Who won?" he yelled out urgently. I was taken aback. Was he talking to me? He was a big friendly guy, but he seemed quite agitated. "Who won?" he shouted again. "I don't know," I shouted back. A look of amazement came over his face. "Come on, man!" he repeated. "Who won? What was the score?" He couldn't believe that I didn't know.

I didn't have to be a detective to realize that a big sports match had taken place that day. It was obviously an important game between Atlanta and its rival. As we shouted across the street, I tried to explain that I'd just arrived from Japan, but he wouldn't accept my excuse. For him, my ignorance was (②). He finally walked away, shaking his head in disbelief.

I tried to imagine (③). Today was the big game. People had been looking forward to it for weeks. It was the big news of the day. Everybody knew the result. How could I not know? Was I an alien? Had I been living in a cave?

My niece had a similar experience with her host family in New Zealand. She began talking about Ichiro, the Japanese baseball hero, but their faces went blank. "I couldn't believe it. They didn't know who he was!" she explained. "Ichiro's famous. He's on TV all the time. Everyone knows him! That's when I realized that (④)."

Each country thinks that it's the center of the universe. And, for the people who live there, it is. Each nation is immersed in news and gossip about people, places and events that "everyone knows" and takes for granted. We all live in a cultural bubble and think that it's the whole world.

That's why foreign travel is so important. It gives us a chance to leave our bubbles, broaden our horizons and learn about other worlds. And that's the first step towards international understanding.

〔出典：The Japan Times ST：March 7, 2014 一部改〕

1 (①)～(④)に入る，最も適切なものを選択肢ア～エより一つ選び，記号で答えなさい。

① ア　I started to take a bath

　　イ　I called a taxi

　　ウ　I decided to walk

　　エ　I wanted to sleep

② ア　incomprehensible

　　イ　contemptible

　　ウ　admirable

　　エ　expected

③ ア　his grading of me

　　イ　why he wanted to know about the conference

　　ウ　how he spent today

　　エ　his train of thought

④ ア　common knowledge in Japan doesn't apply overseas

　　イ　a famous Japanese person, like Ichiro, will be able to become more famous abroad

　　ウ　the well-known things or people in Japan have been accepted in other countries

　　エ　cultural understanding about sports has been developing day by day

2　英文の内容と適するものを選択肢ア～エより一つ選び，記号で答えなさい。

　ア　The discussions about other customs with foreigners might be the best way for international understanding even if we can't go abroad.

　イ　Through overlooking the world from the center of the universe, we can understand the common knowledge in many countries.

　ウ　Each culture will disappear like a bubble without understanding by other countries.

　エ　We take for granted that what is well-known in our country may be known in other countries.

(☆☆☆○○○)

224

【8】 次の記事を読み，あとの問いに答えなさい。

According to linguists (i.e. scientists who engage in the scientific study of human language) there is an important distinction between language acquisition and language learning.

As you may well have noticed, children acquire their mother tongue through interaction with their parents and the environment that surrounds them. Their need to communicate paves the way for language acquisition to take place. As experts suggest, there is an innate capacity in every human being to acquire language. By the time a child is five years old, s/he can express ideas clearly and almost perfectly from the point of view of language and grammar. Although, parents never sit with children to explain to them the workings of the language, their utterances show a superb command of intricate rules and patterns that would drive an adult crazy if s/he tried to memorize them and use them accurately. This suggests that it is through exposure to the language and meaningful communication that a first language is acquired, without the need of systematic studies of any kind.

When it comes to second language learning in children, you will notice that this happens almost identically to their first language acquisition. And even teachers focus more on the communicative aspect of the language rather than on just rules and patterns for the children to repeat and memorize. In order to acquire language, the learner needs a source of natural communication.

The emphasis is on the text of the communication and not on the form. Young students who are in the process of acquiring a second language get plenty of "on the job" practice. The readily acquire the language to communicate with classmates.

In short, we see this tendency in which second language teachers are quite aware of the importance of communication in young learners and their inability to memorize rules consciously (although they will definitely acquire them through a hands-on approach just as they did with their mother tongue).

Unfortunately, when it comes to adult students, a quick look at <u>the current</u>

225

<u>methodologies and language courses available</u> clearly shows that communication is set aside, neglected or even disregarded. In almost all cases, courses revolve around grammar, patterns, repetitions, drillings and rote memorization without even a human interlocutor to interact with.

The very same course that promises you the ability to communicate upon completion of the courses does NOT offer you a single chance to do engage in meaningful conversations. How many times have you bought or read about "the ultimate language course on CD" in which the learner simply has to sit in front of a computer to listen to and repeat words and phrases time and again. That is not communication. That is the way you train a parrot! The animal will definitely learn and repeat a few, phrases and amuse you and your friends, but it will never ever be able to communicate effectively.

How could you be expected to communicate if you are never given the chance to speak with a real person? Language without real communication is as useless as Saint Valentine's day without lovers or Children's day without kids.

In some other scenarios, in which there is a teacher, the work done in class is mostly grammatically oriented: tenses, rules, multiple choice exercises and so on and so forth. Is this similar to the way in which a child "aquires a language?" Definitely not. No wonder why so many people fail in acquiring a second language naturally. Simply because whatever they are doing is highly unnatural and devoid of meaning to them. This is the field of language learning.

Language learning as seen today is not communicative. It is the result of direct instruction in the rules of language. And it certainly is not an age-appropriate activity for your young learners as it is not for adults either. In language learning, students have conscious knowledge of the new language and can talk about that knowledge.

They can fill in the blanks on a grammar page. Research has shown, however, that knowing grammar rules does not necessarily result in good speaking or writing. A student who has memorized the rules of the language may be able to succeed on a standardized test of English language but may not be able to speak or write correctly.

As teachers, it is our duty to make sure that our students "acquire" rather than "learn the language." What can we do to achieve this higher goal?

This is my opinion. What do you think about it?

〔出典：eslarticle.com：by *Julio Foppoli*, July 22, 2012　一部改〕

1　記事によると，第二言語はどのように習得されるべきであるか。「母語」という言葉を用いて，30字以上50字以内の日本語で書きなさい。

2　記事には，下線部の the current methodologies and language courses available が language learning の領域に含まれるとあるが，その理由を二つ取り上げ，日本語で書きなさい。

3　次の質問に英語で答えなさい。

According to this article, what happens to learners' speaking and writing as a result of the grammatically oriented class?

4　以下は，記事を読んだALTのティム(Tim)と中学校教員の江藤先生(Mr. Eto)との会話である。(①)～(④)に入る，最も適切なものを選択肢ア～カより一つ選び，記号で答えなさい。

Tim:　What do you think of this article?

Mr. Eto:　I haven't thought that there is a definite difference between acquiring and learning languages.

Tim:　Which do you think has been taught in your English class, "acquiring" or "learning" a language?

Mr. Eto:　I've emphasized on "learning" in my class. For students, it's (①) to learn basic knowledge first. Also, my students prefer to try some exercises in grammar rather than to communicate with others. Through the exercises they can recognize whether they can understand the grammar or not. When they have correct answers, they

---

seem to understand it.

Tim: I agree with you that students tend to need rules or forms for their tests. But according to this article, grammar is not enough for students to be (②) or to "acquire" the language.

Mr. Eto: Exactly. Although some of my students tell me that they are good at English, many of them are (③) in writing and speaking. They may be good at only filling in the blanks or memorizing the rules of grammar and may not be good at communication in English. I should give students more chances to interact with their friends in English class.

Tim: We should think of activities that are (④) for their age. This article tells it's natural for young learners to acquire languages through the communication.

| ア inability | イ right | ウ important |
| エ contrary | オ communicative | カ weak |

(☆☆☆○○○)

【高等学校】

【 1 】 Listen to the short sentences and choose the best response of the three choices, ア, イ, ウ. You will listen to the short sentences only once.

Q1. The entrance exam is coming soon. I am going to do my best.

ア I think I'm OK.

イ I know. I'll keep my fingers crossed.

ウ I agree with you. You can escape from it.

Q2. I don't have much of an appetite.

ア Really? You should not do that.

イ Really? Why don't you order more?

ウ Really? So, what about food that is easy to digest?

Q3.　Remember, you cannot be too careful when you drive.
　　ア　All right, I will get the driver's license.
　　イ　Even though I was late, I didn't pay a fine.
　　ウ　Sure, I won't forget I'm a newly licensed driver.

Q4.　There is no room for doubt that the man is guilty.
　　ア　Is there any evidence?
　　イ　How did he find it?
　　ウ　Where is it on the map?

Q5.　You have to admit that he deserves being chosen as chairperson.
　　ア　What a coincidence!
　　イ　Just in case.
　　ウ　But he's so vain.

(☆☆◎◎◎◎)

【2】Listen to the dialogues and the questions. Choose the correct answer from the three choices, ア, イ, ウ. You will listen to the dialogues and questions only once.

Dialogue 1
　　W: Long time no see, George. It's so good to see you again.
　　M: Oh, Cathy. What a surprise to see you here!
　　W: I didn't know you were interested in Shakespeare's plays.
　　M: Actually, my girlfriend loves them and brought me here.
　　W: How did you like tonight's performance?
　　M: To be honest, it was really difficult for me not to fall asleep.
　　W: It's a shame you didn't appreciate such a fine performance.

　　Q: How did the man feel about the performance?
　　　ア　It was boring.
　　　イ　It was interesting.
　　　ウ　It was shameful.

229

Dialogue 2

   W: Excuse me. I'd like to buy a ticket for Centrair Airport.

   M: Certainly, ma'am. The next bus leaves in five minutes.

   W: Oh, I won't be ready.

   M: Well, how about taking the train? The fare for the train is the same as that for the bus.

   W: I can get there by train? I didn't know that.

   M: The next train leaves in fifteen minutes.

   W: That sounds good. I'll take that.

   Q: Why did the woman decide to take the train?

     ア　Because the bus takes more time.

     イ　Because the bus leaves too early.

     ウ　Because the bus is more expensive.

Dialogue 3

   F:　Hi, Harry. Have you got a moment?

   M: Sure. What's up?

   F:　Do you have any good topics for our small talk activity?

   M: Oh, for the English club? Well... let me see... How about "If you can get a day off tomorrow, what will you do?"

   F:　That's good! We haven't given them assumptive topics. But wouldn't it be more interesting to give them a more imaginative one?

   M: OK, then...

   Q: What topic would the man probably suggest?

     ア　"What imaginary story do you like the best?"

     イ　"What quality is most important to be a good student?"

     ウ　"What would you do for education if you were the prime minister?"

Dialogue 4

   M: You are good at English. How do you study it? What is the secret of your success?

   F: Umm. I don't know if what I do is the secret of success. I just like English. It broadens my horizons. I like watching American TV dramas. I also like foreign movies with English subtitles. Reading Japanese comics in English also helps improve my English.

   M: I see, I think I can get Japanese comics translated in English in our school library. I will borrow them. I can concentrate on and understand the story! But I don't know if I can do the others.

   F: Hahaha, no pain, no gain!

   Q: Which statement is true?

     ア   The boy wonders how the girl acquires English competence without pain.

     イ   The girl improves her English by reading Japanese comics in English.

     ウ   The boy likes to see Japanese movies with English subtitles.

Dialogue 5

   F: Takashi, what are you doing now? Come here and help me cook dinner!

   M: Oh, no. I'm busy right now. Maybe later!

   F: You've been playing games on your smartphone for three hours now! When I bought you the phone, you promised not to use it so much. You are always playing games on the phone which keeps you away from studying or spending time with us.

   M: Umm, but all of my friends play games, so I need to continue playing to get along with them! We have our own business as teenagers!

   F: As a member of the family, you need to communicate with us and help

us. As a student, you need to study. Those are your responsibilities.
Keep your promise!

Q: Which statement is true?
ア The woman understands the boy's insistence and gives in.
イ The boy and the woman compromise and find a solution on the
matter.
ウ The woman says that she is right and their statements keep
conflicting.

(☆☆☆◎◎◎)

【3】 Listen to the passage about "ukiyo-e" and choose the most appropriate
phrase from the three choices, ア, イ, ウ. You will listen to the passage two
times.

Today we enjoy ukiyo-e works of art as masterpieces at museums, however
they originally were pop art created for the masses during the Edo Period. In
the 17th century, when Japan was unified and peace prevailed throughout the
country, common people had the time and money to enjoy the entertainment.
ukiyo-e was born from these circumstances. The term ukiyo is often directly
translated as "floating world", but within it there are nuances of "the present
age". In this context, art representing the everyday life and interests of
common people characterized the movement.

Ukiyo-e had a big influence on Western painting. Holland, which was
Japan's only Western trading partner during the isolation of the Edo period,
imported lots of Japanese ceramics. Exporters would use paper with ukiyo-e
printed on it to wrap fragile items, and the dynamic compositions, splendid
colors and detailed lines of the artwork fascinated Westerners. After Japan
opened its doors, ukiyo-e pieces were exhibited at Paris Expositions in the late
19th century. Japanese traditional arts were evaluated so highly that the new

expression "Japonism" was made to describe the study of the country's art. Vincent van Gogh, Claude Monet, and even a musician Claude Debussy were inspired by "Japonism".

During Japan's rapid modernization, many ukiyo-e pieces were scattered and lost. This is not surprising as they were not created for permanent ownership. However, it is a pity that three-fourths of ukiyo-e artworks still in existence are held abroad. The value of traditional culture might be hard to recognize when it is so close at hand.

(出典：*Asahi Weekly Sunday*, October 8, 2017)

Q1.　Ukiyo-e works were created (　　) during the Edo period.

　ア　to show outstanding and sophisticated skills of special artists

　イ　as symbols of the peaceful world in that era

　ウ　as popular amusements reflecting ordinary lives for general public

Q2.　Ukiyo-e impressed a lot of Westerners because (　　).

　ア　it was imported secretly and difficult to find in their daily lives

　イ　brilliant colors and energetic compositions were highly valued in Europe

　ウ　items wrapped with ukiyo-e were sensational and attractive

Q3.　Now, we can see (　　).

　ア　almost all of the ukiyo-e works all over Japan

　イ　a lot of ukiyo-e works in foreign countries

　ウ　a number of ukiyo-e works in everyday life

Q4.　Which statement is true?

　ア　Ukiyo-e was considered to be wonderful art by foreign artists, which influenced a variety of arts in Europe.

　イ　Ukiyo-e was so precious in the Edo period that art dealers were trying to import the works.

ウ　As ukiyo-e was becoming popular, people devoted their money to it in the Edo period.

(☆☆☆◎◎◎)

【4】 Listen to the discussion about "AlphaGo (碁)" and choose the most appropriate phrase for each question. You will listen to the discussion two times.

M: Have you heard of AlphaGo? It is an AI program for an ancient Chinese board game. AlphaGo defeated South Korean Grandmaster Lee Sedol and Ks Jie, the world's top player. Do you think it is more perfect than human players?

F: Probably. Actually, in the first contest with Lee in Seoul, AlphaGo made irrational moves, which cornered itself into a disadvantageous position. But, afterwards, in the second contest with Ke, it made much more convincing moves throughout the games. That proves AI has great learning capabilities similar to human brains and it can improve its skills by playing millions of games against itself in order to make improvements. In addition, unlike humans, it is free of fatigue and emotional frustrations. There is no knowing how good it will become in the future. AI seems to be superior to humans, doesn't it?

M: Well, I agree with you only partially. I mean AlphaGo does have a weak point as well. It cannot explain its thinking behind the particular moves it makes. When watching ordinary *go* contests, fans can enjoy listening to analysis by professional players.

F: I can understand that as one of the fans of *go*. But, there is a high possibility that we can apply AI technology used for AlphaGo to other areas, such as developing drugs and taking care of patients through data analysis.

M: You are right. However, the fact that the program made irrational moves

234

during its match with Lee in Seoul shows us that the technology is not error-free. The problem must be resolved before AI is applied to such fields as self-driving vehicles.

F: I see. According to some research, about 50 % of Japan's workforce can be taken over by AI. At the same time, it is said that AI cannot come into the fields where coorperation or harmony between people is needed like art or historical studies. It will be all the more important for us to make serious efforts to cultivate people's ability to think and create while finding out what proper roles AI should play in society.

(出典：*THE JAPAN TIMES ON SUNDAY,* June 4 2017 改)

Q1. Which phrase is the most proper to fill in the brackets 1 & 2 of the following chart?

AlphaGo	
☆Positive Aspects	☆Negative Aspects
・Free of being tired	・No analysis about the reasons of moves
・(1)	・(2)

ア The strength for Asian traditional games

イ The toughness against humans

ウ The ability to learn on its own

エ The active collaboration with people

オ The unreliability of its rational moves

カ The hard work of strong *go* players

Q2. In which field will the know-how from the AlphaGO program be applied to?

ア Medical services

イ Historical studies

ウ Chinese board games

Q3. In the woman's opinion, what should we do to live in harmony with AI?

ア Create a number of programs which people can make for AI

イ Limit the ratio of fields which AI will be applied to

ウ　Develop people's creativity and thinking ability

(☆☆☆☆◎◎◎)

【5】Listen to the passage on teaching English and complete the summary below by filling in the underlined parts. You will have 20 seconds to prepare before listening to the passage. You'll listen to it two times.

When we think of "What are the best kinds of lessons," one of the greatest enemies of successful teaching is student boredom. This is often caused by the predictability of much classroom time. Students frequently know what is going to happen in class and they know this because it will be the same as what happened in the last class ― and a whole string of classes before that. Something has to be done to break the chain.

In his monumental book, *Breaking Rules*, John Fanselow suggests that, both for the teacher's motivation and the students' continuing involvement, teachers need to violate their own behavior patterns. If teachers normally teach in casual clothes, they should turn up one day wearing a suit. If teachers normally sit down, they should stand up. If they are normally noisy and energetic as teachers, they should spend a class behaving calmly and slowly. Each time teachers break one of their own rules, it gives a class a mixture of surprise and curiosity and it is a perfect starting point for student involvement.

The need for surprise and variety within a fifty-minute lesson is also overwhelming. If, for example, students spend all of that time writing sentences, they will probably get bored. But if, in that fifty minutes, there are a number of different tasks with a selection of different topics, the students are much more likely to remain interested. This can be seen most clearly with children at primary and secondary levels, but even adults need variety to keep them stimulated.

However, variety is not the same as chaos. Despite what we have said, students tend to like a certain amount of predictability: they appreciate a safe structure which they can rely on. And too much chopping and changing or too much variety in a fifty-minute lesson can be upsetting. Good teachers find a balance between predictable safety and unexpected variety.

> (出典：Jeremy Harmer (2007). *How to teach English: new edition* Longman 改)

· In order to avoid students' boredom, teachers should ①————————. For example, they can be in a different style of clothes.

· In order to make 50-minute lessons interesting, teachers should ②————— ————.

· In order to avoid chaos, teachers should ③————————.

(☆☆☆☆○○○○)

【6】 Read the following passage and answer the questions below.

· Part Ⅰ

How can we feed the 2.5 billion more people ─ an extra China and India ─ likely to be alive in 2050? The UN says we will have to nearly double our food production and governments say we should adopt new technologies and avoid waste, but however you cut it, there are already one billion chronically hungry people, there's little more virgin land to open up, climate change will only make farming harder to grow food in most places, the oceans are overfished, and much of the world faces growing water shortages.

Fifty years ago, when the world's population was around half what it is now, the answer to looming famines was "the green revolution" ─ a massive increase in the use of hybrid seeds and chemical fertilizers. It worked, but at a great ecological price. We grow nearly twice as much food as we did just a generation ago, but we use three times as much water from rivers and underground supplies.

Food, farm and water technologies will have to find new ways to grow more crops in places that until now were hard or impossible to farm. It may need a total rethink over how we use land and water. So enter a new

237

generation of radical farmers, novel foods and bright ideas.

・Part Ⅱ

How do you free up huge amounts of farmland to grow more food for humans? Easy — switch to commercial algae farms. Algae are simple, single-cell organisms that can grow very rapidly at sea, in polluted water and in places that would normally kill food crops. Major airlines and shipping companies are now investigating a switch to algae oil, and smart clean tech money is pouring in to the nascent technology.

The prize is huge: scientists say that under optimum conditions, commercial algae farms can produce $5,000-10,000$ gallons of oil per acre, compared to just 350 gallons of ethanol biofuel per acre grown with crops like maize. In addition, algae could feed millions of animals and act as a fertilizer. Replacing all US ethanol(biofuel) production with algae oil would need around 2 million acres of desert, but, says Arizona State university professor Mark Edwards, it would potentially allow 40 million acres of cropland to be planted with human food, and save billons of gallons of irrigation water a year.

Algae are at the bottom of the food chain but they are already eaten widely in Japan and China in the form of seaweeds, and are used as fertilizers, soil conditioners and animal feed. "They range from giant seaweeds and kelps to microscopic slimes, they are capable of fixing CO_2 in the atmosphere and providing fats, oil and sugars. They are eaten by everything from the tiniest shrimp to the great blue whales." says Edwards.

・Part Ⅲ

Much of the world is arid, with its only nearby water being the sea.
(a   )

Charlie Paton, a British inventor, has a vision of vast "seawater greenhouses" to grow food and generate power. The idea is simple: in the natural water cycle, seawater is heated by the sun, evaporates, cools to form clouds, and returns to earth as refreshing rain. It is more or less the same in

238

Paton's structures. Here, hot desert air going into greenhouse is first cooled and then humidified by seawater. This humid air nourishes crops growing inside and then passes through an evaporator. When it meets a series of tubes containing cool seawater, fresh water condenses and is then collected. And because the greenhouses produce more than five times the fresh water needed to water the plants, some of it can be released into the local environment to grow other plants.

This is just one of many technologies being developed to enable food to be grown in unlikely places. One of the simplest, but most ambitious plans, may be the long-mooted Great Green Wall of Africa. This linear forest would be 15km wide and 7,775km long, and stretch from Senegal in the west to Djibouti in east Africa. It would, say the 11 countries through which it would pass, help to stop the southward spread of the Sahara, slow soil erosion and wind speeds, help rain water filter into the ground and create micro-climates to allow fruit, vegetables and other crops to be grown.

・ Part Ⅳ

Locusts, grasshoppers, spiders, wasps, worms, ants and beetles are not on most European or US menus but at least 1,400 species are eaten across Africa, Latin America and Asia. Now, with rising food prices and worldwide land shortages, it could be just a matter of time before insect farms set up in Britain.

Not only are many bugs rich in protein, low in fat and cholesterol and high calcium and iron, but insect farms need little space. Environmentally, they beat conventional farms, too. The creatures are far better at converting plant biomass into edible meat than even our fastest growing livestock, they emit fewer greenhouse gases and they can thrive on paper, algae and the industrial wastes that would normally be thrown away.

The advantages of "(b)micro-livestock" farming are great, say the UN and EU, both of which are keen to see if insect rearing could be greatly expanded. The Dutch government is studying how to set up insect farms. But aware of

239

western squeamishness, they have asked researchers to see if they can just extract the protein that many bugs contain.

Meanwhile the EU is offering its member states $3 millon to promote the use of insects in cooking, and has asked food standards watchdogs to investigate their potential to supplement diets.

(出典　*The Guardian*, January 22, 2012　改)

Q1.　What does the author think of algae farming?

ア　It is easy to start, but hard to earn from it.

イ　It has been unknown, but possible to be developed.

ウ　It is starting to develop and promising.

エ　It is everywhere and hard to stop spreading.

Q2.　Choose the most appropriate expression for the blank (　a　).

ア　So how could we create more vegetables and seaweeds using less seawater?

イ　So would it be possible that we generate some energy from rain water?

ウ　So could a technology be found to green coastal deserts using salt water?

エ　So what could we do to prevent soil erosion by filtering seawater?

Q3.　Choose a word from the passage that has the closest meaning to (b).

Q4.　What are the common benefits across the three new ways of farming?

ア　They don't make us pay a great ecological price.

イ　They make good use of seawater.

ウ　They change deserts into farmlands.

エ　They don't stop green revolution from going.

Q5.　What is the most appropriate title for this passage?

ア　A consideration of food in the future

イ　How to fertilize the soil on the earth

ウ　The necessity of the green revolution

エ　A tip for harmony with the environment

(☆☆☆○○○)

【 7 】 Read the following passage and answer the questions below.

Why do so few women end up in physics, mathematics and other fields traditionally associated with "brilliance" ? Part of the answer may lie in what happens to girls by the time they're out of kindergarten.

A study, described in the journal *Science*, shows how early these gender stereotypes begin to affect the self-perception and behavior of girls － which may limit their aspirations and careers into adulthood.

"If we want to change young people's minds and make things more equitable for girls, we really need to know when this problematic stereotype first emerges, and then we know when to intervene to avoid these negative consequences on girls' educational decisions and their future career choices," said lead author Lin Bian, a graduate student in psychology at the University of Illinois at Urbana-Champaign.

The stereotype that men are better at math and science is a pervasive one, difficult to dislodge even at the higher education. A study in the journal *PLOS One* last year found that men in college-level biology classes consistently overestimated the performance of their male peers and underestimated the performance of their female classmates. (The women, by the way, evaluated their fellow students far more accurately in terms of performance, apparently without regard to gender.)

These ideas aren't just a reflection of perceived differences in gender. They're also a reflection of perceived intelligence. "Popular beliefs about ability associate not only specific cognitive processes (e.g., mathematical

241

reasoning) with a particular gender but also the overall amount of cognitive ability," the study authors wrote. "It is commonly assumed that high-level cognitive ability (brilliance, genius, giftedness, etc.) is present more often in men than in women. This 'brilliance＝ males' stereotype has been invoked to explain the gender gaps in many (1) occupations".

These stereotypes may have serious consequences for young women in college and their future careers. For example, the authors point out, previous research has shown that the idea that men are better than women at math actually impairs women's performance and undermines their interest in math-related fields.

But how far back does the stereotype that men are more likely to be "brilliant" start to shape the behaviors of young men and women? To find out, the scientists set up a series of experiments to test the gender perceptions of 5-, 6-, and 7-year-olds.

In one experiment, 96 children were told a story about a person who was "really, really smart" ― but they weren't told the person's gender. The children were then asked to guess which of four adults, two men and two women, that person was. They were also shown pairs of adults ― both women, both men, or a man and a woman ― and asked to pick which adult in each pair was "really, really smart." Finally, they completed puzzles in which they had to associate objects (such as a hammer) or attributes (including "smart") with pictures of men and women.

The scientists found that from ages 5 to 7, children's perceptions of brilliance go through fairly dramatic changes. At 5, boys and girls both associated brilliance with their own gender on roughly the same level. But by 6 and 7, girls were significantly less likely than boys to associate brilliance with their own gender.

Strangely, when asked who got the best grades in school, the older girls were just as likely as the younger ones to pick girls ― and in fact, older girls were more likely than older boys to choose their own gender as getting the best grades.

This was consistent with the reality that girls do get better grades than boys at that ages, the authors wrote. "Nevertheless, there was no significant correlation between girls' perceptions of school achievement and their perceptions of brilliance, thus, girls' ideas about who is brilliant are not rooted in their perceptions of who performs well in school."

The authors also tested whether these beliefs about gender and brilliance affected girls' interests. The researchers had 64 children of 6-and 7-year-old play two games — one for "brilliant" children and one for "children who try very hard." Girls seemed drawn to the "hard-working" game about as much as boys — but they were significantly less interested than boys were in the game for brilliant kids.

"The present results suggest a sobering conclusion: Many children assimilate the idea that brilliance is a male quality at a young age," the authors wrote. "This stereotype begins to shape children's interests as soon as it is acquired and is thus likely to narrow the range of careers they will one day contemplate."

That this shift occurs around age 5 may have to do with children entering more formal school scenarios, where they're exposed to many other people (both children and adults), said Yarrow Dunham, a developmental psychologist at Yale University.

It's unclear which of the myriad social influences happening at the time could be contributing to girls' shift in self-perception, he added. It's possible, for example, that teachers might be unconsciously reinforcing stereotypes by how they respond to boys and girls in the classroom. Or perhaps the exposure to history books that mostly feature men causes children to assume that women are largely absent because they were less intelligent (rather than because of laws and social mores that for centuries treated women as second-class citizens). For now, the complex causes of these stereotypes remain (2).

"It is disheartening and it really calls for some thought about identifying what are the causal variables," Dunham said. "Is it teachers? Is it the kind of historical materials that they are exposed to? Because some of those will be easier fixes than others. And so identifying which is the main causal variable seems pretty important."

Identifying those variables will be the first step to figuring out how to weed out these stereotypes as soon as they take root.

(出典：*The Japan News.* Sep. 3 2017　改)

Q1. According to the passage, which statement is NOT found in the research?

ア　Female students are better at estimating their female peers than male students.

イ　The higher their academic level grows, the less often people are affected by stereotypes about gender.

ウ　It is widely believed that men have higher intelligence in specific cognitive processes.

エ　The belief that men are better at mathematics than women actually prevents women from doing it well.

Q2. Choose the most appropriate word to fill in the blank (　1　).

ア　dishonorable

イ　domestic

ウ　physical

エ　prestigious

Q3. According to the passage, which statement is true about girls?

ア　Many of them choose science careers once they overcome the social stereotypes.

イ　They acknowledge the fact that girls get higher grades than boys in schools.

ウ　They tend to shy away from doing the activities for hard-workers.

エ　At age 5, they start associating themselves with mathematical brilliance.

Q4.　Choose the most appropriate phrase to fill in the blank (　2　).

ア　an open question

イ　a settled question

ウ　an unexpected question

エ　a trivial question

Q5.　What can high school teachers do to prevent students from having these gender stereotypes mentioned above? Write your suggestion in English. Use 2 or 3 lines on the answer sheet.

(☆☆☆☆○○○○)

【8】 Put the words in the correct order and complete the sentences. Write the letter from (a) to (g) that fits in the blanks from (　1　) to (　10　).

Q1.

A: Ms. Tanaka talked with the boss seriously this morning. Do you know what happened?

B: Yeah. She (　　)(　　)(1)(　　)(　　)(2)(　　). If she does, she has to move to another city with her family.

(a)　whether　　(b)　is　　(c)　promotion　　(d)　to

(e)　accept　　(f)　the　　(g)　wondering

Q2.

A: Oh. You don't have your wallet with you? OK. This is my treat.

B: So sorry. (　　)(　　)(3)(　　)(　　)(4)(　　). I'll pay you back someday!

(a)　have　　(b)　to　　(c)　I never　　(d)　pay　　(e)　meant

(f)　the bill　　(g)　you

Q3.

A: I didn't get my mother's signature here! This application for the skiing trip is due today.

B: Well, you could call and ask her to come here and sign it.

A: I guess I should do that. (　　)(　　)(5)(　　)(　　)(6) (　　) her to get here with so much traffic on the streets?

(a)　you　　(b)　it　　(c)　do　　(d)　think　　(e)　take

(f)　will　　(g)　how long

Q4.

A: Have you heard the news that a large shopping mall will be constructed in this neighborhood?

B: Yes. I imagine that (　　)(　　)(7)(　　)(　　)(　　)(8)(　　).

(a)　hurt　　(b)　quite　　(c)　local　　(d)　businesses

(e)　a few　　(f)　will　　(g)　be

Q5.

A: Excuse me. Can I go inside and get the file I left on my desk?

B: (　　)(　　)(9)(　　)(　　)(　　)(10)(　　) the office without your ID card.

(a)　can't　　(b)　let　　(c)　I'm　　(d)　into　　(e)　afraid

(f)　you　　(g)　I

(☆☆◎◎◎◎)

【9】 A debate class will be held in English Expression Ⅱ. The topic is "It should be banned to sell cigarettes and alcohol at convenience stores." The procedure of the debate is as follows. As a teacher you're making a judge sheet with 4 criteria. The first criterion is already shown below. Your task is to create the other 3 criteria and fill in the space from (a) to (f). You need to write more than 15 words for (d)(e)(f).

The time table for debate　(A: Affirmative　N: Negative)

Role	Speaker	Content	Time
Constructive Speech	A1	State the reasons for agreeing with the topic.	2 min
	N1	State the reasons for disagreeing with the topic.	2 min
		Preparation time	2 min
Attack	N2	Refute the opponent from the point of the negative side.	2 min
	A2	Refute the opponent from the point of the affirmative side.	2 min
		Preparation time	2 min
Summary	A3	Prove the superiority of the affirmative argument by comparing and summarizing opinions from both sides.	2 min
	N3	Prove the superiority of the negative argument by comparing and summarizing opinions from both sides.	2 min
		Total time	16 min

The judge sheet

Criteria	Details of Criteria
Teamwork	Each debater plays their own role actively. Debaters support each other by giving advice when in need of help.
(a)	(d)
(b)	(e)
(c)	(f)

(☆☆☆☆◎◎◎)

【10】 Students are going to make a one-minute presentation in Communication English I , as a goal activity or final task of the unit "The Introduction of *Rakugo* to the World". Each of them is required to talk about one of the unique Japanese cultures.

Q1.　Before the preparation for the presentation, you are going to explain what kind of information should be included, for example, the reason why it is or will be popular in the world. Explain the other <u>TWO</u> kinds. You can use about 5 lines.

Q2.　In the classes before the presentations, what kind of small tasks or activities will you do toward the goal, as scaffolding? Explain the procedure and its details of <u>TWO</u> tasks or activities, for (a) and (b). You can use about 4 lines for each. Writing and memorizing the script should not be included.

(☆☆☆☆◎◎◎)

解答・解説

【中学校】

【1】1　(B)　　2　(A)

〈解説〉スクリプトは公開されていない。英文の説明を聞き，説明が表すと思われる語を4つの選択肢から選ぶ。選択肢は問題用紙に印刷されていない。また1回しか放送されないので，集中して聞かなければならない。

【2】1　(D)　　2　(C)

〈解説〉2人の会話を聞き，内容に関する質問に対し，4つの選択肢から正しい答えを選ぶ問題。【1】と同様，選択肢は印刷されておらず，英文と質問も1回しか放送されない。ただしALTとJTEの職員室での会話であり，内容は把握しやすいと推測される。

【3】1　(At) 10：03 (.)　　2　(解答略。本年は問題・解答とも公表されていない。)　　3　C　4　(解答略。本年は問題・解答とも公表されて

いない。)

〈解説〉日本在住のカナダ人のエッセイを聞いて，記述で設問に答えるもの。英文と質問は2回放送される。時間を聞き取ると思われる問いが1問ある。一般的な注意となるが，1回目は，全体の内容を把握し，設問を聞いた後の2回目は，聞き取るべきポイントに注意を払うことが大切である。

【4】(解答例)　Your writing is excellent! I hear you really practice it hard. Now I have some questions. How long have you played it? When will your next game be held? Tell me more next time! (34 words)

〈解説〉できているところ，改善したほうがよいと思われるところを示す。解答例では，現在完了形や受動態を使って質問をしている。さらに盛り込みたい情報を提示する形で生徒の書く意欲を高めたいところである。

【5】(解答例)　I agree with this opinion. I have two reasons. First, there's seldom any urgent need for them to contact with someone. Second, they are likely to spend too much time on social media and that will distract them from their studying. For these reasons, they shouldn't have their own cell phones. (51 words)

〈解説〉題材として与えられているテーマは，難しいものではない。語数が限られているので短時間で端的にまとめる。

【6】(解答例)　I think it's important to ensure students have much time to practice speaking. At the beginning of each class, for example, I'll use 10 minutes for speaking activities. I'll divide them into groups of four and they take turns to make a small speech on a given topic. The listeners are expected to ask questions and make comments. In this way, students can gradually get used to speaking in public. (70 words)

〈解説〉「教壇に立ってから，どのような授業をしたいか」ということは

よく問われる。4技能を統合した指導，または4技能それぞれに重点を
置いた指導について，自分なりの考えをまとめておくこと。更には英
語で準備しおくことが望ましい。

【7】1　①　ウ　　②　ア　　③　エ　　④　ア　　2　エ
〈解説〉1　①　空欄前後の「会議場は私のホテルの近くだった」と「そ
うすれば足を延ばし，そして街を見物できると思った」から，ウ「私
は歩くことに決めた」。　②　空欄後に「彼は信じられないといった
様子で歩き去った」とあるので，ア「(現地の住人である)彼にとって
(試合の結果を)私が知らないということは理解しがたいことだった」。
③　筆者はこのおかしな出来事がなぜ起きたのかを考えている。よっ
てエ「私は彼の思考の流れを想像してみた」。　④　今回の筆者の経
験と筆者の姪の同様のエピソードから，「日本で誰もが知っているこ
とが，海外ではあてはまらないとその時私は気づいた」。　2　エ「自
分たちの国でよく知られていることは他の国でも知られていると私た
ちは当然のように思う」。第1段落の主題文や第8段落の内容に合致す
る。

【8】(解答例)　1　子どもが母語を獲得するように第2言語に接し，有意
義なコミュニケーションを通して習得されるべきである。(48字)
2　(解答例)　・コミュニケーションする機会を提供しないこと
・文法重視の授業であること　　3　Knowing grammar rules does not
necessarily result in good speaking or writing.　　4　①　ウ　　②　オ
③　カ　　④　イ
〈解説〉1　第3段落の内容を端的にまとめて解答する。　2　設問は，
「(大人の学習者に関しては)現在受け入れられている方法論や利用でき
る言語コースがランゲージラーニングの領域に含まれる理由を挙げ
よ」なので，ランゲージアクイジションとは異なる点を書き出す。
3　設問は「この記事によると，文法重視の授業の結果，学習者のス
ピーキングやライティングはどうなるのか」。第11段落の2文目を参照

する。　4　①　ラーニングが強調される授業の特徴としては，ウ「生徒にとってまず基本的な知識を学ぶことが大切である」。　②　文法に対する筆者の考え方を示す文である。オ「文法は，生徒がコミュニカティブになる，即ちその言語を獲得するには十分ではない」。　③　英語が得意であるという生徒の多くは，カ「ライティングやスピーキングは苦手である」。　④　第10段落の2文目「ランゲージラーニングは大人にとっても，若い学習者にとっても年齢に応じたアクティビティではない」を受けて，イ「私たちは年齢に合ったアクティビティを考えるべきである」。

【高等学校】

【1】Q1　イ　　Q2　ウ　　Q3　ウ　　Q4　ア　　Q5　ウ
〈解説〉短文を聞いて，その英文の応答として適切なものを3択で答える問題。一例を挙げると「入試が近いのでベストを尽くします」に対してI'll keep my fingers crossed.「幸運を祈ります」を選択する。英文は1回のみ放送される。

【2】Q1　ア　　Q2　イ　　Q3　ウ　　Q4　イ　　Q5　ウ
〈解説〉対話文と質問を聞いて，答えとして適切なものを3択で答える問題。対話文は1人3回程度，計6回程度のやりとりである。英文と質問は1回のみ放送される。

【3】Q1　ウ　　Q2　イ　　Q3　イ　　Q4　ア
〈解説〉250語程度の英文を聞いて，内容に一致する文や語句を選択する問題。問題用紙に印刷されている選択肢や設問となる英文から，ある程度の内容を予測することができる。英文は2回放送される。

【4】Q1　(1)　ウ　　(2)　オ　　Q2　ア　　Q3　ウ
〈解説〉300語程度の2人によるディスカッションを聞いて，質問に選択肢で答える問題。質問文は印刷されていない。英文は2回放送される。

20秒与えられる準備の時間に，表や選択肢に目を通し，聞き取るべき
ポイントを押さえること。

【5】①　break [their own behavior patternsまたはtheir own rules]
②　have [a variety of tasksまたはdifferent kinds of tasks]　　③　give
students a certain amount of predictability

〈解説〉300語程度の英文を聞いて，問題用紙に印刷されている空欄を補
充し要約文を完成させる問題。英文は2回放送される。基本的にはス
クリプトからそのまま抜き出す形で解答できるので，該当する箇所を
聞き逃さないようにしたい。

【6】Q1　ウ　　Q2　ウ　　Q3　insectまたはbugs　　Q4　ア
Q5　ア

〈解説〉Q1　問いは「筆者は藻類農業をどう考えているか」。PartⅡの第1
段落で，大手航空会社や船会社が燃料として藻類オイルへの転換を検
討していることを紹介したり，第3段落ではすでに日本や中国で食べ
られていたりすることを挙げている。よって，ウ「それはすでに開発
されはじめて，見込みがある」。　Q2　「ほんの近くに海水があるにも
かかわらず，世界の多くは不毛の地である」に続く文。空欄後には海
水温室の仕組みが述べられていることから，ウ「それでは，海水を使
って海岸部の砂漠を緑化するための技術は見つけられるのだろうか」。
Q3　micro-livestock farming「微小家畜を飼育すること」。PartⅣの第1
段落のinsectや，同第2段落のbugsが同義である。　Q4　問いは「3つ
の新しい農法に共通する利点は何か」。PartⅡの第3段落の2文目「藻類
は大気中の二酸化炭素を固定できる」やPartⅣの第2段落の2文目「環
境上，昆虫飼育は従来のものより優れている」などの記述から，ア
「私たちに多大な生態学上の犠牲を払わせることがない」。　Q5　第1
段落の1文目に主題文「私たちはどのようにあと25億人もの人に食べ
物を食べさせることができるのか」とあるように，食糧問題がメイン
アイディアである。よって，ア「将来の食べ物の考察」が正しい。

【7】 Q1 イ　Q2 エ　Q3 イ　Q4 ア　Q5 Teachers can introduce more great female figures, such as scientists, in history. Students can research them and do a presentation.　（別解1）Teachers should nominate more female students as a class representative. They should encourage girls to show their leadership.　（別解2）Teachers should invite women with prominent occupations to school to talk about their career to students. Then girls will see that women are as brilliant as men.

〈解説〉Q1　第9段落で，「5歳では男女ともに，優秀さを自分の性別と結びつけるが，6，7歳になると女子は明らかに男子より，優秀さと自分の性別を結びつけなくなる」と述べている。年齢が進むと（＝学問レベルが上がると），女子は男子のほうが優れていると思うようになることを示している。したがって，イ「学問レベルが上がれば上がるほど，人々は性に関する固定観念に影響されなくなる」は本文とは逆のことを述べているので誤り。　Q2　「ハイレベルな認知能力は女性より男性のほうにあると一般的に思われている」に続く文。この「優秀さ＝男性」という固定観念が，どのような仕事の男女格差につながっているかを考える。よって，エのprestigious「名声のある」。
Q3　第10段落の内容より，イ「学校で男子よりも成績が良いという事実を女子は認めている」。　Q4　第15段落では，女子の自己認知の変化に影響を及ぼす原因について論じている。特定には至っていないので，ア「今のところ，これらの固定観念の複合的な原因は未解決の問題である」。open「決着がついていない」。　Q5　問いは「本文で述べられているような性による固定観念を生徒が持たないようにするために教師ができることは何か。2，3行の英語で書け」。解答例では，「偉大な女性の人物をもっと紹介する，クラスの代表として女性を指名する，卓越した職業に就いている女性を学校に招待し経歴について話を聞く」などが挙げられている。

【8】 Q1　1　(a)　2　(f)　Q2　3　(b)　4　(d)　Q3　5　(a)　6　(f)　Q4　7　(c)　8　(g)　Q5　9　(g)　10　(f)

〈解説〉Q1　whether to ～「～すべきかどうか」。整序すると，is wondering whether to accept the promotionとなる。　Q2　mean to ～「～するつもりである」。have O do「Oに～させる」。整序すると，I never meant to have you pay the billとなる。　Q3　how long(疑問詞)＋do you think ～?「どれくらい～だと思いますか」。整序すると，How long do you think it will take? となる。　Q4　quite a few「かなり多くの」。整序すると，quite a few local businesses will be hurtとなる。　Q5　let O into ～「Oを～に入れる」。整序すると，I'm afraid I can't let you intoとなる。

【9】(a)　Content　(d)　Each argument should be based on facts. Debaters need to make a clear difference between facts and opinions.
(b)　ConnectionまたはRelevance　(e)　Attackers should compare their team's opinions with their opponents'. Their rebuttal should be related to what their opponents said.　(c)　Consistency　(f)　The argument is consistent as a team. The members should focus on the same point.

〈解説〉(a)(d)　別解として次のようにしてもよい。　(a)　Delivery (d)　Debaters should use gestures and have eye contact with the judge. Their voices should be loud enough.　(b)(e)　別解として次のようにしてもよい。(b)　OrganizationまたはStructure　(e)　Each argument should have a topic sentence and supporting sentences to reason it with evidence.

【10】Q1　First, the history of the culture should be included. Students can explain when and where it started. And how it spread all over Japan. Then, they should talk about the present situation of the culture. How do people enjoy it? Is there any special place or event for it? (補足：Students should show any prop or picture for the audience to have the clear image for it. Or they can give their own performance.)　Q2　(a)　Our ALT and I will make model presentations and perform them in front of the students. Students can learn the ideal structure of presentation and how to deliver it by seeing our presentations. If needed, I will give them the scripts so that they can analyze them.　　(b)　Students will do a brainstorming activity. They will break up into small groups and name as many unique Japanese cultures as possible. Then they will talk about which culture will be attractive to people around the world and pick their own topics for presentations.

〈解説〉Q1　問いは「プレゼンテーションの準備前に，どのような情報をプレゼンテーションに含めるべきかを生徒に説明する予定である。『なぜ人気があるのか』以外に含めるべき情報を2つ，5行程度で書け」。解答例では「いつ・どこでそれが始まり，日本中に広がったか。現在，どのように人々が落語を楽しんでいるか。それが行われる特別な場所やイベントがあるか」を挙げている。また，補足として，小道具や写真を見せたり，自身が落語のパフォーマンスをしたりして，聴衆が明確なイメージを持てるようにすることを挙げている。　Q2　問いは「プレゼンテーション前に，目標を達成するため，どのような小タスクやアクティビティをするか。2つのタスクやアクティビティの手順や詳細を，それぞれ4行程度で書け(スクリプトを書くことや暗記することは除く)」。解答例では「ALTと教師が模範のプレゼンテーションをすること」と「ブレーンストーミングで日本特有の文化をグループ内でシェアすること」を挙げている。

【中学校】

【1】【放送問題】

Listen to the description and choose the most suitable word from A to D. The description and choices will be read only once.

1　(A)

　　(B)

　　(C)

　　(D)

2　(A)

　　(B)

　　(C)

　　(D)

(☆☆☆◎◎◎)

【2】【放送問題】

Listen to the conversation. Choose the correct answer for the following questions. The conversation and the questions will be read only once.

1　(A)

　　(B)

　　(C)

　　(D)

2　(A)

　　(B)

　　(C)

　　(D)

(☆☆☆☆◎◎◎)

【3】【放送問題】

　　Listen to the following passage. Answer the questions. The passage and questions will be read twice.

1 _____

2 _____

3 _____

4 ※　解答は横書きとし，句読点は1マス使う。

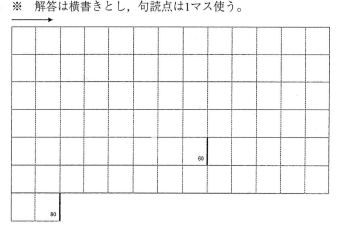

(☆☆☆☆◎◎◎◎)

【4】A先生は，中学3年生の授業で英作文を行いました。テーマは「英語の授業についての感想」で，ある生徒が以下のように書きました。

> When ALT comes to my class, I become very happy.
>
> I can enjoy many English games.
>
> I like speaking English with friends and teachers.
>
> But I don't like writing English.
>
> It's very difficult. I make a lot of mistakes.
>
> What should I do?
>
> I like English so I want to study English in high school and college.

1　あなたはこの生徒に対して，どのようにコメントを書きますか。

英語で書く力を伸ばすための具体的なアドバイスを含めて，英単語30語以上40語以内で書きなさい。

2　A先生は，生徒が積極的にコミュニケーションを図ろうとする態度を身に付けるために，ALTを招いたり，友達同士でコミュニケーションを図ることができるゲームを取り入れたりして授業を進めてきました。

話す活動を通して生徒が積極的にコミュニケーションを図ろうとする態度を身に付けるために，あなたはどのような授業を行いたいと考えますか。その理由も含め，英単語50語以上70語以内で書きなさい。

(☆☆☆☆◎◎◎)

【5】平成29年3月に告示された「中学校学習指導要領　第2章　第9節　外国語」では，「生徒が英語に触れる機会を充実するとともに，授業を実際のコミュニケーションの場面とするため，授業は英語で行うことを基本とする。」と示されています。これを踏まえ，あなたが英語で授業を行うときに，気を付けるべきことについて，その理由も含めて，英単語50語以上70語以内で書きなさい。

(☆☆☆☆◎◎◎)

【6】Read the passage and answer the following questions.

Australian TV channel SBS 2 recently shared a mini-documentary titled "Japan's independent kids" on YouTube, which gives a brief look at the differences between one young Japanese girl's commute to school versus that of a young Australian girl, while examining some of the societal factors that lead to differing expectations regarding independence for children in each country. The short documentary begins by sharing the Japanese proverb "Kawaii ko ni wa tabi o saseyo," or "(　①　)". This saying, which holds that children should learn to take on (　②　) and difficulties from an early stage in life, alludes to the fact that Japanese children are typically socialized into becoming independent and taking care of themselves from a younger age than are many children in Western countries. One striking example of this young independence is in how Japanese elementary school students commute to school on a daily basis.

Viewers next meet the adorable seven year old Noe Ando during a typical day on her commute to elementary school, which she makes alone by train. She even has to transfer once at JR Shinjuku Station, which is the busiest station in the world by number of passengers. Walking through the station can be a harrowing ordeal in itself for an adult, let alone for a tiny child during rush hour. While sending a seven-year-old off by herself to navigate public transportation would be (③) for many parents outside of Japan, Ando's mother shares her own perspective: "Her parents can't always be with her so she has to learn how to solve things herself. If she gets lost or catches the wrong train, she has to figure it out on her own." Finally, we meet the Fraser family from Australia, whose 10-year-old daughter Emily is driven to and from school every day by her father. Fraser is already looking forward to high school, when she will be allowed to walk home and let herself in with a key independently.

The documentary then transitions into a brief discussion surrounding the societal differences and expectations for children in Japan and Australia. As one Australian man comments, "Our society suffers from a paranoia about leaving children on their own." The narrator also reveals that Japan has more than five times the population of Australia, but less than one-fourth the homicide rate. English-speaking Internet users who saw the video shared comments such as, "I think besides the lower crime rate, Japanese communities tend to be a little more collective when it comes to child rearing ...I was raised to be the (④), every stranger is a possible criminal who may want to hurt me." Another commentator says "The girl in the video is not a normal case: she has to travel that far by herself because her parents are sending her to some kind of special private school. It's far more common for elementary schoolers in Japan to walk a short distance to the school nearest to their home. The younger kids rarely walk alone: there are designated spots where they meet up with other neighborhood kids and walk to or from school as a group. The older kids act as leaders for the group." How was your own experience going to school as a child compared with that of the two girls interviewed above?

〔出典－Japan Today *by Krista Rogers, RocketNews24:* September 14, 2015　一部改〕

1　In the blank (　①　) is an English equivalent of the Japanese proverb "Kawaii ko ni wa tabi o saseyo". Choose the most appropriate phrase for this proverb from ア to エ.

　ア　So many countries, so many customs.

　イ　Adversity builds strength and character.

　ウ　Spare the rod and spoil the child.

　エ　When in Rome, do as the Romans do.

2　Fill in the blank (　②　) in the passage with one of the following choices, from ア to エ.

　ア　issues　　イ　challenges　　ウ　responsibilities　　エ　chances

3　Fill in the blank (　③　) in the passage with one of the following choices, from ア to エ.

　ア　unthinkable　　イ　pressurizing　　ウ suspicious

　エ　troublesome

4　Choose the most suitable phrase from ア to エ and fill in the blank (　④　).

　ア　unusual reality

　イ　strongest minded

　ウ　complete opposite

　エ　worst scenario

5　Choose the most appropriate title for this passage from ア to オ.

　ア　A YouTube video observing the safety of life in Japan

　イ　Why do Japanese parents let young kids walk to school alone?

260

ウ A documentary video on the fully independent schoolchildren in Japan

エ Why walking to school is not a safe social experience in Australia

オ Is it really OK to let your children commute to school alone?

(☆☆☆☆○○○○)

【 7 】 Read the passage and answer the following questions.

Service-learning refers to learning that actively involves students in a wide range of experiences, which often benefit others and the community, while also advancing the goals of a given curriculum. Community-based service activities are paired with structured preparation and student reflection. What is unique about service learning is that it offers direct application of theoretical models. Proponents of academic service learning feel that the real-world application of classroom knowledge in a community setting allows students to synthesize course material in more meaningful ways. Common goals achieved by service learning include: gaining a deeper understanding of the course/curricular content, a broader appreciation of the discipline and an enhanced sense of civic responsibility. There are six qualities of service-learning: integrative, reflective, contextualized, strength-based, reciprocal, and lifelong, which are explained below.

1 Integrative: The service-learning experience goes beyond traditional ideas of classroom learning, practicum training or off-campus volunteering. Service-learning holistically integrates class learning objectives, faculty guidance, as well as community perspective and priorities. When engaged in genuine service students participate as both learners and community members. Students demonstrate success both academically and interpersonally.

2 Reflective: "The process of reflection is a core component of service-learning. Service-learning practitioners and researchers alike have concluded that the most effective service-learning experiences are those that provide

'structured opportunities' for learners to critically reflect upon their service experience. Structured opportunities for reflection can enable learners to examine and form the beliefs, values, opinions, assumptions, judgments and practices related to an action or experience, gain a deeper understanding of them and construct their own meaning and significance for future actions." (Moon, 1999, as cited in Conner & Seifer, 2005)

3 Contextualized: Service-learning provides students a unique opportunity to access knowledge and expertise that resides in the context of community. There is opportunity to connect the knowledge of a discipline, as explored in class, to the knowledge in practice, as evidenced in communities. Learning experiences in community settings immerse students in the unpredictable and complex nature of real world situations. Working alongside community members and experienced professionals, the opportunity to construct learning and responses can be immediate and uncontrived.

4 Strength-based: Service-learning draws upon existing community strengths and resources, and honors community members and organizations as co-educators of students. Communities are never built from the outside in. A strength-based approach focuses on the capacity and expertise that exist in every community, rather than on what is absent. By shifting away from a deficit mentality, students learn partnership strategies to identify and develop each community's unique strengths.

5 Reciprocal: The service-learning relationship offers all parties involved some measure of benefits; it is a two way street. Students give time, talent and intellectual capital in order to gain deeper understanding of course material and the nuanced nature of social issues. Course instructors modify their teaching practice to include service-learning and are rewarded with deeper student engagement of course material. Community members and organizations invest time as co-educators and in turn accomplish more toward their mission and goals through the work of students.

6 Lifelong: Service-learning is learning that sticks. By synthesizing theory

and practice, this educational method provides a distinctive, meaningful and influential life experience. Students build relationships, solve problems, value a sense of community and gain self-awareness. Service-learning is beyond memorable; it can influence one's career path and enhance civic responsibility. Service-learning extends learning beyond the academic term; it lays the foundation for continual personal growth throughout the student's academic experience and beyond.

[出典：University of Washington- Center for Teaching and Learning]

1 The sentences below summarize the passage. Fill in the blanks with one of the choices in the box below. Each choice can be used only once.

Service-learning helps deepen students' learning by involving them in a wide range of social and (①) experiences.

The (②) have raised six qualities of service-learning that can help the students achieve goals such as having a broader appreciation of the discipline and gaining an enhanced sense of civic responsibility.

Service-learning goes beyond traditional ideas of classroom learning because it provides 'structured opportunities' for critical reflection; immerses students in the real world situations; enables students to identify and develop community's unique (③); offers all parties involved some measure of benefits; and is the kind of learning that remains with the students and lays the foundation for continual personal growth.

ア strengths　　イ community　　ウ quality
エ proponents　　オ understanding

2 According to this passage, what "allows students to synthesize course material in more meaningful ways" in academic service-learning? Write in English.

3 Explain "the reciprocal quality of service-learning" as described in this passage. Write in Japanese.

4 According to this passage, how is service-learning a lifelong influence? Write in Japanese.

(☆☆☆◎◎◎)

263

【高等学校】

【1】これから問1～問5について，それぞれ短い英文を読みます。それぞれの英文の応答として最も適切なものを，選択肢ア～ウから1つ選び，記号で答えなさい。なお，英文は1回ずつ読みます。

問1　What do you say to having some beer?

 ア　I would like to say so.

 イ　It means "cheers!"

 ウ　Okay, let's.

問2　How did you find the station even though you are a stranger around here?

 ア　I came here alone.

 イ　Because I was lucky to meet a kind old man.

 ウ　It cost me more than I had expected.

問3　After you, please.

 ア　Oh, thank you.

 イ　No, follow me, please.

 ウ　Actually, I'll be there soon.

問4　I'd hate to be a burden on you.

 ア　You're lucky to hear that.

 イ　Please don't say that.

 ウ　I will let you know the date.

問5　I wonder if you could help me move this box.

 ア　No, don't bother, really.

 イ　Where did you put it?

 ウ　Sure. Where to?

(☆☆☆◎◎◎)

【2】これから問1～問5について，それぞれ英語の対話文と質問を読みます。それぞれの対話に関する質問の答えとして最も適切なものを，選択肢ア～ウから1つ選び，記号で答えなさい。なお，対話と質問は1回

ずつ読みます。

問1　M: Where do you want to go for our summer vacation?

　　　F: Well, I'm a bit sick of the hectic city life in New York. I want to visit a place with historic buildings and get away from modern life.

　　　M: I'd rather go to somewhere we can relax and enjoy the beauty of nature.

　　　F: But that sounds boring. Don't you want to experience another culture?

　　　M: I guess you're right.

　　　Q: What will the man and the woman probably see on their vacation?

　ア　Pyramids in Egypt.

　イ　Skyscrapers in Tokyo.

　ウ　Sandy beaches on the Gold Coast in Australia.

問2　F: I can't find my ring. I wonder where it is.

　　　M: You're always looking for something. Try to remember when you last took it off.

　　　F: Well, I wore it to work yesterday. Just before leaving the office, I wanted to put on some hand cream, so I took off the ring and put it in the pocket of my jacket.

　　　M: I took it to the cleaner's this morning. You'd better go and get it now.

　　　Q: What is the woman probably going to do?

　ア　Look for the jacket to clean.

　イ　Clean the jacket.

　ウ　Go to the laundry shop.

問3　F: The school festival is coming soon. Each class is going to give some kind of performance. We should decide what we will do by next Wednesday. Do you have any good ideas?

M: Umm. A drama or a chorus would be a great choice, I think.

F: A chorus seems difficult for our class. The boys in our class are all shy, aren't they? And you, you are not a music person, are you?

M: Don't make fun of us. The boys can't sing well right now, but we have enough time to practice. And I used to play the piano.

F: Really? Then, we have reached an agreement. Our class performance will be a chorus, and you will play an accompaniment.

M: Hum? I will play the piano?

F: What's the matter? You look pale.

Q: Which statement is true?

ア　The class performance will be a drama with the piano.

イ　Most of the boys in the class are good at singing.

ウ　The boy can play the piano but he hesitates.

問4　F: After giving some English instruction for an activity, I always ask students, "Do you understand?" But most of them keep silent. I'm always wondering what I should do.

M: I know what you mean. Only a few students say "yes" in their small voice, but when the activity actually starts, they tend to ask each other, "what are we going to do?" in Japanese. That means they don't understand my English instructions.

F: Yeah, then, what can we do?

M: Umm. I always try to speak English slowly. But I might be giving too much information at one time.

F: I see. Too much information at the same time is certainly difficult for students to understand. Umm. Then, how about giving short and clear instructions in order?

Q: What could the man say after that?

ア　Good idea! We should ask "Do you understand?" after giving instruction.

イ Good idea! We can say things like, "First, you're going to ... ", "Second, you're..."

ウ Good idea! Students should improve their listening ability.

問5 F: Wake up. You will catch a cold if you sleep on the desk.

M: Oh, mom, I can't concentrate on my homework at all. I always feel sleepy after dinner. What should I do?

F: Umm, I know you do your best at club activity every day. And I'm very proud of you. But, you can't make it an excuse. So now, you need a drastic change in your way of studying.

M: How?

F: Give up studying at night. Instead, you can wake up early in the morning and do your homework.

M: Mom, I've tried it once, but, at that time I just didn't wake up, and still felt sleepy. It didn't work for me.

F: You studied in your pajamas! You should change your clothes if you really want to wake up.

Q: Which statement is true?

ア The boy previously tried what his mother suggested but he failed then.

イ The boy always does his homework early in the morning because he is tired at night.

ウ The boy can't concentrate on his homework and he blames the morning club activity for it.

(☆☆☆☆◎◎◎)

【3】これから道路標識に関する英文を読みます。問1〜問4の英文の( )に入る最も適切なものを選択肢ア〜ウから1つ選び，記号で答えなさい。なお英文は2回読みます。英文は20秒後に始まります。

The National Police Agency is set to renew Japan's stop and slow down signs by adding English words to the current designs, ahead of the 2020

Tokyo Olympics and Paralympics.

As the number of visitors from abroad is expected to increase, the new signs are aimed at preventing traffic accidents involving foreign travelers. The National Police Agency will gather public opinions regarding the plan until January 14 next year.

After revising the related laws, the current signs will be replaced with new ones starting in July 2017.

The current "Tomare" stop and "Joko" slow down signs were introduced in 1963. This will be the first change to these displays.

The inverted triangle shapes will stay the same, but the English word "STOP" will be added below "Tomare," and "SLOW" below "Joko".

Stop signs are currently placed in about 1.7 million locations nationwide, and slow down signs in about 1,000 locations. They will be replaced when the renewal period comes, with priority to be given to signs in places where many foreign tourists visit.

According to the All Japan Rent-a-Car Association, the number of foreign tourists who rent cars has sharply increased in recent years, particularly among tourists from Hong Kong and Taiwan.

However, some foreign tourists have complained about the current signs, saying they are difficult to understand.

Furthermore, an increasing number of foreign visitors with an international driver's license have been involved in traffic accidents in Japan, with 216 accidents of this kind recorded in 2015. In response to the situation, the National Police Agency recognized the necessity of English translations for the stop and slow down signs to help prevent traffic accidents.

(出典　The Japan News by The Yomiuri Shimbun December 16,2016 改)

問1　Before renewing the signs, (　　).

ア　the relevant laws will be changed.

イ　the National Police Agency must announce security plans for the Olympics.

ウ　foreign tourists should report traffic accidents when they are involved.

問2　The same shapes will be maintained, but (　　)

　ア　the new colors will be added at the top.

　イ　the English words will be replaced with the Japanese words.

　ウ　the English words will be put below the Japanese words.

問3　There are (　　) now in Japan.

　ア　more slow down signs than stop signs

　イ　almost the same numbers of slow down signs and stop signs

　ウ　more stop signs than slow down signs

問4　According to the National Police Agency, (　　)

　ア　new signs are necessary considering the increase in foreign tourists' traffic accidents.

　イ　the All Japan Rent-a-Car Association should cooperate with the National Police Agency.

　ウ　it's a problem for more foreign tourists to have an international driver's license.

(☆☆☆☆☆◎◎◎)

【4】これから日本の若者の選挙に対する意識調査に関する英文を読み，その後，その内容やあとのグラフや表について質問をします。問1，問2の答えとして最も適切なものを，選択肢ア～エから1つ選び，記号で答えなさい。また，問3の答えとして適切なものを，選択肢ア～オから2つ選び，記号で答えなさい。なお，英文と質問は2回読みます。英文は20秒後に始まります。

The survey asked basically the same questions to junior high school students, high school students and eligible voters aged 18 or older living in the city of Saitama.

When asked who they think influences politics, the top answer from junior high school students was "the people" at 28 percent, while for high school students it was "law-makers" at 22 percent. For eligible voters it was "bureaucrats" at 43 percent. Junior high school students appear to have a strong concept of "rule by the people", but it starts to decrease among high school students and drops to only 8 percent for eligible voters.

What about the level of interest that junior high school and high school students have in politics? According to the survey, about 50％ of both groups of students showed an interest in politics, if the responses "very interested" and "somewhat interested" are combined.

When junior high school and high school students under the minimum voting age of 18 were asked if they would vote once they were eligible, 57 percent of the first-year high school students and 59 percent of the second-year high school students said they would. The figure reached to 72 percent among third-year students under 18 who have classmates aged 18.

Political awareness among third-year students appears to have risen, with the introduction of a new policy that enabled some of their classmates to vote.

When asked about changing the minimum voting age, 52 percent of the junior high school students and 48 percent of the high school students answered that they think it is "just the right age."

(出典　The Japan News by The Yomiuri Shimbun December 20,2016 改)

問1　From the Graph, which is the most suitable combination of categories represented?

ア　A－Lawmakers　　B－The people　　C－Bureaucrats
イ　A－Bureaucrats　　B－Lawmakers　　C－The people
ウ　A－Lawmakers　　B－Bureaucrats　　C－The people
エ　A－Bureaucrats　　B－The people　　C－Lawmakers

問2　From the Table, which is the most suitable combination of numbers represented?

ア　X－50　　Y－59　　Z－72
イ　X－57　　Y－72　　Z－50
ウ　X－50　　Y－57　　Z－59
エ　X－57　　Y－59　　Z－72

問3 Choose two statements which are true about the passage.

ア Lawmakers have the biggest influence on junior high school students.

イ Since some of their classmates have started voting, third-year high school students have increased their awareness of politics.

ウ Most junior high school students think that it's not necessary to change the minimum voting age.

エ There are a lot of differences between junior high school and high school students about interest in politics.

オ About half of the junior high and high school students find it reasonable to vote at the age of 18.

Graph

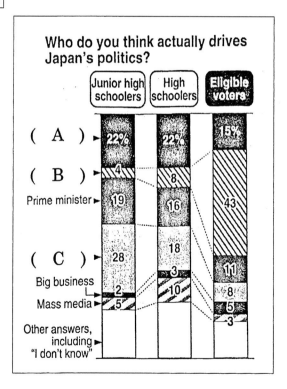

Table

Will you vote after turning 18?

The percentage of the students who answered "YES".

Junior High School	1st-year students	58
	2nd-year students	62
	3rd-year students	67
High School	1st-year students	(X)
	2nd-year students	(Y)
	3rd-year students	(Z)

*Third-year high schoolers limited to those under 18

(☆☆☆☆◎◎◎)

【5】これから読む英文は，学校で第2言語教育を始める時期についての考察を述べたものです。内容のまとめとなるような英文を，次の3つのフレーズをそれぞれ1つずつ使用して，3文で完成させなさい。なお，フレーズにはそれぞれ下線を付すこと。英文は20秒後に始まり，2回読みます。

　　The decision about when to introduce second or foreign language instruction must depend on the objectives of the language program in the particular social context of the school. When the objective is native-like performance in the second language, then it may be desirable to begin exposure to the language as early as possible. The research evidence is fairly strong that only those who begin second language learning at an early age will eventually speak natively.

　　However, even in cases where such high levels of skill are targeted, it is important to recognize certain disadvantages of an early start. An early start in second language means that children have little opportunity to continue to develop their knowledge of their first language. Subtractive bilingualism may have lasting negative consequences. For children from minority-language backgrounds, programs promoting the development of the first language at home and at school may be more important for long-term success in the second language than an early start in the second language itself. Research shows that a good foundation in the child's first language, including the development of literacy, is a sound base to build on. Children who can begin their schooling in a language they already know will have more self-confidence, and will be able to learn more effectively in the early school years.

For foreign or second language instruction where the level of proficiency which is targeted is not native-like performance by all students, the situation is quite different. When the goal of the educational program is basic communicative skill for all students, and where there is a strong commitment to maintaining and developing the child's first language, it can be more efficient to begin second language teaching later. Older children, for example, 10 years old, are able to catch up very quickly to those who began earlier, for example, at 6 or 7 years old, in programs offering only a few hours a week of instruction. This is especially true if the foreign language course includes a period of more intensive exposure to the new language.

(出典：How Language are Learned Pasty M. Lightbown and Nina Spada 1999 OXFORD UNIVERSITY PRESS 改)
・　perform like native speakers
・　disadvantage of an early start
・　basic communication skills

(☆☆☆☆☆◎◎◎)

【6】次の英文を読み，問1～5の答えとして最も適当なものをそれぞれ選択肢ア～エから1つ選び，記号で答えなさい。

Nine families raised children who all went on to extraordinary success. Each of these families is different in thousands of ways, from their ethnicities to their incomes to their sleepover policies. But we set out to find the ways they are the same.

Some of the consistencies are fairly predictable. While none of these children grew up rich, they were privileged in many other ways. They had involved parents and lots of opportunities, and most saw college as achievable, even inevitable. They weren't abused or neglected, and none grew up in abject want. They didn't have an unfair head start, but they were spared some of the most difficult obstacles faced by less fortunate kids.

But other commonalities are more specific, and more telling. Of the nine families, eight had a parent who was an immigrant or an educator, and five had a parent who was both. Many parents were involved in political activism of some kind. Most recall a conflict-heavy family life, but that conflict was rarely between the parents. Many had a strong awareness of mortality as children. And most said they grew up with much more freedom than their friends did.

Here's what they have in common.

On a university campus, Esther Wojcicki was having a pool party. Her husband Stan was chair of the physics department at Stanford, and they regularly hosted barbecues for students and their families. Their daughters Susan, Janet and Anne would interrogate the guests about theoretical physics when they weren't busy passing crackers with cheese to the guests or throwing each other in the pool.

Susan is now the CEO of *YouTube*, Janet is a professor of pediatrics and epidemiology at the University of California, San Francisco, and Anne is a co-founder and the CEO of genetics company *23andMe*. When they show up for breakfast in their childhood home on Stanford's campus, each wears a shirt that belongs to one of the others. They immediately start mocking Anne for bringing her own kale to breakfast, mimicking Janet's high school cheerleading routine and passing around a video of Anne dancing in a hula skirt on a family vacation. "When you have three girls together, it was already a party," Janet says.

Growing up surrounded by their dad's physics buddies had its drawbacks. On their school vacations, the girls were usually dragged to physics conferences, where they would torment the world-famous scientists. They threw paper airplanes during presentations, hurled small objects off hotel balconies and even came up with an elaborate fashion-consulting prank to trick academics into changing their ugly ties.

But the academic environment also instilled a comfort with complex ideas and a confidence in asking questions. "Because we grew up with a lot of strong academics, I think one of the skills we have is not being intimidated," says Susan. "It's never like, 'Oh, this person is so important, I can't challenge him.' "

Esther had begun her daughters' education long before they were peppering Stanford physicists with questions about nuclear particles. After working as a teacher and playground supervisor in the 1960s, she began to suspect that early-childhood education was more crucial than anyone then thought. "My theory was that the most important years were 0 to 5," she says. "It was a gut feeling. So I made everything into a game." She did arts and crafts projects with her toddler daughters, took them to the library every week and taught them how to read, count and swim before they even set foot in a classroom.

Of course, developmental experts have now proved Esther right: the first few years of a child's life are among the most important for learning and brain development. And between Stan's academic universe and Esther's educational parenting, another commonality emerges: seven of the nine families had a parent who was a teacher.

Not all taught at the university level, though three families at least one professor as a parent. The nine families also included parents who were elementary school teachers, a preschool painting instructor, a doctor who taught medical students, a former French teacher and a school administrator who taught a night course on black history.

It may be that (A   ). Parents in these families instinctively understood the importance of at-home instruction decades before researchers established the merits of early education. Their children recalled

275

early supplementary lessons, books read aloud, regular library trips and even at-home worksheets to give them an early boost in school.

This clearly helped the Dungey sisters. *ABC Entertainment Group* president Channing Dungey is the first black president of a major television network, and her sister Merrin Dungey is a well-known actor, with major roles on *Once Upon a Time and Alias*. Their mother had been an elementary-school teacher before Charnning was born, and she applied her classroom skills to raising her two daughters in Sacramento. "She would draw lines of faces, like three happy faces and one sad face, three triangles and one square, and then there's my little crayon marks marking the one that was wrong," recalls Channing, who learned to read when she was 2 years old. "We never went to preschool, because we didn't have to." Merrin adds.

For the Srinivassans, having a parent who was an educator created an unspoken expectation of academic achievement that was almost as powerful as familial love. "You probably have somewhere in the back of your mind that you don't want to disappoint your teachers in the same way you don't want to disappoint your parents," says Sri. "There was just no other way to think."

(出典：TIME 2016 *Ordinary Families. Extraordinary Kids. A Story of nine families* Charlotte Alter　一部抜粋)

問1　According to the passage, which is NOT something in common among any of the children who have achieved great success?

ア　They overcame some difficulties other children couldn't have overcome.

イ　They had parents who were interested in education.

ウ　They took going to college for granted.

エ　They were appropriately taken care of by their parents.

問2　According to the passage, which statement is NOT true about Wojcicki sisters?

ア　They asked questions to academic giants while they were not busy serving food to the guests during the party.

イ They enjoyed imitating each other, wearing the same clothes and eating the same vegetable.

ウ They received early-childhood education, which was not as widely spread as it is now.

エ They grew up in an academic environment, so they wouldn't hesitate to challenge Physicists.

問3 Which phrase is most appropriate for the blank (A)?

ア becoming a university teacher is the way to educate talented children

イ elementary school teachers know more teaching methods than parents

ウ the parents' occupation was less important than the educational mindset

エ teaching students outside the home motivates their own children

問4 According to the passage, which statement is true about Esther's education for her children?

ア She gave her daughters a complete set of literacy skills before school education started.

イ She got her daughters to learn many different things in a fun way.

ウ She started early education due to her daughters' interest in physics.

エ She tried every teaching technique she knew to her daughters.

問5 According to the passage, which statement is most appropriate?

ア To be successful in life, we should go to preschool to receive early-childhood education.

イ Parents should adequately praise their children in order to show their love and care.

ウ Successful teachers are not always parents of successful kids.

エ Though these successful kids were educated from an early age, they also had considerable freedom.

(☆☆☆☆○○○)

【7】次の英文を読み，問1～5の答えとして最も適当なものをそれぞれの
選択肢ア～エから1つ選び，記号で答えなさい。

Teaching English can be very exciting, but at 3:30 on a Monday afternoon, with a whole term ahead of you, it can seem a lot of other things, too.

For the first two years or so in the profession, the demands of getting to grips with subject matter, technique, organization, school politics, not to mention students, can be very stressful and tiring, and it may often feel as if you stand no chance at all of winning through. Ideals and enthusiasm that you started with may fade away as it becomes clear that you can't make every lesson perfect, that some students, some classes simply won't like what you do. And there are the days when you may have to struggle just to get through.

As time goes on, you will probably find that you have more experience to lean on, more tried-and-tested lessons in the bag to recycle endlessly. Then boredom and staleness are the dangers, once the challenge of becoming competent has faded. Twenty years of teaching experience can become no more than two years' experience repeated ten times over. Repeated venturing down well-travelled roads leads sooner or later to boredom, to fossilization of routines, to increasing defensiveness and fear of change. The question becomes not 'How can I survive?' but 'How can I keep moving forward?' or 'How can I become the best teacher that I can be' The more established and safer you are in your job, the harder it can become to take risks, to try something completely different.

The first important steps towards becoming a better teacher involve an increased awareness about what you do now and an openness to the possibility of change.

If you want to move forward, you have to be clear about what it is that you do now. Do you actually know what you are doing in class? Do you ever stop and examine your actions, your intentions, your motives, your attitudes? You keep planning for the next lesson, the next day, but to look back, to recall what happened, to reflect on it: this seems harder to do. What did happen in that class? What were you like as a teacher? Did you enable learning or prevent it? Why did you do the things you did? What were the other options, the ones that you didn't take?

We can teach and teach. Or we can teach and learn. This kind of teaching, a 'learning teaching' , is a refusal to say '(A   )'. Learning teaching is a desire to move forward, to keep learning from what happens. It involves feedback from others and from ourselves about what happened. It involves reflection on what happened, together with an excitement about trying a slightly different option next time. Learning teaching is an aware and active use of the experimental learning cycle in one's own life and work. Learning teaching is a belief that creativity, understanding, experience and character continue growing throughout one's life.

Ask other teachers to come in and observe some of your lessons, and do an exchange observation with them, not to judge each other or score points but to learn from each other. The growth in trust and respect that comes from sharing ideas and skills in this way can really help all involved move forward, as well as having a markedly positive effect on the whole atmosphere of a school.

Even if a colleague cannot come in and observe a lesson, then you could still set aside some uninterrupted time (perhaps fifteen minutes or so) when they will sit and listen to you talk through your thoughts about the lesson. Your colleague could make a 'contact' with you that he or she will not offer suggestions or advice or help or options, but will simply listen and support you. This kind of helping is very simple to describe, but extremely powerful in action. It can be surprisingly beneficial to talk through one's own experience with another person who is really listening.

When you have taught a lesson, it can be tempting to see it completely uncritically in broad shades of extremes either as a huge success or as a complete failure. Teachers sometimes find themselves diving from one extreme to the other in the space of a few minutes.

You may equally be tempted not to think about the lesson at all, to put it away in the back of your mind and forget it, or alternatively to broad over it, picking away at it for hours afterwards, regretting what happened and seeing every possible alternative way of doing things as an improvement on what actually happened.

The alternative (and more difficult option) is to try and take on objective, more balanced view of what happened: first to recall what happened, then to reflect on that and look for what was successful and for what could be improved. Whatever the lesson was like, there will have been good points in it and things that could be worked on. This is true for the most experienced teacher as much as for a beginner.

If you are taking an initial training course, then your tutors may be just as interested in encouraging your own self-awareness as in pointing out success and problems themselves. They could spend the whole time praising what you did, or tearing your lesson into little pieces, but the only thing that is going to move you forward as a teacher is if you yourself become aware of what works and what doesn't.

(出典：Jim Scrivener, *Learnine Teaching,* Third Edition, Macmillan)

問1　According to the passage, which statement is true about the first few years of your career as an English teacher?

ア　It will be the most peaceful part of your career.

イ　You may feel stressed about your classes or the relationship with your colleagues, but your students will cheer you up.

ウ　You may feel as if you were in the middle of a race with your colleagues to be the best teacher at the school.

エ　You may often feel disappointed to find that your lessons weren't perfect.

問2　According to the passage, which is a common situation experienced teachers often fall into?

ア　They want to stick to what they have experienced and become defensive.

イ　They are willing to take risks to try something new.

ウ　They try to rely on other teachers when making lesson plans.

エ　They are inclined to hate routines and look for changes.

問3　According to the passage, which of the fellowing would be the most appropriate to fill in the blank （　A　）?

ア　'Students have a lot of things to learn from us.'

イ　'My class yesterday went quite well. What in particular made it work well?'

ウ　'I know it all. I can relax for the rest of my career.'

エ　'Why did I do it that way? How could I have done it better?'

問4　According to the passage, what is true about teachers doing exchange observations of lessons?

ア　It will be a good opportunity for the teachers to make an assessment of each other objectively.

イ　It will help build a strong sense of trust and respect among themselves and give preferable influence to the whole school.

ウ　It is important to schedule the observations carefully so that all the teachers can come and share ideas and skills.

エ　The most important thing for the teachers is to offer suggestions, advice or help after observing a lesson.

問5　According to the passage, which statement is true?

ア　It is very important that you focus mainly on the positive side of your teaching and try to forget the failures.

イ　It will benefit you greatly if you have your colleagues listen to you, talk about your lesson and ask them to give you alternative ways.

ウ　A tutor in an initial training course of teaching should criticize your lesson in detail so that you know which parts could be improved and how.

エ　Instead of taking extreme views of the finished lesson, it is more profitable to reflect on the lesson objectively.

(☆☆☆☆○○○○○)

【8】問1~5の英文の意味が通るように,それぞれ後の語(句)ア～キを並びかえたとき,(1)～(10)の位置にくる語(句)を記号で答えなさい。ただし,文頭に入る語(句)も小文字で示してある。

問1　A: I'm tired out. I can't run any more.

　　　B: Stand up!(　　　)(　　　)(1)(　　　)(　　　)(2)(　　　), we
　　　　 should never give up. The tournament is coming.

　　ア　practice　　イ　hard　　ウ　matter　　エ　how　　オ　the
　　カ　no　　　　キ　is

問2　A: What a hot day it is! I wish(　　)(　　)(3)(　　)(　　)
　　　　 (4)(　　)planned.

　　　B: You should suggest cancelling it. I also prefer to stay at home and
　　　　 drink something cold.

　　ア　out of　　イ　hiking　　ウ　get　　エ　I　　オ　the
　　カ　Ken's　　キ　could

問3　A: Did you see the car driving crazily on Route 150 this morning? It
　　　　 was like going on a highway.

　　　B: Yes, and you know what? Driving more than (　　) (　　)(5)
　　　　 (　　)(　　)(6)(　　).

　　ア　her　　　　イ　cost　　　ウ　the speed limit　　エ　license
　　オ　the driver　　カ　driving　　キ　double

問4　A: Did you hear the news that the new robot Pepper can do some
　　　　 housework?

　　　B: Really? I can't believe how much robots can do for us!

　　　A: I know. (　　)(　　)(7)(　　)(　　)(　　)(8)(　　)in 50 years
　　　　 from now?

　　ア　like　　イ　you think　　ウ　will　　エ　do　　オ　our life
　　カ　what　　キ　be

問5　A: Why didn't you tell your parents that you want to study abroad?

B: Oh, no. They still think that I am just a little child, so whenever I tell them what I think, they just(　　)(　　)(9)(　　)(　　) (10)(　　)for anything.

ア　count 　　　イ　don't 　ウ　make 　エ　that 　オ　me
カ　my opinions 　キ　feel

(☆☆☆☆◎◎◎◎)

【9】「英語表現Ⅰ」の授業で，「好きな本を持参して英語で紹介し合い，最も読みたいと思った本に投票する」というグループ活動を行いました。ところが，多くの生徒に以下のような課題が見られました。

　　課題1　話し手は原稿を読み上げるだけだった。
　　課題2　話し手は紹介の内容として本のあらすじを述べるだけだった。

　この活動のフィードバックとして，あなたなら生徒にどのようなアドバイスをしますか。アドバイスの内容を3点挙げ，授業中に口頭で説明するという想定で，次の6行以上を使い，英語で書きなさい。なお，前提となる生徒の英語力は自由に設定してよい。

【6行目】

(70％に縮小)
(☆☆☆☆◎◎◎◎)

【10】以下は「コミュニケーション英語Ⅰ」の授業における最初の15分間の様子です。これを読んで，問1および問2に答えなさい。

(Bell rings.)

Teacher: Hello everyone! Today, we are going to start a new lesson, Lesson 3, 'Let's Save the Endangered Animals'. Please read section 1 and answer the True or False questions. You have 5 minutes. Ready go!

(In 5 minutes...)

Time's up!! Now, let's check the answers. What's the answer for No. 1?

Any volunteer?

Students: ....

Teacher: No? Don't be shy! OK, student A. What is your answer?

StudentA: True.

Teacher: That's right. OK, then what's for No. 2? Student B?

StudentB: False.

Teacher: Excellent.

(In the same way, they cheek the rest of the answers)

Teacher: Very good everybody. Let's move on to the next activity.

問1　この授業展開における問題点を，理由を含め2点指摘しなさい。次の5行程度を使い，英語で書きなさい。

問1
【5行目】

(70％に縮小)

問2　問1で挙げたそれぞれの問題点に対して，あなたはどのような提案をしますか。具体的な解決策について，その意図も含め2点述べなさい。次の8行程度を使い，英語で書きなさい。前提となる生徒の英語力は自由に設定してよい。

問2
【8行目】

(70％に縮小)

(☆☆☆☆☆◎◎◎)

解答・解説

【中学校】

【1】1　D　　2　B

〈解説〉スクリプトが公表されていないが，説明文を聞き，指示文にあるように「suitable word」を選択する問題である。名詞または数字などが解答として想定される。放送は1回のみなので注意して聞く必要がある。

【2】1　C　　2　D

〈解説〉スクリプトが公表されていないが，会話文を聞き，指示文にある
ように「correct answer」を選択する問題である。単文程度の解答が想
定される。【1】と同様に，放送は1回のみなので集中して聞く必要が
ある。

【3】(解答略。本年は問題解答とも公表されていない。)

〈解説〉スクリプトが公表されていないが，解答欄から判断すると，1〜3
は【2】よりは長い文が求められ，4の指示文には「句読点」とあるこ
とから，日本語の要約文を60字以上80字以下で記述することが想定さ
れる。放送は2回なので，2回目で点検ができるように聞く必要がある。

【4】1　You write well, but you can write better. For example, you should use
'because' and 'so.' So, you write 'Because it's very difficult, I make a lot of
mistakes.' and 'So, what should I do?' (35語)　　2　Developing students'
practical command of English is needed to enable them to understand English
and express themselves in English. The following are needed: (a) becoming
familiar with the basic characteristics of English and correct pronunciation.
(b) speaking accurately about one's thoughts and feelings or facts. (c) carrying
on a dialogue or exchanging views regarding their listening or reading.
(d) speaking continuously and give a simple speech. (66語)

〈解説〉1　中学校学習指導要領の言語活動のうち，「書くこと」の内容に
ついての設問である。「書くこと」では，主に「語と語のつながりな
どに注意して正しく文を書くこと」と「自分の考えや気持ちなどが読
み手に正しく伝わるように，文と文のつながりなどに注意して文章を
書くこと」が指導事項である。この設問では，後者の観点から解答す
ればよい。　2　問題文に「話す活動を通して」とある点に注意する
こと。学習指導要領や同解説を参考にして「話すこと」の内容を理解
しておくことが必要である。

【5】For the purpose of students' positive use of English, teachers should use English positively in their lessons. Teachers' positive use of English during lessons in principle leads to the chance of students' using English and the real scene of communication through English. What affects greatly to the students' positive use of English is the teachers' attitude for their use of English and their activity during their lessons. (67語)

〈解説〉設問で示された中学校学習指導要領の解説では,「生徒が積極的に英語を使って取り組めるよう,まず教師自身がコミュニケーションの手段として英語を使う姿勢と態度を行動で示していくことが肝心である」という記述がある。また,授業を基本的に英語で行うことのポイントは,「英語に触れる機会」と「実際のコミュニケーションの場面」であるとの記述もある。このような内容をまとめればよい。

【6】1　ウ　　2　イ　　3　ア　　4　ウ　　5　イ

〈解説〉1　アは「十人十色」,イは「逆境が人を鍛える」,ウは「かわいい子には旅をさせよ」,エは「郷に入っては郷に従え」である。設問のことわざは,「幼少のうちにあえて試練を与える」という意味なので,ウが適切である。　2　「困難に立ち向かう」の意味なので,イ「挑戦」が適切である。　3　第2段落第3文は,通学の際の駅や電車内の混雑について述べている。外国人には,このような状況の中を小学生が通学することは信じがたいのである。　4　空欄の直後の部分everyからmeまでに,「知らない人は自分に危害を加える犯罪者かもしれない」と述べている。everyの前にbecauseを補うとわかりやすい。5　第1段落の内容は,日本とオーストラリアの小学生が通学する様子がかなり異なることの導入部分である。第2段落は,日本人の7歳の私立小学生が実際に1人で電車通学する様子と,オーストラリアの10歳の小学生が車で父親に送り迎えをしてもらう記述がある。第3段落では,日本の小学生の通学事情が紹介されている。注目すべきは,第3段落第5文及び第6文である。このような集団登校の仕組みがあるので,親は子どもを1人で通学させるのである。

【7】1　①　イ　　②　エ　　③　ア　　2　(The real-world application of classroom knowledge in a community setting) allows.　　3　学生は時間，才能，知的資産を提供する。地域と関係機関は学生の協働指導者として時間を投資し，次に，学生の活動を通してより多くの使命や目標を達成する。相互関係をもついわば共存共栄的な関係である。　　4　大学在学中だけでなく，個人が継続的に成長する基礎を築き，その影響が生涯にわたって続く。

〈解説〉1　①　第1段落第1文の半ばにあるexperiencesの語に注目する。続くwhichからcommunityまでの文から正答を導ける。　②　第1段落第4文の冒頭のProponentsと，同第6文のThereからservice-learningまでに着目したい。six qualitiesを挙げているのは第4文のProponentsである。③　第5段落第4文後半のstudents以下にcommunity's unique strengths「各地域独特の強み」とある。　2　第1段落第4文に設問の答えがある。that以下settingまでが動詞allowsの主語となる。　3　第6段落第2文では学生側の，同第4文では地域や関係機関の状況を述べている。互いにどのように影響し合っているか述べればよい。　4　第7段落第5文の論旨をまとめる。

【高等学校】

【1】問1　ウ　　問2　イ　　問3　ア　　問4　イ　　問5　ウ

〈解説〉問1　英文は1回しか読まれないので，正確に聞き取れるように注意しよう。「ビールを飲みませんか。」に対して「OK，飲みましょう。」what do you say 〜ingで「〜するのはどうですか。〜しませんか。」という提案の意味となる。　問2　「この辺はよく知らないのにどうやって駅まで来たのか。」に対して「運よく親切な老人に出会ったので。」問3　「お先にどうぞ。」に対して「ありがとうございます。」問4　「あなたのお荷物にはなりたくないのですが。」に対して「そんなことをおっしゃらないでください。」burden on(to)〜「〜のお荷物(負担)になる，足手まといになる」　問5　「この箱を動かすのを手伝ってもらえませんか。」に対して「かまいませんよ，どこへ。」

【2】問1　ア　　問2　ウ　　問3　ウ　　問4　イ　　問5　ア

〈解説〉英文は1回しか読まれないので，選択肢を先に読み何が問われる
か推測することが大切である。　問1　Fは2回目の発言で，「(美しい自
然なんて)退屈だ」と言い，「別の文明を体験しないか」と提案してい
る。　問2　「指輪をジャケットのポケットに入れてしまった」と言うF
に対し，Mは「そのジャケットはクリーニング店に持って行ってしま
った」と言っている。　問3　Fは3回目の発言で「コーラスをやりま
しょう。あなたが(ピアノで)伴奏してね」と言っている。Fの最後の発
言you look pale「顔色が悪い」が示すことをくみ取ろう。Mは「以前ピ
アノを弾いていた」と言ったが，いざ弾くとなるとしり込みをしてい
ることを表している。　問4　Fの3回目の発言の最後の部分に注目し
よう。「短く，明快な指示を順番に」出すことを提案している。　問5
Mの3回目の発言I've tried it onceとit didn't work for meから，「前に試し
てみたけれどその時はだめだった」ことがわかる。

【3】問1　ア　　問2　ウ　　問3　ウ　　問4　ア

〈解説〉ニュースを聞き，内容に合う文章を選ぶ問題である。2回読ま
れるので，1回目に聞き取れなかった箇所を2回目で確認できるようにし
よう。　問1　設問のBefore renewing〜に対応するのは，スクリプトの
After revisingからreplacedの部分であると推測しよう。signsとlawsの位
置を入れ替えているが，解答と同じ意味を示している。　問2　設問
のsame shapes will be maintainedと同義なのはスクリプトの第5段落
shapes will stay the sameである。この後に続く部分が解答となる。
問3　数字を聞き取り，どちらが多いか答える。キーワードであるstop
signsとslow down signsに該当する数字を正しく聞き取ろう。スクリプ
トの第6段落に1,700万箇所と1,000箇所という数字が示されている。
問4　答えはスクリプトの最後の，National Police Agency が見解を述べ
ている箇所にある。キーワードはnew signsであり，これを含む選択肢
はアのみである。

【4】問1　ウ　　問2　エ　　問3　イ，オ
〈解説〉英文は2回読まれる。聞き取った数値をグラフや表の空欄に補充する問題は頻出である。どの数値が何を表すのか明確に区別できるよう，日頃から数値の聞き取りに慣れておきたい。　問1　スクリプトの第2段落に具体的な数値が述べられている。　問2　同じくスクリプトの第4段落に具体的な数値が述べられている。　問3　アは誤り。スクリプト第2段落のthe top answer以下に，中学生の回答は「国民」の28％であると述べられている。イは正しい。第5段落に同じ意味のことが述べられている。ウは誤り。スクリプト第6段落に中学生の割合は52％と述べられているので，「大部分」とは言えない。エは誤り。スクリプト第3段落の第2文で，ともに政治に関する興味は50％と述べられている。オは正しい。第6段落に中学生52％，高校生48％と述べられているので，約半数である。

【5】　・If the goal is to perform like native speakers in the second language, it's better for children to start learning it as early as possible.　・In order to overcome disadvantage of an early start, we need to give children opportunities to develop their knowledge of their first language.　・If the objective is basic communication skills, children can start learning the second language later.
〈解説〉与えられた3つのフレーズを使って，聞き取った内容を要約する問題である。最初のフレーズは，スクリプト第1段落第2文の「ネイティブスピーカーのような能力を望むならば」という箇所をまとめる。2番目のフレーズは，スクリプト第2段落第2文の「第2言語を早期に学び始めると第1言語の能力を発達させる機会がない」と述べた箇所を利用し，「不利な点をカバーする方法」をまとめればよい。3番目のフレーズは，第3段落第2文の「基本的なコミュニケーションスキルと第1言語の発達を目的とするならば」の箇所をまとめる。

【6】問1　ア　　問2　イ　　問3　ウ　　問4　イ　　問5　エ

〈解説〉問1　アは誤り。論旨にはない。イは正しい。第11段落第2文の parents who以下に，親の職業が教育関係であったという記述がある。ウは正しい。第2段落第3文のmost saw以下に，大学への進学は当然のことであったと述べている。エは正しい。第2段落第4文に，子どもたちが育児放棄にも虐待にも遭わず，貧しさで困窮することもなく育ったとある。　問2　アは正しい。第5段落第3文のwould以下に，理論物理学に関して来客に質問したとある。イは誤り。論旨にはない。ウは正しい。第9段落第1文と第5文に，幼い娘たちに家庭で教育を始めたことが述べられている。エは正しい。第8段落第1文にアカデミックな環境で育ったことの利点が述べられている。　問3　第12段落第2文に，「これらの家庭の親たちは，家庭教育の重要性を本能的に理解していた」という記述がある。つまり，「親の職業よりも，親自身の教育的な興味・関心の方が重要である」ということである。したがってウが適切である。　問4　アはa completeからskillsまでが誤り。論旨にはない。イは正しい。第9段落第4文のSo I made以下に，「ゲームとして」とある。ウはdue to以下が誤り。第9段落第2文のMy theory以下に，母親のEstherが早期教育の重要性を感じたとある。エはevery以下が誤り。論旨にはない。　問5　アはwe should以下が誤り。就学前に幼児教室に通わせるべきという記述はない。イはpraise以下が誤り。子どもに褒美を与えるべきという記述はない。ウはnot以下が誤り。親がよい教師であっても子どもが成功するとは限らないという記述はない。エは正しい。第3段落第6文に，他の子どもたちより自由に育ったという記述がある。

【7】問1　エ　　問2　ア　　問3　ウ　　問4　イ　　問5　エ

〈解説〉問1　アはthe most以下が誤り。第2段落第1文に，ストレスがたまって疲れるとの記述がある。イはbut your以下が誤り。同じく第2段落第1文に，ストレスの原因が列挙されている。ウはin the middle以下が誤り。同僚との競争でなく，第2段落第1文の前半に述べられた事柄に

ついて勝ち目がないと感じるのである。エは正しい。第2段落第2文のIdealsからperfectまでにこの内容の記述がある。　問2　アは正しい。第3段落の第4文に、ルーティーンになってしまい変化をおそれて保守的になるとの記述がある。イはwilling to以下が誤り。第3段落第6文のthe harder以下に、経験を積めば積むほど教師はリスクを冒したがらなくなると述べられている。ウはrely on以下が誤り。他の教師に頼るという記述はない。エはto hate以下が誤り。本文の内容とは逆である。問3　第6段落第3文の空欄の直前のrefusalと、空欄に続く第4文で述べている「教え方の学習」とに注目し、どんなことを否定するか判断する。　問4　設問のポイントは「授業の相互観察」である。アは誤り。第7段落第1文のnot to以下に、お互いの授業の評価や採点をするのではないと述べている。イは正しい。第7段落第2文にこの意味の記述がある。ウはItからcarefullyまでが誤り。第8段落第1文で逆のことを述べている。エはto offer以下が誤り。第12段落第2文のbut the only以下に、自分自身が授業の良い点と悪い点を認識できるかどうかであると述べている。　問5　アはyou focus以下が誤り。第11段落第1文から、悪い点にも注目すべきことがわかる。イはask以下が誤り。第8段落第2文に、同僚は提案も忠告も代替案も出さないという記述がある。ウはcriticize以下が誤り。第12段落第2文に、良い点と問題点を指摘すると同時に、自分自身でそれらを認識できるように励ますとの記述がある。エは正しい。前半部分は第9段落、後半部分は第11段落第1文にこの内容の記述がある。

【8】問1　1　エ　　2　ア　　問2　3　ウ　　4　イ　　問3　5　イ　　6　カ　　問4　7　イ　　8　キ　　問5　9　キ　　10　イ
〈解説〉問1　「譲歩」を表す構文で、「いかに～であっても」の意味である。no matter howはhoweverでもよい。no matter how hard the practice is(カ→ウ→エ→イ→オ→ア→キ)となる。　問2　仮定法過去の用法で、空欄4の後にthatまたはwhichが省略されていると考えればよい。I could get out of the hiking Ken's (エ→キ→ウ→ア→オ→イ→カ)である。

292

問3 直訳すると，「制限速度の倍以上で運転したことが運転手に彼女
の運転免許証という代価を払わせた」となる。つまり，彼女は速度超
過で免許取り消しになったのである。語順はdouble the speed limit cost
the driver her driving license(キ→ウ→イ→オ→ア→カ→エである。
問4 「あなたは私たちの人生が50年後にどのようになっていると思い
ますか」の意味である。語順はwhat do you think our life will be like(カ
→エ→イ→オ→ウ→キ→ア)である。　　問5　BのセリフのTheyから
childまでで，両親はBの言うことに耳を貸さないとわかる。語順は
make me feel that my opinions don't count(ウ→オ→キ→エ→カ→イ→ア)
である。

【9】(例1)　There are three ways you can improve your presentation. Firstly,
you need to explain the interesting and wonderful parts of this book. Did you
laugh out loud or cry when reading? Secondly, you should not only read from
your paper, but make eye contact to engage with your audience. That makes
your speech more persuasive. Finally, you should add active parts to your
presentation. Maybe you can open the book and show the pictures, pass it
around your audience and make gestures.　　(例2)　First, you should look
up and try to talk to the audience using gestures. If you do so, you can involve
the audience. Second, you should explain your favorite part of the story and
the reason why you like it. That makes the audience feel more interested in
your book. Third, you don't have to explain everything in the story. You can
focus on some interesting parts and encourage the audience to read the rest of
it.
〈解説〉プレゼンテーションを行う上でのアドバイスを3つ挙げるので，
firstly(first), secondly(second), thirdly(third)のように3つを明確に区別した
上で，それぞれの注意点を述べるとわかりやすい。「英語表現Ⅰ」の
「目標」は，「英語を通じて，積極的にコミュニケーションを図ろうと
する態度を育成するとともに，事実や意見などを多様な観点から考察
し，論理の展開や表現の方法を工夫しながら伝える能力を養う」であ

る。これらの内容に照らすと，(例1)では，最初に，本の感動した点を説明するように指導し，次に，聞き手とアイコンタクトをとるように指導して，最後に，発表にアクションを取り入れるように指導している。上述の「目標」の後半部分「事実や意見などを」以下の内容に配慮していることがわかる。(例2)では，最初にアクションを取り入れるように指導して，次に，好きな箇所とその理由を説明するように指導し，最後に，自分が興味を持った箇所を強調して，その本を読む気を起こさせるように指導している。(例1)とは若干観点が異なるが，「目標」の後半の内容に配慮していることがわかる。

【10】問1　(例1)　First, the lesson has no warm-up activity, so students are forced to read the passage without any background knowledge. Second, the teacher just checks the answers, and students are just saying "True" or "False" without giving any evidence. The teacher doesn't understand how much the students understand the passage.　(例2)　One problem is that the students don't discuss the reasons why it's true or false because they are not given opportunities to talk about them. Another problem is that this class doesn't relate the students to the topic because there isn't any pre-reading (introduction) activity.　問2　(例1)　First, the teacher should plan good pre-reading activities, including a warm-up activity to develop students' interests. Also, the teacher can ask some good questions so that students can be highly motivated to read the passage. With this procedure, the reading activity can be more meaningful.　Second, the teacher should ask students why the answer is true or false. In this way, students can interact with the teacher and the others using English and improve their reading, listening, and speaking skills. Also, the teacher can see the difficulties students have and check whether students truly understand the passage.　(例2)　After the students answer the T/F questions individually, they should be given about 3-5minutes to go over their answers in pairs and talk about the questions to which they have different answers. By doing this, they can check each other's understanding of the text, critically reading through the text together. Before starting reading, the teacher can show some visual aids related to the topic, and ask students about their personal experiences regarding the topic. Accordingly, they will be more engaged in reading it.

〈解説〉問1 「コミュニケーション英語Ⅰ」の目標は,「英語を通じて, 積極的にコミュニケーションを図ろうとする態度を育成するとともに, 情報や考えなどを的確に理解したり適切に伝えたりする基礎的な能力を養う」である。 (例1)では, 第1点として, いきなり授業を始めたので生徒はこの課の予備知識が何もない状態で本文を読まざるを得ないこと, 第2点として, 設問の正誤を解答するだけで根拠を示していないことが述べられている。また (例2)では, 最初に, 各設問の正誤の理由を生徒が述べていないこと, 次に, 生徒に対して新たな課の導入が行われていないことが記述されている。前述の「目標」に照らすと, このような状態では, 生徒は積極的にコミュニケーションを図ろうとすることは難しく, また適切に情報を伝える基礎的な能力をつけることも難しい。 問2 (例1) 新たな課の第1回目の授業なので, 教師には入念な準備が求められる。生徒が新たな題材に興味・関心を持つように工夫された導入のリーディングを実施すべきことと, 生徒に対して理解の程度を確認するために, 正誤の理由をただすべきことが述べられている。 (例2) 設問の正誤について解答した後に, 生徒がペアになって異なる解答の設問について検討する時間をとるべきことと, トピックに関する内容を視覚的に提示すべきことが述べられている。前者については, 客観的な読みにつながる方策であり, 後者については, ICTを用いることで, 生徒の理解を一層助けることが期待できるのである。

2017年度　実施問題

【中学校】

【1】【放送問題】

Listen to the description and choose the most suitable word from A to D. The sentences and the choices will be read once.

1　(A)
　　(B)
　　(C)
　　(D)
2　(A)
　　(B)
　　(C)
　　(D)
3　(A)
　　(B)
　　(C)
　　(D)

(☆☆☆○○○)

【2】【放送問題】

Listen to the conversation and answer the following questions. The conversation and the questions will be read once.

1　(A)　About 8:30.
　　(B)　About 8:35.
　　(C)　About 8:40.
　　(D)　About 8:45.
2　(A)　To participate in an earthquake drill.
　　(B)　To talk with Ms. Tanaka.

296

(C)　To see the homeroom activities.

(D)　To introduce herself to students.

3　(A)　Writing the impression of the evacuation drill.

(B)　Comparing two types of evacuation drills.

(C)　Using the Internet to get some pictures.

(D)　Learning Japanese and English proverbs.

(☆☆☆○○○)

【3】【放送問題】

Listen to the passage and answer each question. The passage and the questions will be read twice.

1 ＿＿＿＿＿＿＿＿＿＿ ％ ＿

2 ＿＿＿＿＿＿＿＿＿＿＿＿＿＿＿＿＿＿＿＿＿＿＿＿

3

・

・

(☆☆☆○○○)

【4】【英作文】

中学2年生の英語の授業で，"Where do you want to go?" というテーマで英作文を行った際に，ある生徒が次のように書きました。

> "Where do you want to go?"
>
> I want to go to New Zealand.
> I like sweets very much. So I want to eat New Zealand sweets.
> I like animals, too. I want to see kiwi birds!
> I want to talk with New Zealand people in English too. But do you think my English is OK?

　あなたはこの生徒に対して，どのようにコメントを書きますか。英語でのコミュニケーション力を伸ばすための具体的なアドバイスも含め，英単語30語以上40語以内で書きなさい。

(☆☆☆◎◎◎)

【５】【英作文】
　中学校学習指導要領　第2章　第9節　外国語には，以下のように示されています。

> ア　3学年間を通じ指導に当たっては，次のような点に配慮するものとする。
> (ア)　実際に言語を使用して互いの考えや気持ちを伝え合うなどの活動を行うとともに，(3)に示す言語材料について理解したり練習したりする活動を行うようにすること。
> ※(3)には，音声，文字及び符号，語，連語及び慣用表現，文法事項など，中学校で扱う言語材料が示されている。
> 「中学校学習指導要領(平成20年9月告示)第2章　第9節　外国語　第2　各言語の目標及び内容等　2内容　(2)　言語活動の取扱い」

　これを読んで，あなたはどのような授業をしたいと考えますか。理由も含め，英単語50語以上70語以内で書きなさい。

(☆☆☆◎◎◎◎)

【 6 】 Read the passage and answer the following questions.

If our children are picky about food, we worry that they won't get enough nutrition and may have problems when they grow up. How can we reduce these strong likes and dislikes in a painless way?

"①(Dislike) of bitterness and acidity is instinctive," said Kansai University of International Studies Prof. Tsuyoshi Horio, an expert on the psychology of taste. Animals avoid stimuli such as bitterness or acidity as a natural biological reaction to protect themselves from danger.

According to Horio, "experiencing various foods and ways of eating them is important" to reduce strong food (②). Recent research has shown that the more different things children taste from an early age, the more kinds of foods they can eat. We should try to put as great a variety of foods on the table as possible.

Worrying too much or forcing your children to eat certain foods is (③). Children tend to sense the pressure and become even more unable to eat them.

Cooking expert Hiroko Sakamoto said: "Children. don't eat foods they're not familiar with. To reduce picky eating, we need to create opportunities for them to learn about food." Sakamoto recommends "reencounters" with foods. Children are shown ingredients before cooking, and encouraged to touch and smell them. According to Sakamoto, developing a fresh interest in the ingredients can create an opportunity to remove feelings of dislike.

Children should also be given the chance to try cooking. Involvement in the process by which ingredients reach the table as food reduces feelings of antipathy toward those ingredients, and children develop a wish to try eating them.

Children should put food on their own plates, too. Even if they do not take much food, we should not interfere but praise them if they eat it all up. This develops confidence, which in turn will have positive effects the next time.

Chopping up hated foods finely and mixing them with other ingredients, then telling your children after they have finished eating, is not recommended because [④]. "Trust your children, and wait until they feel ready to try eating it," said Sakamoto.

If your children have strong likes and dislikes, you may worry whether they are getting proper nutrition. However, Sakamoto advises: "Children can get the same nutrition from different foods. Keep calm!"

〔出典：The Japan News *by The Yomiuri Shinbun*: Decembar 16,2015　一部改〕

1　Find a synonym for the word '①(Dislike)' from the passage and answer in one word.
2　Fill in the blank (②) in the passage with one of the following choices, ア〜エ below.
　ア　preferences　　イ　calories　　ウ　consumption
　エ　leftovers
3　Fill in the blank (③) in the passage with one of the following choices, ア〜エ below.
　ア　affirmative　　イ　counterproductive　　ウ　decisive
　エ　incentive
4　Choose the most suitable sentence form ア〜エ and fill in the blank ④.
　ア　children don't like unfamiliar foods, much less chopped hated food
　イ　parents should use 'the carrot and the stick' to make children eat up meals
　ウ　after taking a bite, children are able to eat foods that they don't like
　エ　it may lead to distrust toward parents
5　Choose the most appropriate title for this column from ア〜エ.
　ア　Healthy food for kids
　イ　Step-by-step guide to reading nutrition facts is important
　ウ　Learning about food helps kids eat healthier
　エ　Children are exposed to "concerning" amount of junk food marketing

300

(☆☆☆○○○)

【 7 】 Read the passage and answer the following questions.

One of our tasks as language teachers is to get students to express their own ideas and opinions both in speech and in writing. This is particularly important in the large multilevel class, where students often feel lost in the crowd and where there are so many students that a teacher might have the tendency to just listen to those who demand attention. Speaking about one's own ideas and outlook makes one feel much more at home in the large forum. Many students, however, are reluctant to express their opinions, partly because they cannot do so adequately in the new language. I learned this the hard way when one of my reluctant speakers once told me, 'You never hear what I say. You just hear the mistakes I make.'

Students in large multilevel classes are also afraid to speak up because they think they will say something stupid in front of an uncaring crowd, or that what they have to say is not important, or that they really have nothing useful to contribute. Students in large multilevel classes have been heard to say, 'Oh, I don't count. I'm just a number here.'

Our job as language teachers is to help students gain competence in language and to provide the support and encouragement that will raise their confidence and motivation. We must assure students that what they think really matters to us more than the way they express themselves. Once people have something to say, they generally are motivated to find the best way to say it.

If we really want to convince our students that their ideas are worthwhile, we should not only pay lip service to such a notion but also structure activities that promote a genuine exchange of ideas and good thinking. As a rule, students are interested in sharing what is on their minds and are waiting for a chance to do so. If our large multilevel class becomes a community, where students feel safe and where their opinions are valued, they will be willing and able to produce relevant language and to exchange opinions with classmates. If we intersperse many idea-sharing activities with strategies that bring about meaningful language, we can hope that language and communication eventually will coincide.

When I structure activities for activation and opinion exchange, I try to keep the following in mind:

- It is not necessary for the teacher to hear everything that is being said or see everything that is being written.
- Students should be allowed to talk about issues of real interest to them.
- The activity should offer many choices of expression.

In large classes, it is important to create activities that will keep the more advanced students interested and at the same time allow the less advanced students to make progress at their own pace. How do we accomplish this? Sometimes students accomplish the task for us by finding their own level in language progression, and this very much depends on the level of their motivation. All of us have had students who conquered material which we thought was way beyond their present level. I have a very fond memory of a beginning student, Maria Lopez, who insisted, against all advice, on joining my advanced *ESL class. The class was reading *My Antonya* by Willa Cather. Maria must have looked up every word in her bilingual dictionary. Then she went home and wrote her book review in Spanish. An advanced student helped her to translate the review into perfect English. She memorized the review and was able to write it in class. Within six months Maria had learned enough English to enroll in a college course and, five years later, she had a Master's degree and was speaking and writing English like a native speaker with only a bare trace of a charming Latino accent on her speech. Maria is not the only one who has decided on where she stands in her language progress and how far and how fast she is willing and able to go.

Many students do this, even if not on such a dramatic scale as Maria's, and in much of our teaching, we can assume that students will drift toward their own level of progress.

However, as we all know, most of our students are not like Maria, but do need to be supplied with challenges that are nearer to their level. This is where multilevel activities are useful and create a more pleasant and accessible climate in our classrooms.

There are basically two ways of modifying activities to make them multilevel — individualization and personalization. When we individualize a task, we allow students to approach it on several different levels. When we personalize a task, we allow students to make it very much their own by giving them opportunities to express their own individual opinions, experiences and feelings as well as working on it on a level appropriate to them.

You can individualize task in two ways — you can use the same material in different ways, or you can use different materials in the same way. You can, for example, take one text, and ask some students to answer difficult inference questions on it, while other students answer simple factual questions. That would be an example of using the same material in different ways. You could also choose two texts on a common theme, making one an unabridged text and the second an abridged text. Later you could give students a set of questions which related to both texts. In pairs made up of a student who read the unabridged text and one who read the abridged text, students would be able to help each other. That would be an example of using different material in the same way.

*ESL：English as a Second Language

〔出典：Natalie Hess, *Teaching Large Multilevel Classes*, 2001　一部改〕

1　The following text is a summary of the first half of this passage.

　　Fill in the blanks ①〜③ with one of the following choices, ア〜オ

below.

Each choice can be used only once.

> Language teachers should try to have students describe their own thoughts.
>
> However, students' language ability varies throughout the class, and many students tend to feel (　①　) about speaking loudly.
>
> Therefore teachers have to help students improve their language ability and assist to raise their (　②　) and motivation.
>
> We can compose activities which create meaningful (　③　) and a way of good thinking.
>
> Also, we can devise ways of preparing material depending on the level of students' language ability.

ア　assurance　　イ　modification　　ウ　fear　　エ　interaction
オ　levels

2　According to this passage, many students in large multilevel classes are afraid to speak up. To avoid that prospect, how should teachers plan classes?

Find a specific phrase within 11-12 words in length that teachers should do.

Teachers should _____.

3　According to this passage, why should teachers modify activities to make them multilevel in the first place? Write in Japanese. Use specific examples presented in the passage to justify your answer.

4　According to this passage, what are concrete examples to individualize a task? Write 2 examples in Japanese.

(☆☆☆☆○○○)

【高等学校】

【1】これから問1〜問5について，それぞれ短い英文を読みます。それぞれの英文の応答として適切なものを，選択肢ア〜ウから1つ選び，記

304

号で答えなさい。なお，英文は1回ずつ読みます。

問1　How soon will the next test start?

　ア　I'm a student here.

　イ　In about fifteen minutes.

　ウ　Every other hour.

問2　Why don't you take a rest and have a cup of tea with me?

　ア　Sounds nice.

　イ　Because I'm tired.

　ウ　That is why.

問3　Do you take this bus regularly?

　ア　No. Only on rainy days.

　イ　No. It hasn't left yet.

　ウ　No. I'm not a regular player.

問4　Judging from his opinion, this evidence can prove her innocence.

　ア　Don't judge by appearance.

　イ　I'm afraid that is not enough.

　ウ　By tomorrow morning.

問5　Mom, can you buy me a new car for my birthday?

　ア　It's raining cats and dogs.

　イ　You eat like a bird.

　ウ　When pigs fly.

(☆☆☆○○○)

【2】これから英語の対話文と質問を読みます。それぞれの対話に関する
　質問の答えとして最も適切なものを，選択肢ア～ウから1つ選び，記
　号で答えなさい。なお，対話と質問は1回読みます。

Dialogue 1

M: Excuse me, which gate does the flight to London leave from? I'm
　wondering if I missed my connection.

F : That flight leaves from gate 15 in Terminal 2. Terminal 2 is to your left, but I see on my screen that it's been delayed by 90 minutes. So you could go to some shops or restaurants instead of waiting at the gate. There are shops in Terminal 3 and restaurants in Terminal 1.

M: Oh, thanks, but I'm not hungry. So I'll do some shopping while I'm waiting.

Question : Where will the man go first?

　　ア　Terminal 1
　　イ　Terminal 2
　　ウ　Terminal 3

Dialogue 2

M: We are going to ride an airplane for almost eight hours on our school excursion, aren't we? It's so long.

F : Yeah, it is. But it took more than twelve hours when I came to Japan last month. I enjoyed some good in-flight movies then.

M: Umm. This time, I will try reading a lot of books I don't usually read, such as Nietzsche, Aristotle, Kant···

F : Are you serious? You will just get airsick if you read such difficult books. That's a bad idea.

M: Do not say that. We are students. Even on trips, we should study a lot.

Question : What will the boy do during the flight?

　　ア　He will read some philosophy books.
　　イ　He will watch some in-flight movies.
　　ウ　He will do some homework.

Dialogue 3

M: Where is Mike? We are supposed to have a meeting in the morning and he is not in his office.

F : I guess he forgot about the meeting. He took the day off to go on a day

306

trip. He hasn't had a day off in a long time. He has been under a lot of pressure.

M: If so, it's understandable. We have been working so hard on this big project. I should reschedule the meeting. I'll call him later.

F : Tom, you have also been so busy. You could use some time off yourself, you know. We know you have been under stress more than usual lately.

Question : What does the woman think Tom should do?
　ア　Take a vacation
　イ　Finish the project soon
　ウ　Call Mike right away

Dialogue 4

F : I'm afraid most of our students are poor at expressing themselves. We need more speaking activities. So, in the next English lesson, how about setting up a theme they will find interesting like "High school students should wear school uniforms"

M: Good idea. Now, we should make the lesson plan. Do you have any ideas?

F : Umm, why don't we make them have a discussion? Through the activity, our students can improve their speaking and listening abilities and deepen their own ideas.

M: For the first grade students, discussion might be too difficult. To begin with, why don't we start off by having each student make a speech. It will be easier for them.

F : Umm, I believe communication ability should improve only through interaction. Discussion is much better.

Question : Why does the woman suggest the idea to have a discussion in the class?
　ア　Because she believes discussion can improve the students' communication ability more than speech.

307

イ　Because she believes making a speech won't improve students' communication ability.

ウ　Because she believes first grade students like discussion.

Dialogue 5

F : I have traveled around Japan quite a lot, and I have found it very easy to move around. The train system in Japan is really excellent.

M: Yeah, I agree with you on this point. The train links are very good in Japan. But I think some famous spots are quite far away from train stations. Moreover, we don't find many directions and signs in English on the way.

F : That's right. The number of tourists visiting Japan has been increasing over the last few years. And Tokyo Olympics will be held in four years.

M: I hope this situation will improve and we can enjoy visiting many more places and communicating with local people.

Question : Which statement is true?

ア　The train system in Japan should be improved.

イ　A lot of Japanese people visit foreign countries.

ウ　Foreign visitors need more help when they visit sightseeing spots in Japan.

(☆☆☆◎◎◎)

【3】これから留学に関する英文を聞き，問1～問4の英文の(　　)に入るのに最も適切なものを選択肢ア～ウから選び，記号で答えなさい。なお英文は2回読みます。英文は20秒後に始まります。

　　Studying in a foreign country can be the adventure of a lifetime. There are four basic stages of studying abroad. The first is the departure stage. You apply to a university overseas. If you're lucky, you get accepted! The next few weeks are busy as you prepare to leave. Soon, it's time to go! Your final days are full of emotions as you say goodbye to your family, friends and relatives.

Finally, you board the plane and take the long flight off to the country where you'll study.

The second stage is the arrival stage. You land in a foreign country, and somehow make your way to your destination. It's exciting to be overseas! Everything seems strange and exotic. But life is busy! There are so many things to do : explore the campus, register for classes, find an apartment, open a bank account ...

This stage is full of new encounters ― meeting your teachers, greeting your neighbors and getting to know your classmates. Your life is full of ups and downs, from moments of homesickness to the thrill of new experiences to embarrassing incidents caused by cultural differences.

The third stage is the study stage. Slowly, you settle down and concentrate on your courses. Your schedule is busy with lectures, seminars and assignments. As your studies progress, you begin to feel at home and start to make friends. Day by day, your language skills improve and you deepen your understanding of the local culture. Each week brings new adventures and new challenges!

The fourth stage is the return stage. Your studies are over and you've finished your exams. Your final days are full of emotions as you pack your bags and say goodbye to your teachers and classmates. There's so much to do but so little time! Finally, you board the plane and take the long flight back to your country. Your family is waiting at the airport. It's great to be home ... but you miss your foreign friends!

Every year, millions of young people study abroad. Overseas students not only gain specialized knowledge in an academic field, they also gain international experience, acquire foreign languages, make cross-cultural friendships and become a bridge between countries.

Please consider studying overseas. And do what you can to support international students here in Japan!

(381 words) (出典 : *The Japan Times ST* November 6, 2015)

問1　The (　　　) stage is full of new encounters.

　　ア　first

　　イ　second

　　ウ　third

問2　In the fourth stage, (　　　).

　　ア　you are not very busy

　　イ　your language skills will improve

　　ウ　you miss your foreign friends

問3　(　　　) occur in the same stage.

　　ア　Homesickness and embarrassing incidents

　　イ　Applying to a foreign university and registering for classes

　　ウ　Opening a bank account and beginning to feel at home

問4　The speaker expects young people to study abroad and (　　　).

　　ア　become a bridge between countries

　　イ　get enough language ability before going abroad

　　ウ　come back to get a job in Japan

(☆☆☆○○○)

【4】これから世界の就学問題に関する英文を聞き，その内容やあとのグラフについて質問を聞きます。問1，問2の答えとして最も適切なものを，選択肢ア〜エより1つ選び，記号で答えなさい。また，問3の答えとして適切なものを，選択肢ア〜カより2つ選び，記号で答えなさい。なお，英文と質問は2回読みます。英文は20秒後に始まります。

The United Nations set a goal that all the children in the world should go to primary schools by 2015. The global number of out-of-school children has fallen considerably since 1990, but the pace of improvement has not been fast enough. Look at Graph 1. Currently, 57 million children of primary school age are out of school, down from 100 million in 2000. Of these, 33 million are in sub-Saharan Africa. This number is about three times larger than that in Southern Asia.

As Graph 2 shows, according to 2012 data, 43 per cent of out-of-school children globally will never go to school. However, the situation is different from region to region. In Southern Asia, around 57 per cent of out-of-school children will never go to school, while in sub-Saharan Africa the proportion is 50 per cent. Gender is also an important factor. 48 per cent of out-of-school girls will never go to school, compared to 37 per cent of boys. On the other hand, boys are more likely to leave school early.

Now, let's move on to another discussion. In countries affected by conflict, the proportion of out-of-school children increased from 30 per cent in 1999 to 36 per cent in 2012. This worrying trend is particularly strong in Northern Africa and Southern Asia. However, recent incidents are not always reflected in the data. For example, in Western Asia the ongoing conflict in the Syrian Arab Republic has had a serious impact on children's education. Data from the Syrian Ministry of Education indicate that the number of children who go to school is decreasing dramatically in 2013. Among Syrian refugee children, those of primary and lower secondary school age in Lebanon, only 12 per cent can go to school.

(出典：*The Millennium Development Goals Report 2015* United Nations New York, 2015)

Graph 1

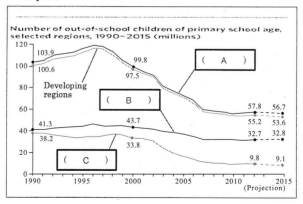

Graph 2

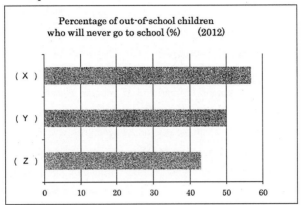

(*The Millennium Development Goals Report 2015*　United Nations New York, 2015 より
作成)

Question 1: From Graph 1, which is the most suitable combination of regions
represented?

ア　A　World　　　　　　　B　Southern Asia
　　C　Sub-Saharan Africa

イ　A　Sub-Saharan Africa　B　Southern Asia
　　C　World

ウ　A　Southern Asia　　　B　World
　　C　Sub-Saharan Africa

エ　A　World　　　　　　　B　Sub-Saharan Africa
　　C　Southern Asia

Question 2: From Graph 2, which is the most suitable combination of regions
represented?

ア　X　World　　　　　　　Y　Sub-Saharan Africa
　　Z　Southern Asia

イ　X　Southern Asia　　　Y　Sub-Saharan Africa
　　Z　World

ウ X Southern Asia   Y World
    Z Sub-Saharan Africa

エ X World   Y Southern Asia
    Z Sub-Saharan Africa

Question 3: Choose two statements which are true about the passage.

ア Almost half of out-of-school girls will never go to school.

イ Girls are more likely to leave school early.

ウ In countries affected by conflict, the proportion of out-of-school children increased from 1999 to 2012.

エ Countries affected by conflict are mostly found in Southern Africa.

オ The ongoing situation in the Syrian Arab Republic has had little influence on children's education.

カ Among Syrian refugee children in Lebanon, 20 percent of them can go to school.

(☆☆☆◎◎)

【5】これから読む英文は，英語の授業で，ある場面に遭遇したときに教師がどうしたらよいのかについて述べられています。英文の内容に合うように，あとの(　　)に適切な表現を英語で書きなさい。なお，英文は20秒後に始まり，2回読みます。

There are occasions in which students use their native language rather than English to perform classroom tasks, such as having a discussion or doing an English-language role-play, and in such circumstances the use of their mother tongue is less appropriate.

When students use their mother tongue in such circumstances, they often do so because they want to communicate in the most effective way they can and so, almost without thinking, they return to their own language. But however much we sympathize with this behavior, we need to have students practicing English in such situations, and so we have to do something to make it happen. Here are some ways of doing this.

No. 1. Teachers can discuss with students how they should all feel about using English and their own language in the class. Teachers should try to get their students in agreement that overuse of their own language means that they will have less chance to learn English. In other words, using their own language during speaking activities denies them chances for rehearsal and feedback.

No. 2. Teachers should also make it clear that there is not a total ban on the students' own language — it depends on what's happening. In other words, a little bit of the students' native language when they're working on a reading text is not much of a problem, but a speaking exercise will lose its purpose if not done in English.

No. 3. Teachers can make it clear by their behavior that they want to hear English. They can ignore what students say in their own language. For example, teachers can pretend that they don't understand the students' native language.

No. 4. Teachers themselves should speak English for the majority of the time so that, together with the use of listening material and video, the students are constantly exposed to how English sounds and what it feels like. Some teachers give their students English names too.

No. 5. Teachers should be prepared to go round the class during a speaking exercise encouraging, or even pleading with the students to use English — and offering help if necessary. This technique, often repeated, will gradually change most students' behavior over a period of time.

(Jeremy Harmer (2007). *how to teach english*: *new edition*. Longman 一
部改)

| No. 1 | Teachers should help students understand (　　　　　　　　　). |
| No. 2 | Teachers should encourage students to keep on using English. |

No. 3	Teachers can only ( ).
No. 4	Teachers should create ( ).
No. 5	Teachers should keep encouraging students to use English.

(☆☆☆○○○)

【6】次の英文を読み，問1〜問4の答えとして最も適当なものをそれぞれの選択肢ア〜エから1つ選び記号で答えなさい。また問5は(A)に入る語を答えなさい。

[1] It has often been said that Japanese authors do not like to give clarifications or full explanations of their views when they write; both they and their readers seem to have greater tolerance for --- and indeed a positive enjoyment of --- ambiguity than writers and readers in English. This difference may be the result of different views in the two cultures about who is responsible for successful communication. English speakers, by and large, see the writer, or speaker, as being primarily responsible for making clear and well-organized statements; if there is a breakdown in communication, it is because the speaker or writer has not been clear enough, not because the listener or reader has not tried hard enough to understand. In Japan, on the other hand, there is a different way of looking at the communication process. In Japan, it is generally thought to be the responsibility of the listener or reader to understand what the speaker or author intended to say. This difference may be illustrated by an anecdote. An American woman was taking a taxi to the Ginza Tokyu Hotel. The taxi driver mistakenly took her to the Ginza Daiichi Hotel. Being from a speaker-responsible culture, she said, "I'm sorry, I should have spoken more clearly." The taxi driver demonstrated his listener-responsible background when he replied, "No, no, I should have listened more carefully."

[2] These different views about who is responsible for successful

communication have noticeable effects on the writing process. For example, whereas Japanese authors frequently compose exactly one draft which becomes the finished product, English-speaking writers go through draft after draft. In this process of writing and re-writing, the writer-responsible author is trying to achieve two things. First, the final text should have unity; that is, the writing should have all its necessary and sufficient parts. Second, the text should be coherent; in other words, the material should be presented in a sequence which is intelligible to the reader. In a writer-responsible tradition, readers expect, and require, landmarks along the way. Transition statements are important. It is the writer's task to provide appropriate transition statements so that the reader can see the logical connections which bind the composition together and create unity.

[3]　In Japanese, on the other hand, transition statements may be absent or much less overt since it is the reader's responsibility to understand the relationship between any one part of the essay and the essay as a whole. The effects of this reader-responsible orientation can be seen in one common way of organizing compositions in Japanese known as *ki-shoo-ten-ketsu*, a rhetorical pattern which may be outlined as follows:

ki　　Begin the argument.

shoo　Develop the argument.

ten　At the point where this development is finished, turn the idea to a sub-theme which has an indirect connection to the major theme.

ketsu　Bring all of this together and reach a conclusion.

[4]　Since the transition to the *ten* section (which has only an indirect connection to the main theme) is often not overtly marked, Japanese readers are required to create the transition for themselves in the course of reading; that is, the responsibility for linking the sub-theme with the main argument lies with the reader. Thus, when such essays are literally translated into English, it is precisely the *ten* section which causes problems for English readers. When a Japanese writer has been developing an argument (let us call

it X) and then, at the beginning of the *ten* section, introduces what seems to be a new and unrelated topic (let us call it Y) without any clear signal of the connection between the two ideas, the English reader becomes confused. This confusion could be cleared up if the writer provided a clear transition statement such as "The following may seem unrelated to the major point, but the connection between Y and X will become clear in due time." However, the key point is that such a statement would be unnecessary for a Japanese reader, and so would be unlikely to appear in a Japanese writer's text.

[5] There are, of course, many examples of reader-responsible texts in English, particularly in literature. In academic writing in English, however, the responsibility for successful communication clearly rests with the writer. A young Japanese person starting to learn how to write academic English can draw several conclusions from this. First, it is important that all the ideas in a composition in English should have a direct connection to the main theme. Second, the logical connections between these ideas should usually be clearly signaled. Third --- and most important --- a single draft of a composition is not enough. Even the most experienced writers of academic prose in English write and re-write in an attempt to remove (A), to provide clarity, to achieve unity, and to sequence the composition in such a way as to make it as intelligible as possible to the reader.

(出典 *First Moves: An Introduction to Acadeinic Writing in English*)

問1 According to the passage, which of the followings would a possible reply of an English-speaking taxi driver in the same situation as the anecdote in paragraph [1]?

ア "Oh, it's my fault. I should have checked the map more carefully."

イ "Oh dear! I took you to a wrong place so you don't have to pay the fare."

ウ "Oh, it's all right. I will take you to Daiichi Hotel right now."

エ "Oh my! I wish you had pronounced the name of the hotel a little bit

317

more clearly."

問2　According to the passage, which statement is NOT true about English texts?

ア　Writers are inclined to write more than one draft in order to be coherent.

イ　It is the writer's task to supply suitable phrases to play the role of landmarks.

ウ　English academic texts will reach their conclusions in any sequence of ideas.

エ　Some English texts require readers to understand the content responsibly.

問3　According to the passage, which statement is true about Japanese texts?

ア　Japanese texts are usually free from unity of readers and writers.

イ　*Ki-shoo-ten－ketsu* pattern includes the sub-theme in the middle of texts.

ウ　Readers are expected to read texts several times to understand the content.

エ　*Ki-shoo-ten－ketsu* pattern is only used for academic texts.

問4　According to the passage, which statement is true?

ア　The author of this passage thinks that Japanese texts should have clear transition statements.

イ　When Japanese essays are literally put into English, it is possible for English readers to be confused.

ウ　In *ten* section in Japanese texts, the idea which is new but overtly related to the major theme is introduced.

エ　Reader-responsible orientation has nothing to do with a Japanese rhetorical pattern.

問5　Which word is the most appropriate for the blank (　A　)? Find the most appropriate word for (　A　) from paragraph [1].

(☆☆☆☆◎◎◎)

【7】次の英文を読み，問1～問5の答えとして最も適当なものを，それぞ
れの選択肢ア～エから1つ選び記号で答えなさい。

Rounding the corner into the nursery school classroom to collect my
daughter, I overheard the nursery assistant tell her, 'You've drawn the most
beautiful tree. Well done.' A few days later, she pointed to another of my
daughter's drawings and remarked, 'Wow, you really are an artist!'

On both occasions, I found myself at a loss. How could I explain to the
nursery assistant that I would prefer it if she didn't praise my daughter?

Nowadays, we lavish praise on our children. Praise, self-confidence and
academic performance, it is commonly believed, rise and fall together. But
current research suggests otherwise ― over the past decade, a number of
studies on self-esteem have come to the conclusion that praising a child as
'clever' (　A　). In fact, it might cause her to underperform. Often a child
will react to praise by quitting ― why make a new drawing if you have
already made 'the best'? Or a child may simply repeat the same work ― why
draw something new, or in a new way, if the old way always gets applause?

In a now famous 1998 study of children aged ten and eleven, psychologists
Carol Dweck and Claudia Muller asked 128 children to solve a series of
mathematical problems. After completing the first set of simple exercises, the
researchers gave each child just one sentence of praise. Some were praised for
their intellect ― 'You did really well, you are so clever'; others for their hard
work ― 'You did really well, you must have tried really hard.' Then the
researchers had the children try a more challenging set of problems. The
results were dramatic. The students who were praised for their effort showed a
greater willingness to work out new approaches. They also showed more
resilience and tended to attribute their failures to insufficient effort, not to a
lack of intelligence. The children who had been praised for their cleverness
worried more about failure, tended to choose tasks that confirmed what they
already knew, and displayed less tenacity when the problems got harder.
Ultimately, the thrill created by being told 'You're so clever' gave way to an

319

increase in anxiety and a drop in self-esteem, motivation and performance. When asked by the researchers to write to children in another school, recounting their experience, some of the 'clever' children lied, inflating their scores. In short, all it took to knock these youngsters' confidence, to make them so unhappy that they lied, was one sentence of praise.

Why are we so committed to praising our children?

In part, we do it to demonstrate that we're different from our parents. In *Making Babies*, a memoir about becoming a mother, Anne Enright observes, 'In the old days — as we call the 1970s, in Ireland — a mother would dispraise her child automatically... "She's a monkey," a mother might say, or "Street angel, home devil," or even my favorite, "She'll have me in an early grave." It was all part of growing up in a country where praise of any sort was taboo.' Of course, this wasn't the case in Ireland alone. Recently, a middle-aged Londoner told me, 'My mum called me things I'd never call my kids — too clever by half, cheeky, precocious and show-off. Forty years on, I want to shout at my mum, "What's so terrible about showing off?"'

Now, wherever there are small children — at the local playground, at Starbucks and at nursery school — you will hear the background music of praise: 'Good boy,' 'Good girl,' 'You're the best.' Admiring our children may temporarily lift our self-esteem by signalling to those around us what fantastic parents we are and what terrific kids we have — but it isn't doing much for a child's sense of self. In trying so hard to be different from our parents, we're actually doing much the same thing — doling out our empty praise the way an earlier generation doled out thoughtless criticism. If we do it to avoid thinking about our child and her world, and about what our child feels, then praise, just like criticism, is ultimately expressing our indifference.

Which brings me back to the original problem — if praise doesn't build a child's confidence, what does?

Shortly after qualifying as a psychoanalyst, I discussed all this with an eighty-year-old woman named Charlotte Stiglitz. Charlotte — the mother of the Nobel Prize-winning economist Jeseph Stiglitz — taught remedial reading in northwestern Indiana for many years. 'I don't praise a small child for doing what they ought to be able to do,' she told me. 'I praise them when they do something really difficult — like sharing a toy or showing patience. I also think it is important to say "thank you." When I'm slow in getting a snack for a child, or slow to help them and they have been patient, I thank them. But I wouldn't praise a child who is playing or reading.' No great rewards, no terrible punishments — Charlotte's focus was on (B).

I once watched Charlotte with a four-year-old boy, who was drawing. When he stopped and looked up at her — perhaps expecting praise — she smiled and said, 'There is a lot of blue in your picture.' He replied, 'It's the pond near my grandmother's house — there is a bridge.' He picked up a brown crayon, and said, 'I'll show you.' Unhurried, she talked to the child, but more importantly she observed, she listened. She was present.

Being present builds a child's confidence because it lets the child know that she is worth thinking about. Without this, a child might come to believe that her activity is just a means to gain praise, rather than an end in itself. How can we expect a child to be attentive, if we've not been attentive to her?

Being present, whether with children, with friends, or even with oneself, is always hard work. But isn't this attentiveness — the feeling that someone is trying to think about us — something we want more than praise?

(出典：STEPHEN GROSZ, *THE EXAMINED LIFE* : 2013)

問1　Which phrase is most appropriate in blank (A)?

　ア　will encourage her to work hard

　イ　may not help her at school

　ウ　should not be avoided

　エ　can give her self-confidence

問2　According to the 1998 study, which phrase is most appropriate to complete the sentence below?

Giving a child admiration (　　).

ア　for his effort can result in him giving up what he is doing

イ　for his intelligence will be a main factor of bringing out more talent

ウ　for his test score can let him show tenacity to the more complicated

エ　for his hard work can enable him to have more confidence

問3　According to the passage, which statement is most appropriate?

ア　Empty praise could be almost the same as showing a strong interest in their children.

イ　Parents should praise their children in order to show how wonderful they are as parents.

ウ　When we give our children thoughtless praising, both their self-esteem and academic performance can improve.

エ　Even though some parents tell their child 'You're excellent', it does not necessarily increase the child's self-esteem.

問4　Which phrase is most appropriate for blank(　B　)?

ア　why a child made a mistake and how she helped that child

イ　how a child spent his ordinary life and how hard that child tried to gain praise

ウ　what a child did and how that child did it

エ　how high a child's test score was and what she gave that child as praise

問5　How can parents help their children gain self-confidence?

ア　They should spend much more time with their children and show a strong interest in their activities.

イ　They should praise their children when they get high scores on tests.

ウ　They should be more aware of the importance of punishment.

エ　They should be with their children to have opportunities to praise their intelligence.

(☆☆☆☆○○○)

【8】設問【 A 】,【 B 】に答えなさい。

【 A 】 問1～問4の英文の( )に入れるのに, 最も適当なものを選択肢ア～エから1つ選び, 記号で答えなさい。

問1 It is said that the new tax will be ( ) over two years.

ア phased in イ carried on ウ bumped into エ taken up

問2 A: Where is Emily? I wonder if she has got into an accident.

B: You shouldn't ( ) the possibility that she is just lost. I'm sure she is safe.

ア giv out イ map out ウ carry out エ rule out

問3 Foreign people who visit Japan often find that Japanese people do not show their opinion clearly, so they sometimes say behaving ( ) is one of the characteristics of Japanese people.

ア purposefully イ humbly ウ unconsciously

エ recklessly

問4 Choose the appropriate word for the ( ) blank.

ア respectful イ respectable ウ respecting

エ respective

【 B 】 問5～問7の英文の意味が通るように, それぞれあとの語(句)を並べかえたとき, (1)～(6)の位置にくる語(句)を記号で答えなさい。

問5 ( ) (1) ( ) ( ) ( ) (2) ( ) ( ), she has been playing an important role as a main bookkeeper in our office.

ア deep イ advantage ウ her エ of オ of

カ taking キ accounting ク knowlege

問6 I couldn't understand ( ) ( ) (3), ( )( )(4)

( ) in German.

ア which イ most ウ was エ what オ wrote

カ of キ Ken

問7 Shizuko will be praised ( ) ( ) (5) ( ) ( ) (6)

(　　) her strong disapproval of bullying to the whole class.

ア　of　　　イ　showed　　ウ　the great courage　　エ　in

オ　she　　カ　bacause　　キ　expressing

(☆☆☆◎◎◎)

【9】「英語表現Ⅰ」の授業で，「小学生に自分自身の携帯電話を持たせて
よいか」の賛否について，自分自身の意見を100語程度で書かせる指
導を行います。その際，生徒にどのようなことを留意させればよいで
しょうか。生徒が英文を書く上での留意点を3つ挙げ，あなたが授業
で生徒に口頭で説明するという想定で，次の6行以上を使い，英語で
書きなさい。なお，前提となる生徒の英語力は自由に設定してよい。

【6行目】

(70％に縮小)

(☆☆☆◎◎◎)

【10】以下の2人の英語教員(TeacherA，TeacherB)による会話を読んで，問
1および問2に答えなさい。

①　TeacherA　「『思い出の品物を紹介するスピーチ』は，次単元の
まとめの活動ですね。例年通り，1人ずつ前に出て発表させましょ
う。」

② TeacherB 「全体の前で1人ずつではなく，少人数のグループの中で生徒が順番にスピーチをする形式にするのはどうでしょうか。」

③ TeacherA 「1人がクラス全員の前で話すよりもリラックスした雰囲気でできそうですね。数人の生徒のスピーチを聞くのであれば，生徒同士の相互評価も集中してできそうです。どんな評価項目を示しましょうか。」

④ TeacherB 「前回のスピーチは下を向いて原稿から目を離さず，ぼそぼそと早口で話す生徒が多くみられました。アイコンタクトと音声の明瞭さは評価項目に入れたいですよね。」

⑤ TeacherA 「他にも，スピーチの内容を評価項目に入れるのはどうでしょうか。思い出の品物にまつわる出来事がどんなことだったのかがきちんと伝わる必要があります。3つの評価項目について生徒にA・B・Cで評価させましょう。互いに評価し合えば責任を持ってきちんと聞こうとする姿勢が自然と要求されますから。」

⑥ TeacherB 「なるほど，でも，生徒同士が相互評価をするのにA・B・Cと書くだけで十分でしょうか。もっと生徒たちが主体的に話を聞く姿勢を育成したいのですが・・・。」

問1 ①〜⑤の会話の内容を，次の5行程度を使い，英語で要約しなさい。

【5行目】

(70％に縮小)

問2 Teacher Bの⑥の発言に対して，あなたはどのような提案ができますか。具体的な工夫について理由も含め2点述べなさい。次の8行

程度を使い，英語で書きなさい。前提となる生徒の英語力は自由に
設定してよい。

【8行目】

(70％に縮小)

(☆☆☆☆◎◎◎)

解答・解説

【中学校】

【１】１　(D)　　２　(C)　　３　(A)

〈解説〉英文は1度しか読まれず，しかも選択肢が問題用紙に示されてい
ないので，英文および選択肢の要点を聞き取る力が必要になる。特に
英文に出てくる数字，人物名，地名は集中して聴き取り，選択肢を吟
味することが大事である。

【２】１　(B)　　２　(A)　　３　(B)

〈解説〉質問文は文頭の疑問詞を聞き逃すと，問題に対処できないので，
最初の2，3語は特に集中して聞き取る。　１　時間を聞き取る問題で

は，複数の出来事とその時間が言われたり，出来事の予定変更や何分
後に行われるなどといった表現が予想されるので，リスニングの際に
は臨場感を持ってその場面に入り時系列で把握する練習を日頃から心
がけたい。 2, 3 選択肢の英語を理解して予測して聞くことになる
が，earthquake drill, evacuation drillのようなよく似た意味の語句や複
数回出てきている語句には注意を払いたい。また，Ms. Tanaka,
homeroom activities, Internetなど，人名やなじみのある語句も心に留め
て内容把握に役立てたい。

【3】1 46.7 2 大都市の水道水はまずい 3 ・水道管から水が
もれることがほとんどない。(20字) ・浄水の技術が高い。(9字)
・設備のメンテナンスがよい。(13字) から2つ
〈解説〉1 数字を答える問題は簡単な計算を伴うことがあるので，意識
しておくとよい。また，小数点が絡む数字の聞き取りにも注意を払い
たい。解答の46.7％は，forty six point seven percentと読む。
2 1行の短い日本語になるという予測がたつので要点を簡潔に書く。
3 20マスの解答欄が2つ示されているので，20字以内の日本語で2点
を解答する問題と推測される。やはり，何がどうなのかを聞き取って
素早くメモするようにしたい。

【4】It is good to begin your essay with the place you want to visit, but you
should make clear how many reasons there are before writing them. It would
be better if you write them using 'firstly, secondly, and thirdly.' (40語)
〈解説〉行きたい場所(国)は明示できているが，その理由のはじまりが示
されていないので，I like sweets very much.が唐突に聞こえる。理由が
いくつあるのかということを伝えて，順序よく述べるようにすればバ
ランスのよい英文になるというアドバイスでよいと思われる。

【5】Firstly, I will give several model sentences including important
grammatical items. After getting used to the pronunciation, meaning, and

usage of the words and idioms, students should be given a topic and make a short passage about it using those sentences. Finally they should express their opinions by turns in the small groups. With these steps I can let them work on the fields of speaking, writing, and listening. (69語)

〈解説〉中学校学習指導要領解説外国語編(平成20年9月，文部科学省)によると，「実際に言語を使用して互いの考えや気持ちを伝え合うなどの活動を行うに当たっては，それを支える言語材料についての理解や定着のための練習が不可欠である。(中略)また，これとは逆に，言語材料について理解したり練習したりする活動に終始し，その結果，言語を使用する活動そのものが不十分になることのないように配慮する必要がある」としている。これを踏まえた授業計画とする。具体的には，①授業での既習事項を含んだ英文をいくつか用意しその中の単語・熟語の理解を発音とともに確認する。②英文には異なる文法事項が入っているようにすると幅広い復習となる。③音声を重視しながら英文に慣れたあと，1つのテーマを与えてそれについて自分の考えをまとめさせる。そのときは，必ず与えられた英文の構造を使うことを条件にする。その後，④グループ内で順番に考えを発表し，可能なら互いに質問や感想を交換する，という流れを考えたい。

【6】1　antipathy　　2　ア　　3　イ　　4　エ　　5　ウ

〈解説〉1　下線部①のDislikeは「嫌いなこと。嫌気。反感」という気持ちを表している。同様の意味の単語を探しながら読み続けていくと，第6段落2文目にantipathy「反感」がある。　2　strong food (　②　)は第1段落2文目のstrong likes and dislikesと関連するから，「何かを優先的に好むこと」という意味のアが正解である。　3　「悩みすぎたり，無理矢理食べさせること」がどういうことかを問うているが，そのあとの英文を読むと，それは子どもにとってマイナスであるということがわかる。選択肢のうちア「肯定的」はプラスの意味，ウ「決定的」，エ「刺激的」は中立的な意味であり，イが「逆効果の，非生産的な」というマイナスの意味で正解となる。counter-という「反対・対立」を

表す接頭辞に注目してほしい。 4「嫌いな食べ物を細かく切り刻んで他の食材と混ぜ合わせてやっと子どもが食べたあとに，そのことを子どもに言うことはよくない」ということの理由を考える問いであるが，そのあとのTrust your children, and wait …の内容も考慮に入れて考えたい。ア「馴染めない食べ物もそうだが，細かく刻んだ嫌いな食べ物はもっと嫌い」，イ「the carrot and the stick(あめとむち)を使って食べさせるべき」，ウ「嫌いな食べ物も一口食べたら食べられる」はどれも第7段落からの内容と照らしても理由として通らない。エ「そうすることが親に対する不信につながる」が第7段落のconfidenceや空欄④のあとのTrustという語とも呼応し，要旨に合うから正解。
5 ア「子ども用の健康食品」，イ「栄養に関する事実を段階的に読み取っていく指導が重要である」，エ「子どもたちは(親が)困るほどの大量のジャンクフード市場にさらされている」は本文の主旨に合致しない。ウ「食べ物について学ぶことで子どもたちは健康に食べられる」というのは第5段落の内容，とりわけ最初の1～2文に注目すれば正解だとわかる。

【7】1 ① ウ ② ア ③ エ 2 (Teachers should) structure activities that promote a genuine exchange of ideas and good thinking.
3 多人数クラスでは，学びが進んでいる生徒の興味を維持しつつ，同時に学びの進みが遅い生徒が，自らのペースで進展していける余地があるように活動を作ることが重要だから。 4 ・一つの文章を取り上げて，ある生徒には推論を要する難しい質問に答えるよう求め，一方で別の生徒には単純な事実に関する質問に答えるようにする。・ある共通のテーマに関する，要約されていない文章と要約された文章の二つを選び，生徒に両方の文章に関係する一連の質問を出す。
〈解説〉1 ① 第1段落後半から第2段落を含めた英文の内容から「生徒たちの多くは自分の意見を述べることへの懸念・恐れを抱いている」ということがわかるので，ウが入る。第1段落5文目のreluctantと，第2段落1文目のafraidに注目。 ② 第3段落1～2文目を参照。confidence

はassuranceと同義。　③　第4段落1文目but以下を参照。structureは
composeと，exchange of ideasはinteractionとそれぞれ対応している。
2　第3段落で「生徒たちが思い切って自分の考えや意見を述べるよう
にするためにどのような授業活動をつくるか」ということに触れてい
る英文を探すと「自分の考えが価値があると確信して」話そうとする
ような授業のことだから，第4段落1文目で授業活動の構成のことが書
かれているところを語数条件を考慮してまとめる。　3　第5段落には
授業活動を構成していくときの筆者の留意点が書かれており，箇条書
きの3つ目でoffer many choices of expressionとあるが，これが問題文の
make them multilevelと対応する。よって，そのあとの第6段落1文目を
参照すればその理由がわかる。　4　第9段落1文目にYou can
individualize task in two waysとあるから，その2つを簡潔にまとめれば
よい。同段落2〜3文目のThat would be an example of using the same
material in different waysまでと，4文目から最後の文のThat would be an
example of using different material in the same wayまでのそれぞれをわか
りやすくまとめる。

【高等学校】

【1】問1　イ　　問2　ア　　問3　ア　　問4　イ　　問5　ウ
〈解説〉問1　How soon 〜?が何を問う疑問文であるかがわかれば，時間
の経過を表すinを用いた表現のイが正答となる。　問2　Why don't you
〜?は「〜してはどうか」「〜しないか」といった提案や勧誘を表すの
で，それに対する応答となる。　問3　質問は「普段定期的にこのバ
スを利用しているか」という意味で，現在形で日々の習慣的行為を表
している。　問4　Judging from 〜「〜から判断すると」は聞いてすぐ
に理解できないと，アの「外見で判断するな」を除外できなくなる。
「この証拠が彼女の無実を立証できる」という考えに対する否定的な
応答であるからI'm afraid (that) …が使われている。evidence, prove,
innocenceが一度に1つの意味として聞き取れるようにしたい。
問5　誕生日に新しい車をねだる子どもへの応対。動物を使った慣用

表現はたくさんあるので，機会をみつけて覚えたい。ア「どしゃぶりだ」，イ「少食だね」，ウ「豚が空を飛んだらね」→「まさか，ありえない」となる。仮定法表現でI could eat like a horse.「腹ぺこだ」や，a snake in the grass「目に見えない敵(危険)」など文脈から判断できるものもあるので，そういうものから習得していくことを勧める。

【2】1　ウ　　2　ア　　3　ア　　4　ア　　5　ウ
〈解説〉限られた時間で各問の選択肢から聞き取るべきポイントを予測すること。英文も1回しか読まれないので，選択肢から内容を予測しキーワード，キーフレーズを頭に入れながら聞く。英文後の質問においてもキーワード，キーフレーズに素早く反応したい。　1　選択肢からTerminal 1, 2, 3の違いを聞き取ろうとすれば，質問のWhere, go firstに対応できる。飛行機が出発する15番ゲートがあるのはTerminal 2，男性が待ち時間に寄ろうとしているショップがあるのはTerminal 3，飲食店があるのがTerminal 1となる。　2　選択肢を限りなく突き詰めると，books, movies, homeworkになるから，これらの3つがどうなるのかを聞き取ろうとすれば，質問のWhat, do, during the flightの解答が導ける。airsick「飛行機酔い」。　3　選択肢の3つの行動がどういう内容として出てくるのかを聞き取る。本問がやや難であると思われるのは，質問がWhat, Tom should doだけを意識すると，reschedule the meeting, call himにとらわれてしまう。the woman think, Tomを聞き逃さず対応すべきである。英文を聞きながら登場人物がだれなのかが自然に聞き取れていると問題はない。　4　選択肢3つに共通する語句はBecause she believesであり，2つに共通するのはdiscussion, improve, communication ability, speechである。それを意識し予測して聞けば，質問を聞くとき，Whyよりもsuggest, have a discussionへうまく反応できるであろう。　5　本問では英文を聞きながら内容を要約できないと正解は難しい。ただ，選択肢そのものに注目すれば，正解以外は聞きながら除外できていくので，残っていく選択肢が要約になっているかを的確に判断してほしい。

【3】問1　イ　　問2　ウ　　問3　ア　　問4　ア

〈解説〉英語をより正確に聞き取る能力，聞き取った内容を頭の中に留め
ておく能力，質問文と選択肢を素早く読み取り正誤を判断する能力が
問われる問題。本問では，留学に関する英文であると明示されている。
また，選択肢からstageが少なくとも4つあると予測できる。英文を2回
聞けるので，それぞれのstageでの出来事やキーワード，キーフレーズ
を選択肢の語句と照らしながら聞き取るようにすれば対応しやすいと
思われる。　問1　new encountersがどういう内容のところに出てくる
かを聞けばよい。ただ，encounterが「(予期しない)出会い，遭遇」と
いう意味であるとわかっていれば，The first is the departure stage.と聞い
たときに除外できる。　問2　the fourth stageを聞き取りながら選択肢
を見ていけば，ア，イは除外され，you miss your foreign friendsが聞き
取れたらウを導ける。　問3　「AとBが同時に起こる」という質問のA，
Bにあたる内容を聞き取る問題である。常識から判断してもイ，ウが
不自然であると考えられるが，英文の流れのなかでhomesickness，
embarrassing incidentsが出てくるのが，the fourth stageの内容の前なので，
正解は2回目に聞いたときに確定させればよい。　問4　質問の内容が
まとめに近いので，後半から終わりにかけて選択肢の語句を意識して
聞き取りたい。

【4】1　エ　　2　イ　　3　ア，ウ

〈解説〉1　選択肢とGraph 1を見れば，World，Southern Asia，Sub-
Saharan Africaという3つの地域の音には敏感に反応することと，グラ
フの特徴を述べる部分がどの年代の数値を語っているかを聞き取りな
がら確定したい。第1段落1文目のin the world，2文目のthe global
numberという語句に反応しながら，3文目のLook at Graph 1以降に集中
して聞き取る。Currently(現在)と57 millionでAが確定すれば，33
millionとsub-Saharan Africa，それに続くthree times larger ～ Southern
AsiaでB，Cは確定となる。　2　1と同様，3つの地域の語句に意識し，
第2段落冒頭のAs Graph 2 shows以下の内容に集中すれば，43 per cent，

globallyでZが確定。あとは，Southern Asia，57 per cent，sub-Saharan Africa，50 per centでそれぞれX，Yが確定する。　3　選択肢それぞれにおいて，キーワード，キーフレーズに印をつけて英文を聞き取りながら照らしていくとよい。英文は2回聞けるので，オのinfluenceは英文ではimpactになっていることを聞き取る必要はあるが，それ以外はそれほどの難度は感じられない。　イ　第2段落最後の文参照。girlsではなくboysに関する記述である。　エ　第3段落3文目参照。Southern AfricaではなくNorthern AfricaとSouthern Asiaで強まっている傾向である。　オ　第3段落5文目参照。serious「深刻な」影響を及ぼしている。カ　第3段落最後の文参照。20％ではなく12％である。

【5】No. 1　the importance of using the target language in class

No. 3　listen to what is said in English / respond to what is said in English

No. 4　an environment where English is mostly used

〈解説〉問題文から英語の授業の場面に関する英文が流れるという心構えをし，設問のNo. 1〜No. 5までの英語を確認する。特にNo. 2とNo. 5から生徒への英語使用を求める内容であることを意識したい。その前提があれば英文の始まりからスムーズに内容に入れるだろう。英文の途中でNo. 1という英語が聞けたとき，設問への解答の仕方に気づくが多少の混乱もあるかもしれない。ただ，英文が2回流れるから不安にならず，英文の聞き取りに集中してNo. 2，No. 5の内容と問題に示された要約の英語を確かめたい。　No. 1　help students understand …だから，「生徒たちに英語(学ぼうとしている言語)を使い，日本語使用を少しでも減らすことの重要性，必要性，意義」をわからせるという英語であればよい。　No. 3　they want to hear English, they don't understand the students' native languageという英文が聞けたら，「授業の中では日本語じゃなく英語を聞きたい」という内容の表現にして入れるとよい。No. 4　英文の最初の部分が聞き取れたら解答はぶれることはない。Teachers themselves should speak English 〜や，あとの…English names …から，解答以外にEnglish atmosphere by using English themselvesという

のも考えられる。

【6】問1　エ　　　問2　ウ　　　問3　イ　　　問4　イ　　　問5　ambiguity
〈解説〉問1　第1段落は，successful communicationを達成する際の中心的
責任が英語文化においてはthe speaker (the writer)にありthe listener (the
reader)にはないが，日本語文化においてはその逆であるという内容で，
同段落7文目から始まる日本人のtaxi driverとお客であるan American
womanとのエピソードに関してである。到着したホテルが間違ってい
たときの反応で，間違いに対する責任を感じているその女性に対して，
日本人のtaxi driverはlistenerである自分に責任を帰す。もしこれがan
English-speaking taxi driverであれば，the speakerに責任があるとするか
ら正解はエとなる。　　問2　文章を書く場合に，英語文化においては
どのようなプロセスになるかを問う問題で，間違っている記述を選ぶ。
第2段落2文目draft after draft，5文目のcoherent(首尾一貫した)よりアは
内容に一致。また，6文目のreadersが文章の中にlandmarksを求めると
いうことからイは内容に一致。ウのEnglish academic textsのことは第5
段落に記述があるが，その段落の最後の文にto sequence the composition
in such a way as to make it as intelligible as possible to the readerとあるの
で，決してin any sequence of ideas(どんなふうであれ一連の考えの流れ
で)ではないから内容と不一致，よってこれが正解。また，同段落1文
目にThere are ～ many examples of reader-responsible texts in English…と
あるので，エは内容に一致している。　　問3　日本語の文章について
内容である。アのunity of readers and writersに関して本文に記述はない。
第3段落2文目から始まるki-shoo-ten-ketsu以下のところのten(転)の定義
に合致しているのでイが正解。第4段落のtenの内容に関する記述も含
め，Readers are expected to read texts several times to…という記述はない
のでウは不正解。エについても本文に記述はない。　　問4　アはこの
英文が英語文化，日本語文化における文章構成の「違い」を述べてい
るだけで，決してどちらかがshould ～(～すべきである)と言っている
のではないから不正解。イは第4段落2～3文目の記述と合致するので

正解。第3〜4段落の*ten*に関する記述のan indirect connection to the major(main) themeとウのovertly related to the major themeが不一致である。エは第3段落2文目の記述と不一致である。A has nothing to do with B「AはBと関係がない」を確認しておきたい。 問5 第5段落の内容はacademic writing in Englishに関してであり，(A)を含む英文にみられるclarity, unity, sequence, intelligible to the readerを確認し，第1段落1文目から，writers and readers in Englishが耐えられず，楽しめないのはambiguityであることがわかれば正解を導ける。

【7】問1 イ 問2 エ 問3 エ 問4 ウ 問5 ア
〈解説〉問1 第2段落においてI would prefer it if she didn't praise my daughter. と筆者自身の考えを表明している。それが第3段落2〜3文目のPraise,〜 suggests otherwise というこの段落の要旨につながっているから，それに沿った意味の英文を選べばよい。「賢いねと子どもをほめることはその子にとって何の役にも立たない」というイが正解。問2 選択肢をみると，アのhis effortとエのhis hard work，イのhis intelligenceとウのhis test scoreはそれぞれ同じことである。第4段落の内容から，his effort, his hard workをほめることに関しては6文目a greater willingness to work out new approaches，7文目more resilienceという語句にあるようにプラスの効果がある。his intelligence, his test scoreをほめることについては，8文目worried more about failureと less tenacity(tenacity「粘り。不屈」)という語句からマイナスの効果があるということ。ア，イ，ウはそれぞれ逆の効果につながるということになっている。よって正解はエ。 問3 第7段落3〜4文目で筆者は「empty praiseはひと世代前の親が行ったthoughtless criticismと同じで，結局どちらもindifference(無関心)と同じだ」と言っている。つまり，a strong interest in their childrenの反対なので，アは不正解。同段落2文目では「親が声高に子どもをほめることは親として自分がいかに素晴らしいか，いかに素晴らしい子どもを持っているかをまわりに示そうとしているにすぎない」と言っている。だから，イの「親としての素晴

らしさを示すために子どもをほめるべき」というのは合致しない。同様にthoughtless praisingによってtheir self-esteemやacademic performanceがimproveすることはないからウは不正解。エは2文目後半のbut it isn't doing much for a child's sense of selfというこの段落の要旨と合致するので正解。　問4　第9～10段落の内容を参照する。アの「なぜ子どもが間違いをしたか」とか「どうやってその子を助けたか」という記述はないので不正解。また、「子どものtest scoreがいかに高いか」とか「彼女がpraiseとして何を子どもに与えるか」という内容はないのでエは不正解。第10段落にあるようにpraiseを期待している子どもに対して何事もないかのように話しかけるCharlotteの様子からイのhow hard that child tried to gain praise は合致しない。さらにそのあとの最後の2文but more importantly she observed, she listened. She was present.という記述からウが正解となる。　問5「子どもが自信(自己肯定感)を獲得するのを親はどうやって助けることができるか」というこの英文の本旨を問うている。イのhigh scores on testはintellectをほめることになり，エのintelligenceをほめることと同様マイナスの効果につながるので除外する。ウのpunishmentはひと世代前の親のthoughtless criticismであるからindifferenceにつながるので不正解。第10段落最後の文と，第11，12段落のそれぞれの1文目であるBeing present ～の内容を参照してアが正解となる。

【8】A　問1　ア　　　問2　エ　　　問3　イ　　　問4　エ
　　B　問5　1　イ　　　2　ク　　　問6　3　オ　　　4　ア
　　問7　5　ウ　　　6　エ
〈解説〉A　問1　ア be phased inで「段階的に導入される」。英文は「新しい税が2年にわたって段階的に導入されるだろうと言われている」という意味。イ「がんばって続ける」，ウ「偶然出会う」，エ「取りかかる」。　問2「Emilyの不在」を「事故に遭ったのではないか」というAに対して，Emilyの無事を信じるBが「ただ道に迷っているだけということもあるじゃないか」と言っている。「道に迷っているという可能

性を除外するな」ということから，エ「除外する」が正解。ア「〜を発表する。発する。配る」(他動詞用法)，イ「〜を地図に示す。作成する」，ウ「〜を外へ運び出す。実行する」。　問3　「自分の意見をはっきりと表さない」日本人の様子は「どういうふうな態度」と表現するのかを考える。ア「断固として，故意に」，イ「謙遜して」，ウ「無意識に」，エ「無鉄砲に」で，イが正解。　問4　英文は「それぞれの空所に入る適切な語を選びなさい」という意味。ア「礼儀正しい」，イ「立派な」，ウ「〜に関して」，エ「それぞれの」で，エが正解。B　問5　並べ替えるとTaking advantage of her deep knowledge of accounting(カ→イ→エ(オ)→ウ→ア→ク→オ(エ)→キ)となる。接続詞がなくカンマだけで2文が結ばれていることから分詞構文と推測して，accounting「経理」，bookkeeper「簿記係」の単語から意味を考える。問6　並べ替えるとwhat Ken wrote, most of which was (エ→キ→オ→イ→カ→ア→ウ)となる。接続詞はないが，カンマの位置からwhich，whatが関係代名詞として使用されているという見当のもと意味を考える。what Ken wroteがwhichの先行詞であると判断できたら正解が見えてくる。　問7　並べ替えるとbecause of the great courage she showed in expressing(カ→ア→ウ→オ→イ→エ→キ)となる。選択肢カにbecause があるので，「彼女が賞賛される」理由が述べられているのではないかと推測し，名詞表現のthe great courage からbecause of とshe showed the great courageを結びつける方向に考えれば正解に至る。

【9】(例1)　First, you should decide whether you agree or disagree with the topic. That way, readers can easily understand what you will write about. Second, brainstorm for ideas. Write down as many reasons as possible that support your opinion. Finally, you should be careful about the structure. It should contain an introduction, a body, and a conclusion.　(例2)　There are three points that you need to follow when you write an English essay. Firstly, make sure whether you are for or against the topic. By so doing, readers can have some idea of what they should understand. Secondly, describe a few reasons for your opinion. You can add some experiences to each reason. Thirdly, end the essay by repeating your opinion in different English.

〈解説〉生徒が自分の意見を英語で書くときに留意してほしい点を3つ挙げて伝えるということであるから，First(ly), ～. Second(ly),～. Third(ly)(Finally),～.という定型の列挙の仕方で明確にやるべきこと，やってはいけないことを示す。可能ならその理由や意味を簡潔な英文で補足的に伝えると生徒にとってはわかりやすい。留意点の例としては，「テーマについての自分の立場，賛否を明らかにする」，「ランダムに考えを出しながら自分の立場を支持するような理由づけを作る」，「理由に代わるものとして自分の経験を述べる」，「最後に全体の文構成に配慮して，序論・本論・結論の流れを確認する」，「最後に他の表現で自分の意見をまとめてみる」などである。なお，「6行以上」は，50語以上が想定される。

【10】問1　（例1） They are discussing how students can evaluate each other in a speech activity. The students will work in small groups so that the speakers can relax. In order to help the students listen to their peers' speeches more carefully, the evaluation sheet should include three viewpoints: eye-contact, voice clarity, and content of speech.　（例2） Two teachers are talking about the next lesson's goal activity. Both teachers agree that students deliver a speech by turns in a small group because it would allow students to be relaxed and evaluate each other with concentration. Then they talk about how to evaluate the speech and decide three criteria; eye contact, clarity of voice, and content of speech. Teacher A proposes students grade each other's speech using three ranks; A, B and C.　問2　（例1） First, we could let the students choose the best speaker in their groups. Through ranking other speakers' performances, they will find ways to improve their own speeches. Second, the students could write questions while listening and ask the speakers orally after each speech. They will be able to think what kind of information should be included in a speech.　　(例2)　Shall we have a rule that all students must make comments such as good points or bad points and ask at least one question after each speech of the other group members?　To do this, they have to listen to the other students' speech attentively and the students who are asked need to answer those questions.　That is, they inevitably have to exchange opinions with each other.　Besides, how about setting another rule?　Each student has to write the best speaker's name in the group and the reason why they choose that student.　Thus, they can judge whose speech is best from different viewpoints.

〈解説〉問1　①，②，③からは，まとめの活動として生徒1人ずつにさせるスピーチを全体の前か，少人数グループ内かの決定とその理由，さらにそのスピーチの評価について話し合われていることがわかる。④，⑤からは，スピーチを評価する場合の具体的な項目と方法が話し合われていることがわかる。以上の内容をまとめる。なお，「5行程度」は，60〜80語程度が想定される。少人数グループだとリラックスしてスピーチをすることができるし，集中してスピーチを聞いて評価できるということと，具体的な3つの評価項目は必ず要約に入れたい。　問2　⑥から，スピーチを聞いたあと，評価としてただA，B，Cと書くだけにならないように工夫すること，集中して主体的に聞く必要が生じるような方法を考えることが求められている。聞いたスピーチについて必ず英語で質問をすることと，話者は必ず英語でその質問に答えることを活動のなかに入れるとか，質問と感想を英語で言ったり書いたりするとか，自分の一押しのスピーチのgood pointsを英語でまとめて意見交換をするなどのやり方と，そのメリットをいっしょに考えたい。なお，「8行程度」は，60〜100語程度が想定される。

●書籍内容の訂正等について

　弊社では教員採用試験対策シリーズ（参考書，過去問，全国まるごと過去問題集），公務員試験対策シリーズ，公立幼稚園・保育士試験対策シリーズ，会社別就職試験対策シリーズについて，正誤表をホームページ（https://www.kyodo-s.jp）に掲載いたします。内容に訂正等，疑問点がございましたら，まずホームページをご確認ください。もし，正誤表に掲載されていない訂正等，疑問点がございましたら，下記項目をご記入の上，以下の送付先までお送りいただくようお願いいたします。

> ① 　書籍名，都道府県（学校）名，年度
> 　　（例：教員採用試験過去問シリーズ　小学校教諭 過去問　2025年度版）
> ② 　ページ数（書籍に記載されているページ数をご記入ください。）
> ③ 　訂正等，疑問点（内容は具体的にご記入ください。）
> 　　（例：問題文では"ア～オの中から選べ"とあるが，選択肢はエまでしかない）

〔ご注意〕
○ 電話での質問や相談等につきましては，受付けておりません。ご注意ください。
○ 正誤表の更新は適宜行います。
○ いただいた疑問点につきましては，当社編集制作部で検討の上，正誤表への反映を決定させていただきます（個別回答は，原則行いませんのであしからずご了承ください）。

●情報提供のお願い

　協同教育研究会では，これから教員採用試験を受験される方々に，より正確な問題を，より多くご提供できるよう情報の収集を行っております。つきましては，教員採用試験に関する次の項目の情報を，以下の送付先までお送りいただけますと幸いでございます。お送りいただきました方には謝礼を差し上げます。
（情報量があまりに少ない場合は，謝礼をご用意できかねる場合があります）。

◆あなたの受験された面接試験，論作文試験の実施方法や質問内容

◆教員採用試験の受験体験記

- -

送付先	○電子メール：edit@kyodo-s.jp
	○FAX：03-3233-1233（協同出版株式会社　編集制作部 行）
	○郵送：〒101-0054　東京都千代田区神田錦町2-5
	協同出版株式会社　編集制作部 行
	○HP：https://kyodo-s.jp/provision（右記のQRコードからもアクセスできます）

　※謝礼をお送りする関係から，いずれの方法でお送りいただく際にも，「お名前」「ご住所」は，必ず明記いただきますよう，よろしくお願い申し上げます。

教員採用試験「過去問」シリーズ

静岡県・静岡市・浜松市の
英語科 過去問

編　集　Ⓒ 協同教育研究会
発　行　令和5年11月10日
発行者　小貫　輝雄
発行所　協同出版株式会社

〒101-0054　東京都千代田区神田錦町2 - 5
電話　03－3295－1341
振替　東京00190－4－94061
印刷所　協同出版・POD工場

落丁・乱丁はお取り替えいたします。